Evolution
of the
Feminine Mystique:
Searching For Happily Ever After

Malia Litman, R.N., J.D., *S.H.M.

*Stay-at-Home-Mom

Cover Art by Patti Rye, Advertising Design

ISBN-13: 978-0692525197
ISBN-10: 069252519x

DEDICATION

This book is dedicated to David, my Prince,
and to my kids, Zach, Anna, and Katie,
the very best part of my
"Happily Ever After"!

ACKNOWLEDGEMENTS

Several people have provided an assist to me in getting this book to publication. I will be forever grateful to Jeanette Cates for her technical expertise and hours of work on the technological aspects of this e-book. My mother, and Prince Charming provided an assist with editing. Patti Rye of Advertisingdesign1.com (**patti@advertisingdesign1.com**) and Cindy Rolen shared their invaluable talent in the design of the cover. For the multitude of people who posted videos on YouTube that made this journey so much fun, thank you. Most of all, thank you to everyone reading! It is through your support that I have found my HAPPILY EVER AFTER as a woman's advocate.

TABLE OF CONTENTS

"What is a woman's place in this modern world? Jasnah Kholin's words read. I rebel against this question, though so many of my peers ask it. The inherent bias in the inquiry seems invisible to so many of them. They consider themselves progressive because they are willing to challenge many of the assumptions of the past.

They ignore the greater assumption—that a 'place' for women must be defined and set forth to begin with. Half of the population must somehow be reduced to the role arrived at by a single conversation. No matter how broad that role is, it will be—by-nature—a reduction from the infinite variety that is womanhood.

I say that there is no role for women—there is, instead, a role for each woman, and she must make it for herself. For some, it will be the role of scholar; for others, it will be the role of wife. For others, it will be both. For yet others, it will be neither.

Do not mistake me in assuming I value one woman's role above another. My point is not to stratify our society—we have done that far too well already—my point is to diversify our discourse.

A woman's strength should not be in her role, whatever she chooses it to be, but in the power to choose that role. It is amazing to me that I even have to make this point, as I see it as the very foundation of our conversation."

—Brandon Sanderson, Words of Radiance [1]

FOREWARD

Women are dying, figuratively and in fact. On this chilly fall day I was glad to be spending my time to support a friend with whom I had shared so much. As I sat in a somber Catholic Church on a hard wooden pew discolored from age, I scanned the multitude of people dressed in black. Although many of the mourners were strangers to me, I was glad to be counted among them. The deceased and I had met only a few times. Dorothy's daughter, Deborah, started in the litigation section one year after I did. In spite of the fact that I had conversed with Dorothy on only a few occasions I knew her well. Dorothy's life and personality had been the subject of many lunchtime conversations with Deborah.

Dorothy was a member of my mother's generation. They had many things in common. They had never met, even though both knew that their daughters were best friends. My mother and Dorothy knew their daughters were ambitious and shared a passion for the law. Deborah and I enjoyed success and respect from our male counter-parts. Our moms didn't have male-counterparts. Men respected women of our mothers' generation if they raised polite children, were accomplished in the kitchen, and wore pretty dresses.

My mother never worked outside the home. Dorothy had always worked to supplement her family's income. Five children, cleaning, and cooking kept my mother busy. Dorothy was equally busy raising two children and working as a teacher. Mom and Dorothy were taught that women could be teachers or nurses if they had to work to help their husband cover the family's expenses. In the 1970's teachers and nurses were almost exclusively women. That fit nicely with the image of nurturing women who needed to be home with the kids at the end of each school day, greeting them with fresh cold milk and steaming hot chocolate chip cookies. Both of our mothers would have liked to have had professional careers. Both were adept at making cookies.

Deborah became a teacher and I became a nurse. Perhaps to distinguish ourselves as outstanding in our fields Deborah became a special-ed teacher and I became an ICU/Burn Unit nurse. Yet, both of us knew quickly that in spite of our accomplishments we wanted more. We were each too ambitious to be satisfied with our chosen careers. The men we had out-performed in high school had gone on to become engineers, doctors, and lawyers. Those men would enjoy financial independence, security, and respect. Deborah and I, as a teacher and nurse, would have been lucky to afford a modest home by the end of our careers. The Principal at the school where Deborah taught was a man. The doctors with whom I worked were men. We were destined to be viewed as subordinates. Men would have always controlled our success if we had chosen to remain in those fields. As a nurse or a teacher there was no independent path towards professional success. Our success would have always been dependent on a man's evaluation and approval of our performance.

Deborah and I attended different law schools. Yet in each we were considered unusual. Of course it was unusual for any law student in the late 70's to be a woman. What was hard for some to understand was that we were both exceptional students. Deborah was the Editor-in-Chief of the Southern Methodist University Law Review. I was only one of several editors on the University of Oklahoma Law Review. However, I was also the Moot Court Champion. Deborah had been married and divorced. I had never been married. At the outset of our careers Deborah and I each aspired to "have it all." We expected to become senior partners, the wife of a man who adored us, and to have a family with adorably cute, well-mannered, and brilliant children. Both of us loved to cook. Neither of us belonged to a feminist group. Both of us expected to be treated fairly by the men for whom we worked. As attorneys if we ever perceived that we were treated unfairly, or paid unfairly, we always had the option of working for ourselves.

Deborah's brother stood and spoke to the silent mourners. With tears in his eyes he shared stories that made us cry and laugh out loud. Most of the stories had a common theme. Dorothy was a great chef. Many memories of her were inextricably connected to her achievements in the kitchen. Dorothy was famous for her scrumptious desserts. Everyone loved her chocolate mousse but her soufflés were legendary. As her son reminisced about his memories of Dorothy in the kitchen I realized that she defined her success through success in the kitchen. As I thought about my mother I realized that she too defined success by the culinary delights she conceived. For my mother cooking provided purpose, validation, and an escape from a particularly bad day. Nothing provided relief for mom like the enjoyment derived from watching the family fight over the last piece of one of her exquisite cakes. If we ran for the antacids after eating too much beef stroganoff mom was fulfilled. In some perverted way the fact that all of my siblings and I have struggled with our weight is a testament to just how competent mom was in the kitchen. When mom wanted to do something special for a member of the family she'd make our favorite dessert. Our teachers at school always anticipated receiving a loaf of her famous pumpkin bread at Christmas. On special occasions mom would cook for a multitude of people including church groups, bridge clubs, and dad's colleagues. If the meal was a success, mom was a success.

In my teenage years there was hope that I too might one day be a success. At age thirteen I won a blue ribbon in the Tulsa State Fair for my cherry pie, using mother's recipe. Cakes, pies, cookies, and other sweets were among my award-winning accomplishments. One of the special gifts my mother gave me is a three-ring binder with all of her favorite recipes. To this day I find that cooking for someone is a way to convey to them that they are special to me. At age 16, I baked a pie for my dentist who performed an emergency root canal on my front tooth so that my family could proceed with our family vacation. At age 25, I baked a pie for my Prince Charming as the finale to the first meal I prepared for him. At age 28, I baked a birthday cake for the Senior Partner who entrusted me with research on a case for his most important client. At age 33, I baked and decorated Valentines cookies for the Valentine's Day party at Zach's preschool. At age 37, the green smoking witches brew I made for the dozens of children attending the Halloween party at our house was a big hit. At age 44, I made a chocolate sheet cake for David to take to his office for the holiday luncheon. At age 47, I made Snickerdoodle cookies for Anna's debate team and custom decorated basketball cookies for each of the girls on Katie's basketball team. At age 51, I made Obama cookies to thank the people in my precinct who had worked with me on the campaign. At age 57, I made brownies for the staff at the hospital that treated me with a new therapy for Multiple Sclerosis.

Baking is a way to say that I care. No matter how busy I am, no matter how disabled I am from Multiple Sclerosis, and no matter how financially secure we are, home-made treats are always a way to convey that I personally care. Nothing says "you are special" or "thank you" like a homemade birthday cake, a custom decorated cookie, or a warm gooey brownie fresh from the oven.

In addition to being a great cook, mom inspired me to be a professional. Mom encouraged me to achieve success in the kitchen and in school. Simultaneously she was a role model for me. Through her example she taught me to be a loving, devoted, mother and wife. Deborah's mother did the same for her. What our mothers couldn't know was how hard it would be to achieve success professionally and domestically. Deborah and I wanted to be able to bake like our mothers, and achieve success professionally like our fathers.

Deborah and I are each in our late 50's. We are each happy with our paths in life, even though we ended up in very different places. We started in the same firm, in the same department. Our goals, both personal and professional, were similar. Thirty years ago our definitions of success were virtually identical. Today Deborah and I both are happy, satisfied, and feel a sense of pride in our achievements. Even though we have chosen different paths we still have the same character, determination, persistence, ambition, intellect and compassion. I am married. She is not. I have children. She does not. Deborah has served on the Texas Supreme Court. I have not. Deborah now runs her own law firm and is one of the premier appellate attorneys in the state. I am not. I no longer practice law and never had my own firm. Business people across the state seek Deborah's counsel. Mothers of kids from school still ask me for my sugar cookie recipe. Deborah has earned millions of dollars providing legal advice to her clients. I don't get paid in dollars when I give legal advice to my husband and his business partner.

Deborah and I each achieved the status of "Senior Trial Partner" before our paths diverged. I developed Multiple Sclerosis. Deborah did not. We both still like to cook. Deborah's table is set with elegant china. Mine will one day be set with plastic Disney dishes when my grandchildren come to visit. Deborah's table is complete with sterling silver flatware. Mine is stainless steel. Deborah's guests are treated to fine wine in Waterford Crystal. My guests are lucky to have a Wal-Mart water glass that doesn't have a chip in it. All of the guests at both tables enjoy chicken. Deborah's guests might be treated to Chicken Cordon Bleu, while mine would likely prefer chicken fingers. At the conclusion of the meal Deborah may surprise her guests with a Gran Marnier Soufflé. The kids around my table will be treated to Halloween cupcakes with black icing and green oozing eyeballs. The differences in the tables will not be the result of different financial resources. Deborah and I each could afford the Waterford crystal. We both appreciate its elegance. We both understand why kids would love cupcakes with green oozing eyeballs. The difference in our choices relate to our individual perceptions of our "happily ever after."

Deborah and I are each happy and satisfied with our lives. Both of us feel successful and gratified as we look back over the past 30 years. We are still the best of friends and respect the choices each has made. This is the story of my journey towards achieving success. If you lose it all, while trying to have it all, happiness can never be achieved. Inherent in the notion of having it all is the recognition that having it all means finding a way to achieve happiness with whatever choices you make. Women are afraid that when our days are numbered we will be remembered for our scrumptious desserts and little else. We are afraid people will think the reason for our choice to enrich the lives of the people in our families may suggest we weren't smart enough, or ambitious enough, to have a profession. We are fearful that our lives will be defined by the different desserts we made, instead of the differences we made in people's lives or by our professional accomplishments.

Deborah will be remembered for her professional successes. Her life and career will be celebrated by friends and colleagues. Few would even mention or care that she never had kids. I'll be remembered for the play centers I built in the preschool including the castle complete with a pulley-operated drawbridge, the underground cave with a moving conveyor belt that transported real pebbles, and the aluminum-foil covered space ship. My life will be celebrated by family and friends. One day my granddaughter may peruse her mom's basketball scrapbook. Katie, my daughter, might explain that grandma made scrapbooks for each member of her high school varsity basketball team. That scrapbook will teach my granddaughter to appreciate her mother's basketball talent. She'll also understand just how dedicated her grandma was to her family. Few will remember that I was ever a registered nurse who saved patients' lives. Most wouldn't remember me as a Senior Trial Partner at one of the most prestigious firms in Dallas, who was a board certified litigation specialist.

For a time Deborah felt disappointed that she didn't have children. There was a time that she was still searching for her "happily ever after." However because she didn't have children and was twice divorced her choices were more limited than mine. It was easier for her to set her professional priorities without a husband to satisfy, or children to nourish. I had a more complicated mix of conflicting demands on my time. I came perilously close to "losing it all" when I became overwhelmed with the challenge of balancing a husband, children, and a demanding career.

We have both evolved. The definition of success for each of us is now very different. Our definitions for success started out as virtually identical. Over time our definitions for success changed as each of us found ourselves confronted with circumstances that were unanticipated when we initially embarked upon our journeys. Our accomplishments are polar opposites, but we each celebrate the success of each other. Deborah and I both will be recognized for being successful but the type of success will be very different.

My hope is that by sharing my journey you will come to understand, appreciate, and respect that success for each woman is necessarily different. One type of success is not better than another…just different. Our biggest challenge is to define the success that will truly make us happy. Then we must have the courage to make the choices that will make it happen. Once you identify what your "happily ever after" is, you can plan your journey. Women can't begin their journey toward happiness until we identify the destination we seek.

It is a new awakening for women in the 21st century. No longer do companies hire women because it is the politically correct thing to do. Women are hired because we are good at what we do. People use a small business not because it is owned by a woman but because it best suits their needs. When somebody in the family needs bypass surgery we don't select the best female surgeon we can find. We select the very best cardio-vascular surgeon in town. It doesn't matter if that surgeon is a woman, what kind of a chef she is, or whether she has children. We simply want the best. Women don't become stay-at-home moms because we don't have any other choice. We choose that life because raising the next generation is quite simply our priority. Raising children may be more difficult than pursuing professional success. The hours are longer and the financial rewards are non-existent. As a professional our hard work typically means increases in salary and promotions. Typically if we work hard in our professions we can predict success. As mothers we have less control of the outcome. We know that in spite of our best efforts, children may turn to drugs and alcohol. Professional acclaim is more predictable. If we are successful at raising strong, independent children, they will grow up and leave home. Instead of a corner office at the end of her career, a mother may find herself all alone in a rocking chair in the corner of the family room. Instead of identifying our occupation on our Medicare application as Managing Senior Partner, we might list our occupation as a S.H.M.

For the last century women fought for the choice to have a profession, a family, or both. Now that we have the right to choose, we must have the courage to make the best choice for ourselves and our family. If we become unhappy with our first choice, we have the ability to make a different one. When our circumstances in life change, we must be pro-active in determining what new choice might better suit our lives, given our change in circumstances. Women have had the ability to *have it all* for a long time. The real problem is not having a professional life, or a home life, but how to make choices that make both manageable. If we make the choice to lean in to our careers, we receive reinforcement through promotions, professional recognition, and financial rewards. However if we choose to lean in to our families, and forgo the professional accolades, we must recognize that there will be little support or recognition. Our personal satisfaction must be its own reward. It is time for society, and especially women, to recognize and respect the choice of women to lean in to our marriages and children. The rewards are different, but no less satisfying. Women enhance our society through our choices to be professionals and mothers. Both are essential for society and for our families. If we are to live "happily ever after," it is imperative that women stop disparaging other women for making choices different than their own.

Because my journey has been long and difficult, I hope that the insights I have gained along the way will be helpful to other women in redefining success for themselves. My goal is for more women to gain respect and to develop an appreciation for the different choices of other women. In doing so, we improve the likelihood that each woman will choose a path that will allow her to live happily ever after. If women can't respect other women for the choices we make, women will never gain respect from men. If we are successful in redefining success for ourselves, men might also learn from our example. While success should never be dependent on the approval of another, the support and recognition of achievement of our goals by those about whom we care, enhances our feeling of satisfaction. Ultimately if the struggle of women leads to losing it all, then we have not adapted effectively. Evolution is based on the premise of survival of the fittest. Our very survival depends on our ability to identify the path that provides the greatest chance for happiness. If we are to eliminate the possibility of losing it all we must set our priorities and make choices to maximize the likelihood of achieving them. Every woman must assess her unique situation and determine the right course for herself.

This book is a compass. It is not intended to be a map with a predetermined destination. It is only a tool to help you find your way. This is the story of my journey. I hope it helps you with yours.

*"Women are not
thinking about
'having it all.'
They're worried about
Losing it all..."*

- Sheryl Sandberg, Lean In [2]

CHAPTER I: LOSING IT ALL

A. Too Late

Where was I? How did I get here? It was as if I was awakening from a dream but I couldn't remember the dream. Instead of being wrapped in my threadbare comforter, providing warmth and security during a night of power sleeping, it was the seat belt of my car that was holding me tightly. The light ahead was red and my car was stopped. Instead of the soft downy pillow under my head, it was the hard leather seat back of my car that supported my head. Instead of the faint hum of the ceiling fan above my bed, the CD player in my car blared the familiar melody of Chicago's famous song, *Searching*.[a] In August of 1994 the Dallas North Toll Road terminated at the Spring Creek exit. I was at the light at Spring Creek. Nobody was honking. My car was perfectly positioned parallel to the lane lines for the right turn lane. The air conditioning vent was pointed toward me and a pleasant breath of air cooled my face. The thermometer for the outside temperature read 97 degrees. The digital display on the dashboard indicated it was 11:17 a.m. There were no children in the car, but evidence remained that each had recently occupied the 1990 grey Chevy Suburban stopped at the intersection. A plastic mottled purple Brontosaurus lay motionless in the back seat where Zach usually sat. The 14 inch Barney lay face down in Anna's seat. Katie's car seat wasn't in the car but one of her pacifiers lay on the floor next to the flat, brown-crusted, McDonald's ketchup packet.

The last thing I could remember was the sweltering heat as I opened the car door in the driveway of my home at 10:48 a.m. I remember fastening my seat belt. Is this what a stroke feels like? If I had suffered a stroke would I still be able to hold Katie while I gave her a bottle? I could still lift the over-due volume of the *Little Engine That Could* resting on the passenger seat next to me, so surely this wasn't a stroke. Perhaps I had died? No… surely in heaven I'd drive a nicer car… there wouldn't be mud in heaven on the soccer shoes resting on the cloth floor mats. In heaven, pacifiers wouldn't be needed because babies would never cry. I had heard about a "brain-fart," so maybe this is what that feels like. … No, that seemed unlikely. I couldn't smell anything except fruit gummies that had fallen between the seats. I could still sing along with tunes on the CD player so I hadn't lost my memory,…totally. Perhaps I was suffering from amnesia? No…I had no swollen or painful lump on my head. I still remembered the date of my last mammogram, my last colonoscopy, and my last menstrual period. I knew I had three kids…somewhere…a husband of 10 years with dark curly hair and a mustache, three filthy dogs, two birds that squawked when the kids tried to remove them from their cages, a chinchilla that would bite the tiny fingers of any child that might dare try to pet it, at least 5 immortal salt-water fish, and a gluttonous spotted eel.

---

[a] https://www.youtube.com/watch?v=eHD7KekkSLs

I knew that I used to *have it all* because I'd just come back from a three week trial in Shreveport Louisiana. I was such a great trial attorney that I was a Senior Partner with one of the largest firms in Dallas. My client loved my work so much that he asked me to help another attorney in Louisiana with a case similar to one I'd successfully handled in Dallas. I was such a great mother that I had established myself as capable of producing children that were both prolific in number and substantial in size. All three of my kids weighted close to 10 lbs. at birth. The children had survived to ages five, two, and 6 months, so my aptitude in the field of protective instincts was also impressive. I was also good at balancing my personal and professional life. I had a nanny who came to my house so the kids could nap in their own beds. I had a housekeeper who came once a week to clean. I had a secretary who devoted 100% of her time to my schedule. I had a legal assistant of 11 years who would give me a full report on the rest of my docket that had been unattended for the last three weeks. I had all the help I needed from young trial attorneys hoping to learn from my example. I had a husband who loved me, the last time I saw him. Surely I still had it all. Had something changed? Did I need another person to help me manage my trial docket, my kids, my husband, my responsibilities at home, and the physical and mental health that I'd been neglecting?

I didn't know what was happening. Instead of being confident and in control, I felt scared and vulnerable. Suddenly life was moving in slow motion. The last 20 minutes of my life had just evaporated. I don't think I had really understood the concept of a void, until that moment. All I could feel was a profound emptiness. I didn't even remember why I had driven to the end of the Toll Road. Would it be safe to drive home? Could I remember the way home? Should I call the police? Should I call the mental hospital? Did I need an internist or a psychiatrist? Perhaps I had simply forgotten to sleep? Maybe I just had low blood sugar and needed some sustenance? Would my husband and kids recognize me when I returned? Would they be able to tell I was losing it? I knew I was exhausted but I thought if someone was tired they'd fall asleep while driving. It had never occurred to me that a person could be awake but lose all memory of the immediate past.

I was making a six-figure income in 1994 so I could afford a nice car to impress clients. However the Suburban I sat in on this particular day was chosen to transport a multitude of children on field trips and to soccer games. Today I wondered if it would adequately protect me on the treacherous journey home. Since my husband was enjoying success running one of those dot.com companies, if I died on the way home my financial contribution to the family would probably never be missed. But who would take the time to put jokes in Anna's lunch box? Who would make sure that Katie had the right ointment for the eczema on her arm? Who would hunt fossils with Zach? Who would make cherry pie for David? What would they say at my funeral or my commitment hearing? Would they laud my devotion to my profession and my family…until the day I died? Would David marry again? Would the kids like their step-mom better than me? FOCUS. FOCUS. I had to focus on driving home and worry about the rest of my life if I made it home.

As I headed home it was hard to focus on driving instead of all the details of the next 24 hours that I was supposed to remember. I hadn't gotten birthday gifts for my sister, brother, and niece who had birthdays coming in August. While out of town in trial I had missed the birthdays of my two best girlfriends, so I owed them lunch. I was behind in scheduling my teeth to be cleaned. Mary, the nanny, would be taking vacation for two weeks in August and I hadn't found a substitute for her. Zach would be starting kindergarten next month and he had outgrown his shoes. Anna was supposed to go to a birthday party for her best friend next weekend but I hadn't wrapped the gift. We were out of milk. The dryer was making a funny noise. What would the kids eat for dinner tonight? Anna was old enough to be potty trained, but I'd been lazy. It was so much more convenient to just change her diapers than to run for the restroom when she announced it was time. Lucille, the housekeeper, kept putting the flannel sheets on the bed. I was behind in getting the oil changed. Zach needed a haircut before school started. It was time for Katie's 6 month checkup. This week was our turn for snacks for Anna's preschool class and I hadn't gotten anything. Soccer sign-up started in one week. I had to get Zach on his best friend's team. I didn't even know what to worry about at the office, as I'd been gone for three weeks. If I'd taken a three-week vacation at least I'd be returning refreshed and energized. Instead I was returning worn out, sleep-deprived, and needing to re-establish relations with my children and husband. Is this what a mental breakdown feels like?

I remembered that David and I were supposed to go to a cocktail party that night. When people asked what I did I could proudly tell them that I had just returned from a grueling three-week trial out of state. I could explain that I successfully balanced the needs of my husband and young children. If someone asked me what I'd been doing today I could account for most of my activities. I just wouldn't mention the part that I couldn't remember. If asked about how I could leave my 6 month old baby for three weeks I would explain that I had a nanny, a husband, and I saw Katie on the weekends. If asked how I could leave my 2 ½ year old daughter, I'd explain that having me gone was really good for her. I served as a role model for her. If she followed my lead, she could strive to be just like me. I was teaching her to be independent and self-reliant. If asked about how my five year old boy reacted when I left, I'd explain that I had always worked during his life-time so he knew I would return. He was accustomed to being left. If asked about whether my husband resented my absence I'd have a chance to explain that he was pre-occupied with running an extremely successful internet company. A babysitter for the evening had already been arranged so I knew the kids would get the care they needed. But who would care for me? I remembered thinking that I had it all, but on this particular day I felt as if I had already lost it all!

If I wasn't able to remember driving down the toll road, how could I ever be trusted to drive my children anywhere, ever again? If I couldn't handle the supervision of another attorney in trial, how could I handle my own cases? Would my husband love me if I had to be institutionalized? Would my kids come to visit me? I had convinced myself that my kids were fine and that having a "professional" mother would give them an example of the success for which they could aspire. When they were bigger, if they worked really hard, they too could achieve success like me. They could leave their children too. They could tell my grandchildren about the professional accomplishments of their deceased grandmother…the one who died in that terrible accident on the Dallas North Toll Road. When the kids cried as I left for work each day, I convinced myself that they were just trying to manipulate me. They would be stronger and more independent if they had to depend on themselves for comfort. I was really doing them a favor. When my husband was feeling abandoned and lonely, I reminded him of my contribution to the family income. If I was short with the kids, I told myself that they should learn that parents are people too. Everyone has bad days. When I couldn't be home with Zach when he had an ear infection I reminded myself that I had gotten him those special ear drops to ease his pain. He'd sleep most of the day because his fever was so high. The nanny could measure the dosage of Tylenol as easily as I could. She'd only forgotten his medicine once. If I couldn't handle having it all, there must be something wrong with me. Other women could do it, so why couldn't I? I worried that if I quit my job I'd never get another. In my mind giving up my job meant giving up being an attorney. If I wasn't an attorney who would I be? It didn't occur to me that I could stop working for a short time and later re-evaluate whether I was happy. I didn't realize that just because I quit my job wouldn't mean that I quit being an attorney. I worried that if I didn't quit my job, my marriage would end in divorce and my kids would become delinquents. I was worried that if I didn't quit that my children would contribute to society by being the leaders of their therapy groups in prison rather than winning Nobel prizes. How could I give up all I had worked so hard to achieve professionally? How could I abandon my husband and children when they were the most important parts of my life? If I got married and had children, didn't that mean that I had made them a priority in my life? If I spent seven years in college preparing to be an attorney and twelve years perfecting my skill as a trial attorney, surely I wouldn't simply quit, giving up all the hard work of the last 19 years of my life? For God's sake, I had devoted over half of my life to arrive at this point professionally. Surely I wouldn't just quit? If I didn't have a profession would I become addicted to soap operas and bon-bons? Why was this so hard?

In 1963 Betty Friedan wrote the Feminine Mystique. She identified a problem commonly faced by women that had no name. In 1963 I was a naïve six years old. My only problems in my sixth year of life related to what we were having for lunch in the school cafeteria and how I would survive one more day with three intolerable brothers. My problems all had names: Frank, Steve, and Phil…and grits.

I never faced a silent question. When I experienced dissatisfaction it wasn't hard to give it a name. It might be a physically dominant brother, a misogynistic doctor, a lecherous old judge, or a clueless husband. When I decided that I aspired to be more than a nurse, I didn't feel I was taking a stand for women's liberation. I just wanted to be independent. I wanted to be in control of my life. I wanted the same type of opportunities that less ambitious, stupid boys had. I knew what I wanted. It was called equality. It wasn't some amorphous feeling that had no name. It was a compelling passion to be the best that I could be in all that I did. It was an overwhelming sense of indignation that anyone would suggest that I wasn't mentally equipped to do anything a man could do.

As I sat at the end of the Dallas North Toll Road reality set in. My problem was not wondering if this was all. Instead I was wondering if I had lost it all. My problem was not living a life that revolved only around my home and children. My problem was that my life was no longer revolving around one or two things. It was spinning out of control, trying to revolve around too many different things in one 24 hour cycle. I needed more time! I was not dissatisfied because I lacked challenge in my life. I was dying because there were too many challenges in life. I felt I was a failure as an attorney, a mother, and a wife. Without question my husband, my kids, and my clients all needed more time from me. The problem was not that I lacked the talent or ability to do a good job both professionally and personally. The problem was that because I had the talent and ability to do it all, I thought I could do it all... at the same time.

Survival is a powerful instinct. I was fortunate that my instinct for survival guided me home from the end of the Dallas North Toll Road. It was my instinct for survival that guided me to the managing partner's office on the next business day to announce my resignation. A choice had to be made. Realizing that my children were more important than my career, the decision was clear. It was my good fortune to be unconstrained by the financial burden of supporting my family. It almost would have been easier if financial considerations for our family dictated that I must work because then there would be no choice. If my income was required to support the family then I wouldn't have to worry about giving up my career. My life might have been harder if money was tighter. However, I wouldn't have felt the need to choose. If I wasn't the perfect mother, because I had to devote time to being a great attorney, it would have been alright. If money was a problem, then making money would have been a way of being a good mother. If my income was essential for our family, then doing a good job at work would have been a way to demonstrate my commitment to my husband and children. If my income was essential to support the family then my husband would also not have had a choice. He would have had to help more with the kids and domestic chores because he would know that we were dependent on my income. Because my financial contribution was not essential to the support of the family, I had to choose. Because my husband's potential income was greater than mine, it was my job that would be compromised if something had to be sacrificed. Ignoring societal pressures to remain a successful female attorney, I resigned. Feeling that I was a complete failure, defeated, and out of control, there seemed no alternative. I knew that one day I might regret opting out of my career. However, I also knew that if I didn't opt out immediately, I wouldn't live long enough to regret my decision.

Over time I learned to say I was retired, instead of saying that I "quit". Everyone, except my children, was disappointed with my decision. "How could you give it all up?" my mother asked while choking back tears. She would have loved having a professional career but having five children made that an impossible choice. Having achieved the success of being named a Senior Partner, people were astonished that I would so easily discard the distinction and achievement for which other women worked so hard. Younger women in the trial department expressed their disappointment with words of defeat and hopelessness. If I couldn't make it work who could? The firm had given me three months of maternity leave after giving birth to each child. I should strive to work harder to pay them back and to convince them that giving young women maternity leave was a good idea. I had received nine months of pay from the firm without fulfilling my obligation to devote my life to the practice of law with that firm. It was fear of falling into an abyss, out of which I could never climb, that caused me to choose to stay home and devote myself to my marriage and to my children. I was so desperate to catch my breath that it was clear that I had to prioritize survival and worry about the rest later.

Twenty years later I know that I made the choice that saved my life, my marriage, and my children. In hindsight, contrary to advice of family and friends, I was the only person who could weigh the considerations of my unique situation to reach the right decision for me and my family. I considered both the demands of my career and of my husband's business. I considered the relative income that would likely be derived from each occupation. I considered the needs of my three young children. I thought about my inability to function on five hours of sleep. I considered my perceived need to do more for my children. It was clear that I needed to make a dramatic change.

Even Prince Charming was trying to be supportive and encouraged me to try to find a way to remain a professional. He knew how much I enjoyed the practice of law and the respect that came with it. He knew how hard I had worked during seven years of college and twelve years of practice to be the very best trial attorney I could be. David knew how much I enjoyed beating arrogant male attorneys in court. David knew what a kick I got out of being a lecturer at state-wide CLE conferences where I was the only female trial attorney on the roster. I'd worked so hard to gain the confidence of clients. Having a full docket of cases sent to me by my own clients was certainly the sign of a successful trial partner. Yet it was clear I was at the breaking point.

My Prince Charming still loved me but he was unable to compromise his business success to come home early to cook dinner or pick up children from school. He didn't even know the name of the pediatrician. David didn't know which child was allergic to sulfa, that babies require immunization shots more than once, or that children can have ear infections without fever. David didn't know the names of Anna and Zach's preschool teachers, where their classrooms were located, that peanut butter could not be part of the snack he should bring on snack day, or what food to pack in the kids' lunch boxes to ensure that they would have nutritious meals. He could have made pot roast for dinner, but that would require knowing where the recipe books were located. He could have changed Anna's sheets after she threw-up in the middle of the night, but he didn't appreciate the importance of her pink Power Ranger sheets. He might have laughed when Anna explained to him that she would absorb special powers from those sheets. He could have given Katie a bottle now that I was no longer breast feeding but he might have mistaken her crying as a desire for more formula, rather than simply needing to burp. David knew that Zach loved dinosaurs, but he didn't know what a Hadrosaur looked like, or whether it was an omnivore or herbivore. David was smart enough to educate himself about the mundane parts of parenthood but I knew he wouldn't make the time.

Strategically I waited to have children until I made Junior Partner at the firm. After Zach was born I announced I would go part-time. The result was that the firm was glad to pay me half of my salary but I billed as many hours as I had when I was full-time. After returning to full-time status and making Senior Partner, I gave birth to Anna, our second child. Realizing that part-time simply wouldn't work, I determined that I could operate on less sleep. Becoming more efficient in all that I did, I eliminated any miniscule amount of time previously devoted to myself. David also agreed to do the grocery shopping. The problem was that I was still trying to have it all at the same time…except for grocery shopping. When Katie was born there was nothing left to eliminate. Every part of my life became imperiled. I'd waited too long to recognize my limitations.

In the years after I left my job I was diagnosed with Multiple Sclerosis, an autoimmune disease of unknown cause. Now I realize that the most likely cause of my M.S. is the stress of trying to do too much in a short period of time. My health was the victim of attempting to have it all. In the year after I quit my job, my dad developed brain cancer and died. Zach was diagnosed with severe dyslexia. Within three years of quitting, Anna and Katie contracted a horrible bowel infection or parasite causing Katie to miss three weeks from school and Anna five. During those five weeks, Anna awoke in the middle of the night writhing in pain. As I held her tightly I knew sleep deprivation would be a problem the next day. But because I was now a stay-at-home mom, my sleep deprivation would only result in forgetting to add an ingredient to the chicken casserole I was making for dinner rather than forgetting the crucial question in the expert's deposition. When Katie developed an inability to walk, due to some undiagnosed condition, I was able to rush her to the E.R. The doctors sent us directly to a different hospital for an emergency bone scan. I could focus on her illness instead of worrying about missing that critical expert's deposition. When David came home stressed and unhappy from a challenging day at the office, I was less inclined to explain why my day was far worse than his. Instead I was more inclined to simply give him a back rub. When I missed the satisfaction of winning a case I taught myself to find success in different ways. Instead of devising the winning argument in a multi-million dollar lawsuit, I was devising adorable bulletin boards featuring the unique art work of children. I created imaginative costumes for school plays and extravagant spook houses sure to delight even the most apathetic of 4th graders. Instead of leaning in to my job, I leaned into my family.

Over the last twenty years I have struggled to understand why it was so hard to quit my job. Why did I feel like such a failure? Didn't I know how rewarding it would be to build scenery for the 4th grade play? Why could other women do it all and I couldn't? Didn't I know that when Katie was playing basketball in college I would want to travel every weekend to see her games? I couldn't take three-day-weekends throughout basketball season and manage an active trial docket. Wouldn't everyone choose to quit work if they could? The answers remained elusive until I considered that the image of mothers has evolved over the course of my life.

B. The Price of "Having it All"

Julia Ormond in the movie Sabrina explained that: "More isn't necessarily better; it's just more." [3] Gandhi gave similar advice when he said: "There is more to life than increasing its speed." [4] The lesson for women is that you make yourself miserable by trying to do all the things that bring you joy at the same time. It's like the child whose favorite candy is Reese's Peanut Butter Cups. When that child went trick-or-treating, she might have been elated to find 15 Reese's in her bag. The dilemma she faced was whether to enjoy eating all of them that night, or to enjoy one cup every day. If she ate them all at once she'd feel horrible, throw up, and be incapacitated for the rest of the evening. However, if she ate only one each day she wouldn't get sick. She'd look forward to each day. She'd have a pleasing taste in her mouth every day. She'd be pleasant to be around. She'd accomplish a variety of things each day. Women, like the child with too much candy, must realize that we must be patient. If we try to enjoy everything at once, we might spoil the best part of our all. We must take control of our desire to consume too much, too fast. Even if we have great kids, a terrific job, and a loving husband, the challenge of enjoying all of them at the same time might be too stressful. Even if getting a new home, getting a new better paying job, getting married, and having a baby might each be wonderful events, they are stressful. The combination of all four events at the same time might be the recipe for disaster.

Women now make up over half of the professional and technical workforce in the United States.[5] Women tend to feel more stressed at work than their male counter-parts.[6] Unfortunately, women also feel stressed at home, at higher rates than men. Women still do the lion's share of housework despite increasing numbers of women working outside the home. Women spend three times as long as their male counterparts on domestic chores. One in five men admit that they do nothing around the house. The average woman spends 17 hours each week on household chores compared to less than 6 hours spent by men.[7] Therefore it is not surprising that "stress" is on the rise in women. Married women feel even more stress than single women. Women are more likely than men to report that their stress levels are getting worse.

Recent research on women who *have it all* documents that: [8]

- Women are more likely than men (28% vs. 20%) to report "having a great deal of stress" in their life.

- Only 35% of women report success in their efforts to manage stress (compared with 69% who believe this is important).

- Women (49%) more often than men (39%) reported that their stress has increased over the past five years.

- Married women report higher levels of stress than single women. Single women (22%) report that they have experienced a "great deal of stress in the previous month. In answer to the same question, more married women (33%) reported a great deal of stress. Similarly, more married women report that their stress has increased over the past five years. Single women are also more likely than married women to say they feel they are doing enough to manage their stress.

- Married women are more likely than single women to report that they have experienced the following due to stress in the past month:

  - feeling as though they could cry (54% vs. 33%);

  - feeling irritable or angry (52% vs. 38%);

  - having headaches (48% vs. 33%); and

  - experiencing fatigue (47% vs. 35%).

- Women are more likely than men to say that having a good relationship with their families is important to them (84% vs. 74%).

- Nearly half of all women (49%) say they have lain awake at night in the past month because of stress. Yet the majority of men (58%) and women (75%) identify getting enough sleep to be "extremely" or "very" important.

- Only 33% of women report being successful in their efforts to get enough sleep.

- Only 36% of women report success in their efforts to eat healthy (compared with 64% who believe this is important).

- Only 29% of women are successful in their efforts to be physically active (compared with 54% who believe it is important).

While these statistics are important for all women, the most revealing information is the heightened levels of stress internalized by married women. The clear implication is that stress levels in women are highest when we are trying to balance a marriage, children, professional success and domestic chores. It appears that women view a husband as another person who increases the demands on them, instead of a person to help share the load. It is not clear that men actually expect a woman to do it all. Husbands may simply be happy that we are willing to concurrently handle all the domestic chores and pursue a career. Who would object if a partner took responsibility for all the annoying domestic chores, while contributing significantly to the financial stability of the family?

Stress Induced Illness and Diseases are on the Rise in Women

Illnesses that are stress-related occur nearly twice as often for women as men. Job stress has been linked to heart disease, muscle/bone disorders, depression, and burnout.[9] Women who have experienced stressful events are much more likely to develop dementia in later life.[10] Scientists have also identified increase in women's stress levels to be related to an increase in autoimmune diseases.[11] For example, women develop Multiple Sclerosis, an autoimmune disease, almost twice as often as men. Nobody has ever told me that I have M.S. as a result of trying to have it all. However, my diagnosis of M.S. was made within 2 years of the day that I quit my job due to overwhelming stress. Isn't it ironic that the salutation for a liberated female is Ms.? It is tragic that a woman who is miserable due to stress in her life is ashamed to opt out of her job. If she leaves because of a heart attack, she is pitied. If she is smart enough to quit before she has the heart attack, she is labeled a "quitter" and "too weak" to handle her job.

Heart disease is accelerated and intensified by stress.[12] The impact on women of stress is unmistakable. One in four women will die of heart disease.[13] Famous female celebrities have suffered from heart disease, including Rosie O'Donnell, Star Jones, Barbara Walters, Toni Braxton, Miley Cyrus, Jennie Garth, and Elizabeth Taylor. [14] The desire to have it all and the resulting increase in stress have been directly linked to more heart disease in women. Women are more likely than men to have microvasculature disease, which leads to heart attacks. Death rates from heart disease have dropped in the last 30 years due to advancements in medical science. However, the rate of heart disease in women isn't dropping as fast as it is in men. In addition women are more likely than men to suffer from a medical condition called BHS, or stress-induced cardio-myopathy. BHS is a condition resulting from "extreme emotional stress" which can lead to severe heart muscle failure.[15] As stress in a woman's life increases, so does her chance of developing heart disease.

The American Heart Association reports that heart disease is the #1 killer of women, resulting in the death of a woman every minute. More importantly, heart disease in women is increasing. In 1997 heart disease claimed the lives of 30% of women who died. By 2009, that percentage had increased to 54%. Heart disease claims the lives of more women than the combined total of all deaths from all forms of cancer, chronic lower respiratory disease, Alzheimer's, and accidents.[16] The type of profession of a woman may also exacerbate her potential for heart attack. Women who reported having highly demanding jobs were nearly twice as likely (88%) to have a heart attack than women who didn't have such stressful jobs. The women with stressful jobs were also 43% more likely to need a bypass procedure. Overall, women have a 40% greater risk of heart disease if their job is "high-strain."[17]

Stress has been shown to result in bad habits including smoking, eating an unhealthy diet, and failure to exercise. Stress triggers reduced blood flow to the heart, promotes heart irregularities, and increases the likelihood of blood clotting. If a woman already has atherosclerosis or high blood pressure, stress can make these conditions worse. [18] Thus the increase in heart disease in women can be directly linked to trying to do too much at the same time.

The increase in pathology in women caused by stress is likely also a significant factor in the death of women. A 2012 report found that women were dying younger than we were 10 years ago! Women in 737 counties across America realized a DECLINE in life expectancy. That is the largest decline in life expectancy since the Spanish Flu epidemic of 1918.[19]

Not surprisingly, quality of life for women has declined as well. More than ever before, women are binge drinking (defined by five or more drinks at a single occasion) and abusing illegal substances.[20] More women are obese, have diabetes, suffer from high blood pressure, and are testing positive for Chlamydia, a sexually transmitted disease.[21] Unbearable levels of stress and anxiety have been identified as a contributing cause of this increase in pathology of women. "It is ludicrous to admonish them (women) for not exercising, cooking healthy meals, taking supplements, or chilling out at the spa when they can barely put food on the table. Far too many women today are living on the edge of economic and psychological survival."[22] By 2008, 23% of women, ages 40–59 years, were taking antidepressants.[23] Women experience twice the rate of depression as men, regardless of race or ethnic background. An estimated one in eight women will experience "major depression" in her lifetime.[24]

Female Prison Population Is Increasing

The prison population of women is rapidly increasing, at 1.5 times the rate of men.[25] The number of women arrested for DUI is just one indicator of the problem. Between 1998 and 2007 the number of women arrested for DUI **increased by 28.8%.** During the same period the number of men arrested for DUI **declined by 7.5%.**[26] That represents a gender gap of 36.3% in a nine year period of time. The next question must be why? This increase in DUI arrests for women has been linked to stress at home and work. Depression, anxiety and biological issues may each have an impact. When a man and woman, of the same weight, have the same amount of alcohol, the woman will have a higher blood-alcohol level. Women metabolize alcohol slower than men.[27]

Women Need More Sleep

Women are profoundly affected by lack of sleep, and more so than men.[28] Women who sleep poorly, or not enough, are more likely to have heart disease, type-two diabetes, hypertension, and psychosocial distress. Scientists report that sleep-deprived women tend to wake up "more miserable than men."[29] What the scientists can't know is whether the women in the study are more miserable than men simply because they are sleeping less, or whether the reasons that they are sleeping less is causing them to be miserable. Maybe having it all is so hard because getting less sleep is only one of many reasons we are constantly exhausted.[30]

The average adult, age 25-55, needs 8 hours of sleep. When people are sleep deprived, bad things happen. Sleep deprivation played a role in the 1989 Exxon-Valdez oil spill, the Challenger space shuttle disaster, and the Chernobyl nuclear accident.[31] If having it all means that we expose ourselves to a nuclear accident, then we should probably settle for more happiness, more sleep, and a little less all. Sometimes the smarter, safer, more satisfying course is to settle for less all. Women should stop talking about opting out and instead, we should be talking about happily ever after. If we fall asleep while trying to master the third wave of feminism, we'll drown.

Professional Women are Losing Custody

If a woman has a child, the presumption is that she wanted to be a mother. Surely if she went through nine months of pregnancy, she wanted to spend time with her child. If the mother is a professional, working outside the home during the day, then nights and weekends with the child (children) become even more vital to the mother's ability to enjoy her children. For most women, having a baby and pursuing a career, will inevitably result in stress caused by the conflicting demands of each. If the father volunteers to stay at home to care for the child, the mother may be relieved to have a solution to the challenge of balancing a career and a family. However that professional woman might be surprised several years later if things didn't turn out as anticipated. Her husband will necessarily become dependent on her financial support. Her husband might have the time to have an affair. What if the couple divorces? In a divorce proceeding, the court would likely award custody to the parent who spent the most time with the children, the husband. The wife would likely be required to pay the husband child support and alimony. The reality is that this situation happens with alarming frequency.[32] In 2009, there were over 2 million women in the United States who were non-custodial parents.[33]

Today it seems a commonly accepted principle that women are capable of having it all, but we don't have enough hours in a day to do it all. Ironically, our new problem is that we risk losing it all if we try to do too much at the same time. Like the old problem that had no name, our new problem is also "taking a far greater toll on the physical and mental health of our country than any known disease." [34] Instead of feeling empowered we are feeling tired. Instead of feeling successful at home and work, we are feeling frustrated that there is never enough time to do all that needs to be accomplished personally and professionally. We are competing with men in the work place who don't have similar responsibilities in their homes. Professional women are competing in their personal lives with mothers who stay at home, who don't have the distractions and stress of demanding professions. Whether by divorce, loss of custody, depression, physical illness, addiction, mental illness, and/or sleep deprivation, the new problem for women is the danger of losing it all.

"When men are oppressed,
it's a tragedy.
When women are oppressed
it's a tradition."

— Letty Cottin Pogrebin
[35]

CHAPTER II. TRADITIONAL ROLES OF WOMEN

Understanding how we arrived at this point in our evolution is a critical starting point for every woman hoping to achieve happiness. In 1975 I graduated high school. The United Nations identified 1975 as the year of the woman. Over One Thousand delegates attended the first World Conference on Women, held in Mexico City that year. Participants at the conference worked to enhance the legal recognition of women and promote the role of women around the world. The United Nations chose a song by Helen Reddy, *I am Woman*, as the theme song for the Year of the Woman.[b]

Ms. Reddy's song became a symbol of female empowerment and the enduring anthem for the women's liberation movement. The opening stanza of *I am Woman* uses the powerful image of a tiger roaring:

> "I am woman, hear me roar
> In numbers too big to ignore
> And I know too much to go back an' pretending
> 'Cause I've heard it all before
> And I've been down there on the floor
> No one's ever gonna keep me down again
>
> Yes I am wise
> But it is wisdom for the pain
> Yes I paid the price
> But look, how much I gained
> If I have to
> I can do anything
> I am strong
> I am invincible
> I am woman"

Forty years later, in 2015, Katy Perry was selected to perform her hit *Roar* at the Superbowl.[c]

> "You held me down, but I got up (HEY!)
> Already brushing off the dust
> You hear my voice, you hear that sound
> Like thunder gonna shake the ground
> You held me down, but I got up (HEY!)
> Get ready 'cause I've had enough
> I see it all, I see it now

---

[b] https://www.youtube.com/watch?v=MUBnxqEVKlk
[c] https://www.youtube.com/watch?v=18612NwFRA0

[Chorus:]
I got the eye of the tiger, a fighter, dancing through the fire
'Cause I am a champion and you're gonna hear me roar
Louder, louder than a lion
'Cause I am a champion and you're gonna hear me roar
Oh oh oh oh oh oh oh
Oh oh oh oh oh oh oh
Oh oh oh oh oh oh oh
You're gonna hear me rooooooar"

The lyrics and images created by Helen Reddy's hit song *I am Woman*, and Katy Perry's song *Roar*, are strikingly similar. Both involve the image of a powerful roaring feline. Both describe the fact that someone was trying to hold the tiger down, but she refused to be repressed. When I first heard Helen Reddy's song it reminded me of the attempt of my three brothers to "hold me down" and my refusal to be restrained. I wasn't thinking about women who were being treated badly in the work-place. I was focused on the male members of my household who felt that I should be their subordinate.

 In 2013, when Katy Perry's song was released, it didn't occur to young women that the same symbolism of *Roar* had been used for the last forty years. Young women listening to Katy Perry's song weren't alive in 1975. They had no way to fully appreciate the women who paved the way for them. As young women watched the Super Bowl in 2015 they probably didn't think about how remarkable it was that a strong woman was chosen to perform at half-time during the most watched man's sporting event in America. Women born after 1975 wouldn't remember that Super Bowl shows were previously performed by marching bands. The 1975 Super Bowl half-time show was performed by the Grambling State Marching Band, an all-male band.[d]

Just as the Super Bowl, and its half time shows, have evolved, so have the women watching. Helen Reddy was born in 1941. In 1984, when Katy Perry was born, Helen Reddy was 43 years old. I wonder if Helen Reddy has ever heard Katy Perry's song *Roar*? Ms. Reddy is in her '70s now and has never been happier. She is still strong, wise, and invincible.[e]

When I was young I didn't have time to read books about the women's movement. I was devoting 110% of my time to being a part of it. I didn't belong to women's groups focused on empowering women. I was busy attending Law School learning how to empower myself. I didn't go to Law School because I wanted to set an example for other women or to prove that women could appeal to a jury as well as a man. I wanted to become an attorney to improve my

---

[d] https://www.youtube.com/watch?v=fzgZJlg63aI
[e] https://www.youtube.com/watch?v=1xhVxpx7aCQ

personal chances for professional success and achieve fulfillment that I would never find in nursing.

Once in Law School I joined moot court, not because of my gender, but to learn to be the best litigator I could be. I didn't leave nursing because it was a female dominated profession. I left because I couldn't achieve my goals. My goal was not to be rich but to be more financially comfortable than I would have been as a nurse. I didn't expect to be treated with respect simply because I was an attorney. However, I wanted the chance to prove that I was worthy of respect. When I became an instructor of Business Law in my third year of Law School I didn't make more money than I had earned working in the ICU of the local hospital. What attracted me to the job was the sense of independence and respect I enjoyed. Three other law students and I were selected out of 20 who tried-out for 4 positions. Suddenly I was evaluated on an equal footing with men. The standard for measurement was performance in the "try-out" rather than whether we had the preferred reproductive organs. Each of us earned the respect of the Head of the Business School because of our demonstrated mastery of the law and our ability to communicate with students. The other three instructors were men. All the nurses at the hospital were women.

The students in my Business Law class respected me because I was a Third-Year Law Student. That sense of respect came, not because I was a woman, but because of what I had accomplished. The test of my success as a teacher was not based upon my appearance, my gender, or the flaky crust of my cherry pie. I was no longer in a female-dominated job. My students respected me because of my ability to teach rather than because of the curves of my legs. I didn't have to report to a male superior who assumed because I had ovaries that I was less than his equal.

So why was it so important for me to be evaluated for my performance instead of my gender? Maybe I never resolved my need to be treated equal to my three brothers. Even my parents didn't think I could ever accomplish as much as my brothers. My father told me I could do anything if I tried my best. In his mind, what he was trying to do was to inspire me to be a really good teacher or nurse. When my mother told me to practice my trumpet every day, she hoped I'd be good enough to play in the band. She never expected me to be the first-chair in a section of 22 boys. My parents didn't think that I was weak, stupid, uneducated, or that I lacked motivation. They simply forgot to tell me that I was supposed to be less intelligent, to have less education, or to be less motivated than my brothers.

A. Miss America

What is a training bra anyway? Is the idea that if young girls wear them they will train girls' breasts to grow bigger and more voluptuous? Is the idea that those minimally enlarged nipples need to be trained to stand erect? The truth is that in 1968, at 11 years old, I had no need for any kind of a bra. I just wished that I did. The absence of a bra strap across my back was like an acknowledgement to the world that there was nothing to train. I wished I had something in need of being pushed-up. Boys didn't even fantasize about putting their hand up my shirt. Rubbing my chest would have been more like giving me a back rub…without the shoulder blades.

Miss America had wonderfully perky breasts. Even in her swimsuit the weight of those pendulous breasts never caused them to sag. It was a miracle of modern science that they remained parallel to the ground, no matter the cup size or girth. Amazingly, there was no evidence of nipples. Was it a marvel of evolution that women could grow stupendous breasts that were void of nipples? I knew the chances of ever having such spectacular breasts, like those of the women in the pageants, was simply a fantasy. However having breasts large enough to require a bra was a goal that seemed reasonably attainable.

To be a success, Miss America needed other qualities. She had to have a tiny waist. Mine at 11 was already as large as those of the 18-year-old contestants. Miss America had to have talent. She could sing, play the flute, or perform gymnastics. When I sang people gave their condolences to my parents. The only dance I knew was the Hokey Pokey. The only gymnastic feat I had mastered was a forward roll. My gym teacher gave me an "E" for effort as she was impressed that I tried so hard to stay on the mat. My size 9 feet would have been considered an asset for some types of monkeys and sloths, but they didn't seem particularly helpful to me. Those two-inch toes could curl around the narrowest of balance beams. Big feet are an asset when trying to stick a landing. However before you can stick a landing you have to be fast enough and strong enough to mount the uneven bars, the beam, or the vault. I could handle the dismount, which could be accomplished by falling. However, the mount was a greater challenge. My only gymnastics event would have been the floor exercise. On the floor exercise I could perform my signature move, a somersault. The added benefit of floor exercise is that when I fell, the distance traveled wasn't quite so far. By the 8th grade I had perfected both the lateral jump and the somersault.

Since I couldn't sing or perform gymnastics, if I aspired to one day be chosen as Miss America my only option was to play a musical instrument. Mom tried to get me to play the flute. Her choice of instruments would have allowed me to compete in a pageant one day. The flute was a dainty, feminine instrument. The flute would satisfy the desired image for Miss America. That shiny, delicate, woodwind instrument had no spit valve. A flautist could showcase the newest shade of lip gloss and matching nail polish, while sending soothing waves of soft whimsical melodies through the airwaves. Saliva never drips from the end of a flute.

Being the savvy intellect that I was, I chose the trumpet over the flute. Any one-eyed moron could see that the flute had many more fingering configurations than the trumpet which had only three valves. Trumpets often take the lead in the band. Most trumpet players wouldn't be caught dead with nail polish on their rugged, masculine fingers. Trumpets are bold, brass instruments, with spit valves to prevent that annoying gurgling of saliva. Emptying a spit valve onto the runway of the pageant might cause a contestant to slip and fall. A trumpet would be offensive to the tender sensibilities of the contestants. The trumpet fit my personality. While the trumpet was capable of creating soothing melodic refrains, it could also be harsh, assertive, and dominant. It was of no consequence to me that all the other trumpet players were boys. I did wonder why so many girls chose not to play the trumpet.

I didn't know when making my selection of instruments that girls were supposed to play only woodwind instruments. The bold, brass, bigger instruments were supposed to be played by boys who were bolder, bigger, and stronger than girls. Boys weren't afraid to take the lead. The trumpet had three valves so I presumed it was the easiest instrument to play. I wasn't trying to make a feminist statement. I made my choice of the trumpet for the wrong reason; thinking it would be easiest to play. I made my choice to continue playing the trumpet into college for the right reason; I loved it. Neither had anything to do with my perception of feminism. Both had to do with what seemed logical at the time.

For weeks before the Miss America Pageant every year I would carefully plan my schedule so that all homework and chores would be completed by that magical night. I learned about each contestant. I knew who was favored to win. I picked my top 5 contestants and cheered them on during the 3 hour television spectacle. By my 11th birthday our family had a color television. The swim suit competition was even more fun to watch due to the multitude of colors of the swim suits that covered those phenomenal bodies. With only one television in the house it was imperative that I secure viewing rights for the evening. Fortunately, my mom had one rule about the television. If a child started watching a show, they had the uncontestable right to finish watching that show before any other child could change the channel. Of course that rule only applied to children. The selection of shows by the parents always took precedence over that of the children.

Fortunately for me in 1968 on the evening of the Miss America Pageant my parents were going out. Thus creating a distraction for my parents was unnecessary. Strategically planning for my evening of pageantry, I made sure that my older brother was eating cake at the commencement of the Pageant. I turned on the television one minute before the introduction by the host, Bert Parks.[f]

Realizing that the music from the opening ceremony might alert Frank to his fate, I adjusted the volume to a level that was almost inaudible. As I strained to hear the sounds of the pageant, sitting against the 36" console cabinet of the Motorola, it never occurred to me that there would come a day when televisions wouldn't need picture tubes, the channels would be changed remotely, or that most women wouldn't care which state Miss America called home.

Just as the opening ceremony concluded, Frank took the last bite out of his Chocolate Bundt Cake. Until that moment, Frank had been oblivious to the rest of the world, consumed with gastronomic satisfaction. As the pleasing flavor of cake dissipated he re-directed his focus to the source of all things entertaining, the television. As Frank entered the den, Miss Colorado was just being introduced. The realization that a beauty pageant might consume his entire evening was enough to cause the Bundt cake to re-emerge in his throat. He didn't care who was crowned the "Queen of Femininity." Without thinking he lunged at the channel dial. In his deep, brusque voice he yelled "NO WAY!" My older, bigger brother, would not tolerate being tortured for three painful hours of any beauty pageant. It didn't matter to him that the rules of the house were on my side. Frank was older, stronger, and bigger than I. He changed the channel. Try as I might, I was totally unable to return the television to its rightful channel. I was outraged that the strength of a boy was being used to unjustly impose his will on me. He was breaking the rules! He knew it. There was nothing I could do to get the channel back to the pageant. I yelled and screamed defiantly, without effect.

This was war! Realizing that I could not win this war through physical means, I considered my options and identified a new goal. I selected the form of retaliation that was sure to be of the greatest annoyance without earning the castigation of my parents. Ironically it was the trumpet. The very instrument that might have prevented me from being a real contender in the Miss America Pageant provided the perfect form of retribution. Nothing irritated Frank more than being forced to endure the blare of my bold, brass horn. Its sounds were inescapable. The wall between my room and Frank's was no match for the blare of my trumpet. Frank felt as if he was listening to the charge of the cavalry each time I sat down to practice. My brother was irritated and annoyed for 30 minutes every day while I practiced. Mom praised my dedication to excellence in trumpet playing by practicing every day. There was no solitude for Frank anywhere in the 2000 square foot house when I was practicing my chosen musical instrument. Try as he might, there was no escaping the "toot, toot, diddle-deda" of my trumpet.

Retrieving my trumpet from the quiet solitude of its case upstairs, I positioned myself next to the television. As Frank tried to enjoy the sounds of WWII

---

[f] https://www.youtube.com/watch?v=V6RJY5Isv4Y

airplanes engaged in a dogfight, I treated him to the most annoying rendition of Stars N' Stripes that I was capable of producing. Because there was no sheet music to assist in this endeavor there were many errors which simply amplified the impact of this form of terrorism. For the next three minutes Frank's eyes remained fixed on the scenes from WWII. Frank didn't look at me. He didn't move. He didn't acknowledge that my trumpet was blaring. Then without warning, without the exchange of typical insults or colorful aspersions highlighting the pimples on my face, or the braces on my teeth, Frank grabbed my arm in his vice-like grip. He dragged me kicking and screaming across the shag carpet, up the stairs, and into my room. The captain's chair in front of my desk was not intended to be used as a tool to hold a young girl captive. Yet Frank determined that it was the perfect place to restrain me. He thwarted my attempts to annoy him by securing me to the chair with a rope. He tied me to the captain's chair. Consumed with anger I wasn't able to focus on the knots he tied in the rope or the location of younger siblings who might have come to my aid. Tears of anger welled up in my eyes as Frank departed my room. He was satisfied that the war with his younger sister had come to an end. He returned to the war on the television. He was comforted to know that he could dominate our entire relationship simply by relying on brute force.

The longer I sat in that chair the more resolute I became to exact my revenge. Rules had been broken. Physical force had been used to inflict the will of the enemy. I would have restitution. Because Frank was not too adept with a rope I knew that I could easily break free. However the dramatic effect on parents walking into the room of their young innocent daughter, only to find her physically restrained, would be the thing about which books would someday be written. The shock and horror of my mother upon her arrival home was epic. Forty years later I would give anything for a picture of mom's clenched teeth as she ascended the stairs and beheld her precious daughter unable to free herself from the ropes of bondage. Frank was grounded for a week. Mom baked me a pound cake. Frank was not allowed to have any. I chose the television shows for the entire week.

I don't know who won the Miss America pageant in 1968. It never occurred to me to even ask. Suddenly it became apparent that men judging women for their attractiveness and talent was highly offensive. The lesson of Frank controlling me and being in charge was intolerable. The realization that I could exact revenge was life changing. Never again did I aspire to become Miss America. From that night on, it was fundamentally important, in all my relationships with the opposite sex, that boys and men respect me. Never again would I put myself in a position where a man could impose his will on me. From that night forward I learned that I should never expect to dominate a man physically. But I could compete on equal footing, or even win, if the weapon of choice was wit. The cunning of my passivity was more powerful than my brother's grip. I possessed a weapon that was much stronger than any known to my brother.

The idea that a male judge in a beauty pageant set the standards for judging a woman was particularly offensive. Even worse was the notion that the most important criteria for judging a woman was her appearance. Worst of all was that for years the only judges of the Miss America pageants were men. Suddenly I realized that I was a woman, living in a man's world. My brother could dominate me with his physical strength. Simultaneously women were entering pageants which contemplated that men determined each woman's self-worth. It was a man who determined which woman would wear the crown. The judges didn't try to determine how intelligent, ambitious, or educated the girls were. Instead the appearance of the women in the swimsuits seemed to tell them all they needed to know. The irony of the pageants was that a scholarship would be awarded to the winner. Academic achievement and intelligence were not part of the criterion for winning the pageant! It was as if a beautiful woman was presumed to be in need of intelligence.

■ ■

A day came when I sold my silver trumpet. I gave it all up but I never gave up my love of music. Just because we move on to another phase of our life, we don't lose the experiences of our past. They become an integral part of who we are.

Babe Ruth is often identified as the best hitter of all time.[36] When Babe Ruth quit playing baseball he didn't stop being regarded as an icon. It didn't change who he was, but only what he was doing at the time. Like Babe Ruth I didn't stop loving music when I quit making music with my trumpet. Just as Babe Ruth never forgot the thrill of hitting a home run, I never forgot the thrill of taking the lead.

When we competed for the first-chair trumpet position, we sat behind a curtain so that the assessment would be objective. If I beat a boy it was because I was simply the better trumpet player. I loved music. I loved being treated equally to my male counterparts. While I always appreciated the beauty of every instrument in the band, the trumpet remains my favorite. No other instrument offers the diversity of the trumpet. Its role may be accompaniment, or it may take the lead. Although the trumpet is usually played by men, a woman can play it just as well. It may be soft and soothing, or bold and brash…much like me. While women were fighting in the 60's for the right to be treated as equal to men under the law, I was fighting a different battle. I didn't worry about earning the same salary as a man, for the same job. I just wanted my brothers to be treated like me and have to do the dishes after dinner. If I performed the best in trumpet tryouts, I expected to be first-chair. If expecting to be treated equal to boys in trumpet try-outs, or washing dishes, caused me to be a feminist, then I surely was. From the first day my brothers thought it wasn't their job to do the dishes, I was a feminist. When I realized that boys thought girls couldn't play the trumpet as well as a boys, I became a feminist.

B. Cinderella

In addition to the Miss America pageant, there was another annual television viewing event that was sacrosanct. Every young girl in America in the 1960's, was glued to her television the magical night of the re-run of Cinderella. In the late 60's and 70's, "DVD" and "VHS" were not yet part of our vocabulary. Watching a movie was limited to those movies that the television Gods deemed to be worthy of reruns. Of course the TV Gods were all men, so Cinderella and the Miss America pageant were the type of shows men thought that women would like to watch repeatedly. Cinderella, not the Disney animated version, but the Rogers and Hammerstein 1965 version with Leslie Ann Warren, epitomized all that I could hope for as a young girl.[37, g] After all, Cinderella had to sweep and dust her house as I did. Cinderella had three ugly step-sisters, and I had three brothers that were equally disgusting. However there were other attributes of Cinderella that I did not possess. Leslie Ann Warren had the voice of a nightingale. I could only carry a tune with my trumpet. Cinderella had a figure that would rival any woman in the Miss America pageant. I didn't own a training bra.

Cinderella was petite and dainty. She wore glass slippers that were slip-ons. I was 5'9" and my size 9 saddle oxford shoes had to be secured with laces. They were black and white. Worst of all they smelled. Cinderella's glass slippers highlighted her soft delicate feet that were only suited for gracefully gliding across a ballroom floor. Cinderella's feet were probably incapable of sweating. My normal feet had roughly 250,000 sweat glands, so sweating half-a-pint-a-day was to be expected.[38] The Prince, in search of his Cinderella, would never have allowed the glass slipper to be exposed to my sweat-laden feet. If my path had crossed his, you can be sure that the Prince would never have offered to let me get close to that dainty glass slipper.

My dirty saddle oxfords were designed to correct flat feet. I wore saddle oxfords for 4 years. My feet are still flat. Every pair of saddle-oxfords I wore retained that putrid smell better than any other type of shoe made. My saddle-oxfords served only one useful purpose. Nothing was more effective at leaving a divot in some obnoxious boy's shin bone than my saddle-oxfords. Cinderella would never have kicked anyone, either because she never experienced anger, or boys were never obnoxious to Cinderella. I'm sure she never owned a pair of saddle-oxfords. She was probably born without sweat glands in her feet.

Prince Charming was tall, dark, and handsome. I think he was Christian because he didn't wear a yamukah. They didn't serve hot dogs the night of the ball. Imagining my Prince Charming, I never considered the possibility that he might not be Christian. When I fantasized about falling in love, and having that love

---

g https://www.youtube.com/watch?v=VtFhREtPdiE

returned, it was the Rogers and Hammerstein Prince Charming that I envisioned. In the movie Prince Charming was handsome. His voice could melt even the coldest of hearts. Whether he was funny, ambitious, loyal, or a good father never occurred to me. At 11 years old, I assumed that when I met the man of my dreams, like Cinderella, I would know immediately. He would immediately fall in love with me, and I with him. It didn't occur to me that on our first date, I would drive the Prince home in my Ford Granada, rather than being whisked off my feet on his tall stallion. I never imagined that my Prince Charming would live in a run-down house, furnished in its entirety with garage sale furnishings that cost a total of $250.00. Instead of whisking me off my feet on his strong steed, David arrived in a Volkswagen Rabbit, occasionally infested with fleas from the dogs that shared his house.

As I watched Cinderella sweep the floor, and dust her house, it never occurred to me that one day I would expect my Prince Charming to help with those mundane tasks. Prince Charming in *Cinderella* was a "prince." His job was to love Cinderella, and to look handsome. Cinderella and Prince Charming never talked about their religious differences. There was never an issue about whether a priest, rabbi, or judge would marry them. Cinderella would have had one grand and glorious wedding and reception, unlike the three receptions I had in order to accommodate friends in Dallas, Jewish family in New York, and Christian family in Oklahoma. Cinderella and Prince Charming never had to struggle with decisions about whether Cinderella should quit her job to care for their children, or who should do the grocery shopping. Cinderella never worried about being treated as an equal to Prince Charming. It was clear that he was royalty, and she was not. She was lucky to have been loved by such a handsome fellow. She would spend the rest of her life trying to find a way to thank the Prince for saving her from a lonely life of cooking and cleaning for others. Cinderella had only beautiful clothes, and a figure to match. If she became the queen one day it would only be because she married the Prince. It was the Prince who elevated Cinderella to the status of royalty. Otherwise she would remain a peasant. In essence Cinderella owed her entire future to Prince Charming. Curiously, both Cinderella and her fairy-god-mother wore crowns. The reason for the crowns was never given. They were probably both award winners in the Miss America pageants at some time in the past.

Nothing about my marriage to David was as expected. He was Jewish. I was Catholic. He came from a family of four. I came from a family of seven. He has brown eyes. Mine are blue. His hair is dark and curly. Mine is straight and auburn. David went to an Ivy League Law School. I went to O.U. David had lived in New York, Dallas, and London. I lived my entire childhood in Tulsa, Oklahoma. David was athletic. I could do a summersault. David was worldly. I was naïve. David had taken a wine tasting class in college. I didn't know the difference between a cheap Chardonnay and an expensive Fume Blanc. David had traveled extensively through Europe, by himself. I had been to San Diego in the back of a station wagon, with my 4 siblings, depositing dirty diapers in road-side restrooms along the way. David had been to the opera in London with his parents, where they had separate restrooms for men and women. I had been to the drive-in movies with my entire family. If we had to use the restroom while at the drive-in, we had a handy plastic potty bowl from our home potty seat, immediately available in the back end of the station wagon.

When Prince Charming arrived at the law firm for his first day of work, he represented the solution to my problem. One week before the Prince began his clerkship. I had accepted a dinner invitation from a young single attorney at the firm for the upcoming Friday. The attorney wanted to bring a date, so I agreed to bring a date too. At the time I had been seeing a guy for over a year, so I thought that getting a date wouldn't be a problem. The only problem was that on the Sunday before the Prince arrived at work, I decided that I would not be sharing any more dinners with that boyfriend. Upon my arrival at work on Monday morning, I realized that I desperately needed a date for the upcoming Friday. I didn't need Prince Charming. I just needed a male escort. Any man would do. It was just about that time that David was being introduced around the firm by his advisor on the first day of his clerkship. Since the new clerk wasn't looking for the owner of some pathetic shoe made of glass, I wasn't worried about appearing bold or aggressive. I was focused on my career as an attorney at the firm. Any responsible associate should be capable of getting a date if she indicated she would bring one.

The minute the introductions of the new summer clerk were over, David found his desk. Just as he was about to sit down in his new chair for the first time, I renewed my welcome and invited him to dinner for the upcoming Friday. It didn't matter that I didn't know the Prince. It didn't matter that he didn't have a car, or whether he could correctly pronounce my name. He was available and would qualify as a date. If I was really lucky, Lowell, the attorney who invited me, would be grateful for the opportunity to entertain two clerks for the price of one. David and I didn't speak the rest of the week. On Friday afternoon, while arranging plans to pick him up in my car, I tactfully reminded him of the correct pronunciation of my name.

Lowell was not even remotely attractive. However he was a brilliant attorney. Although he was young, he already had the hairline of an unemployed Rogaine model. His face would have given nightmares to the most callous of dermatologists. Lowell was awkward in his demeanor and appearance. He spoke as if he had just exited the outhouse of his home in the hills of Tennessee. I wondered what type of woman would be his date.

To my amazement Lowell's date looked like a dancer from the *Climax Strip Club.* Her breasts were as large as twin sea otters. The halter top she was wearing covered only the noses of the otters. Her hair was longer than Ariel's. The bleach required to achieve that degree of blonde could have disinfected an entire public restroom. The cheap gold chains around her neck were only surpassed by those of Mr. T.[h] Worse yet, Miss Teen Carolina[i] surpassed her intellectually by a factor of about 30%. Lowell's challenge was to refrain from drooling over her monstrous breasts. My challenge was not to comment on the amount of liquor she was consuming.

The Prince's reaction to this woman was much like mine, only David seemed unafraid of offending Lowell. Sarcasm, insults, and offensive remarks, at her expense, comprised 98% of David's conversation at dinner. The amazing thing was that Lowell was too focused on the sea otters to notice David's remarks. The female dancer was too ignorant, or drunk, or both, to notice. I think I fell in love with the Prince that night. His remarks conveyed not only his sense of humor, but also his utter disdain for the appearance and lack of intelligence of this woman. Over the next three years I learned that there was much more to love about the Prince than his sense of humor. I knew from the outset that his attraction to a woman would never be based on appearance alone.

David and I couldn't be married in a church or synagogue due to the differences in our religions. Cinderella would have been married in a castle or St. Peter's. David and I were to be married in the bar of a hotel, with the party to immediately follow. Cinderella would have been married at least by a Bishop, and maybe even the Pope himself. David and I were married by a Federal Judge with a sense of humor. Mom decided the day before the wedding that we should use the last unoccupied ballroom in the hotel for the service, instead of the club where the party would be held. Cinderella's church would have been reserved years in advance.

David's parents weren't speaking, so a traditional rehearsal dinner was not even considered. My mother decided we should economize and have the "rehearsal dinner" at my house. Cinderella wouldn't even need a "REHEARSAL" as she would innately know what to do when getting married. It was hard to decide what to cook for the 35 people who came to my small gingerbread-style house. I finally decided on spaghetti. I was worried that the annoying rumble of the dryer and the spin cycle of the washing machine, as I washed my clothes for the honeymoon, might bother some guests. Fortunately my suitcase was still in the attic so it didn't interfere with the traffic flow of the party. Cinderella didn't have to wash her clothes the night before her wedding. Her fairy god-mother waived her wand and Cinderella had brand new clean clothes.

When Cinderella married the Prince, her hair was magically perfect. The hairdresser mom brought from Tulsa did the Queens' hair before Cinderella's. After all they were the queens. The hairdresser didn't start working on my hair until AFTER the service was supposed to begin. At Cinderella's wedding the entire kingdom attended the ceremony, throwing rose petals along the walkway,

---

h https://www.youtube.com/watch?v=7_rBidCkJxo
i https://www.youtube.com/watch?v=lj3iNxZ8Dww

with a glorious sunset in the background. The people attending my wedding were stranded in one of the worst thunderstorms to hit Dallas in 20 years.

Having gotten only a few hours of sleep the night before the wedding, the "honeymoon" suite began to take on more importance; not because of the wild sex we could have after the wedding, but because it had a bed where we could sleep. At 6:00 a.m. on Sunday morning after the wedding my father knocked on the door of the honeymoon suite. He offered David a beer. Dad announced we should leave for the airport. What were we thinking? Cinderella didn't have to arise early the next morning after her wedding. Cinderella didn't have to meet the Prince's side of the family with circles under her eyes. Cinderella probably never had circles under her eyes, even when she stayed up all night. How would the new Catholic bride of David be greeted by the all-Jewish side of the family in New York, the day after the wedding, if she looked like she'd just been run over by one of those stampedes in Texas?

After the reception in Long Island, we rode in Great Uncle John's car headed for the Grand Central Expressway. I questioned the wisdom of having the reception in Long Island. We knew John would drive us back to his apartment in Queens to stay the night. We knew John and Teachers' Scotch were inseparable. We knew John couldn't see well at night, even when sober. We knew all the people honking at us, as we swerved from lane to lane, could see better than John. Cinderella's carriage driver was never allowed to drink, and nobody would dare honk at her. Cinderella wouldn't arise in the morning until she was well rested. She'd be greeted by the Prince and they would enjoy an intimate breakfast together. I'd be awakened at 5:30 am so that the Prince and I could enjoy breakfast at a New York diner with 20 of John's closest friends. What were we thinking?

It was 6:00 p.m. before we arrived at our honeymoon hotel in Montreal, Canada. If Cinderella had just arrived at her hotel for the first real night of her honeymoon, Prince Charming and Cinderella would surely have made passionate love all night and greeted the dawn with wistful glances as they held each other in the quiet solitude of their honeymoon suite. Instead as David and I entered the Hyatt in downtown Montreal, David and I had one objective: SLEEP. Delusional from 8 hours of sleep in the last 72, the line of 80 conventioneers waiting to register at the front desk of the Hyatt didn't even slow me down. We passed their line as if they were non-existent. Very calmly and politely, I explained to the front desk clerk that I was a new bride and that I was about to have a nervous breakdown in her lobby. I calmly explained that if somebody didn't get me to a room immediately, an exorcism might be necessary. Whether it was the tremor in my voice, the circles around my eyes, or the unavailability of the exorcist, the saint behind the desk gave us the key to room 637, and said she'd get our credit card later. I couldn't get on my Christian Dior baby-doll nighty fast enough. Cinderella and Prince Charming would have made time for a romantic dinner before retiring to the honeymoon suite. David and I were too tired to even eat.

There is an interval between sleep and waking where your brain isn't sure if you are dreaming or actually experiencing an event in real time. I found myself in just such a predicament at about 2:00 a.m. that next morning. As a child I had a recurring dream, facilitated by my father's obsession with John Wayne. Over and over I dreamed that Indians were circling my house, waiving spears and tomahawks in the air, whooping it up, as they planned to set fire to my house. It had been at least 10 years since I stopped having that dream. It had been at least 10 years since I stopped calling Native Americans, Indians. However, at 2:00 a.m. on my honeymoon, in Montreal, Canada, I thought the Indians had returned to set fire to my house. "Whoo-whoo-whoo, whoo-whoo-whoo" was the chant echoing through my room. Drums and rattles were synchronized with the chants of what sounded like hundreds of Indians. It had to be a dream! Montreal Canada wasn't inhabited by Indians. I was far from the plains of Oklahoma. John Wayne was dead. Yet the more I awoke, the more real the war whoops seemed. Prince Charming seemed to be unaffected. He, like John Wayne, was unafraid of the savages that were about to set fire to our hotel room. Shaking the Prince from his slumber, I asked in a panic if he too heard the Indians. As the Prince rolled over he simply pulled the pillow over his head and moaned.

I was a damsel in distress, but there was nobody interested in rescuing me. My adrenalin was running and my heart was pounding. Now I was wide awake. The chants were real. They were coming from directly outside our hotel room door. Somebody had the nerve to wake Cinderella at 2:00 a.m., on her honeymoon night when sleep was more important than sex! Without bothering to reach for my glasses, or cover my bare legs, I shot out of bed and flung the door open. "What the hell is going on out here!" were the words that erupted. I was outraged! Even without my glasses, I could see the images of the back-sides of at least 20 Indians kneeling on the floor, dressed only in war paint, loin cloths, and head-dresses. These were the same conventioneers who previously stood quietly in line hours ago. Their serenade of my neighbor across the hall came to an abrupt halt as they each turned to view the indignant Princess, clad in nothing but a very short nighty. Their drums went silent. Their mouths dropped opened. Their eyes widened. Their chants were replaced with drunken laughter. Realizing that I was not in my business suit, or my Cinderella Ballroom dress, and realizing that there was a reason civilized men don't wear loin cloths, I slammed the door shut. Still outraged I grabbed the phone to share my indignation with the front desk. Surely they would be mortified that Cinderella had been awakened from her slumber.

"I know you are not going to believe this, but there are Indians outside our door!" I exclaimed. Instead of disbelief, the front desk clerk shouted "WHAT!!! They're on the sixth floor TOO?!!"

The perfect wedding came to a perfect conclusion as we arrived home after the reception in New York, our reception in Tulsa, and honeymoon complete with conventioneers in loin cloths in Canada. As we pulled in the driveway of our home in Dallas, we were greeted by the rental car of David's new business partner who had already arrived to live with us. I knew that David and Bob planned to start their new business after our wedding. I just didn't realize that it would be IMMEDIATELY after the wedding. I did realize that it made no sense for Bob to have to pay rent when he wasn't married. He didn't have a spouse to support him. Bob didn't have income to justify paying rent. After all Cinderella was in no position to make demands on the Prince. The Prince had just made Cinderella his wife, promising to love her for richer or poorer, in sickness and in health. The Prince had saved Cinderella from cleaning houses for the rest of her life. Besides, our house had three bedrooms so we still had an extra even with Bob there. We only had one bathroom. However, I had experience sharing a bathroom with filthy brothers, so Bob was a step up. David and Bob had saved money for their business for the last two years, so why would I expect Bob to waste that hard-earned money on something as trivial as rent? I was making enough as an attorney to make the mortgage payments and buy the groceries for all three of us, so why wouldn't I? We didn't expect the new business to turn a profit for some time, so all three of us had to have reasonable expectations for the immediate future.

What seemed logical at the time probably today seems inconsistent with the image of a liberated young woman. Many people thought I was a fool for supporting David and his partner. Bob always respected me and valued my advice. Thirty years later, David and Bob are still partners. Even though both are attorneys, they never found it necessary to draft a partnership agreement. When Bob comes to town, he still stays with us. He still appreciates my counsel. The only difference is that now Bob's in the guest room with his own bathroom. He has never forgotten that I'm an attorney. He never asks when I'm going back to work.

My wedding and life were dramatically different than Cinderella's. My Prince and his partner were dependent on me for support as they began their careers as entrepreneurs. We didn't live in a castle. I didn't ride in a carriage. David was not a stay-at-home dad, but I provided the financial support for our family. When he quit his job as an attorney to start his own business, nobody thought less of him. If anything, business acquaintances envied him because he chose to attempt that which they were afraid to try. Nobody asked him how he and Bob could give it all up. Nobody asked David if, now that he was married, he was really quitting to start a family? Nobody cautioned him about the dangers of becoming dependent on his wife for support. David was perceived at the time to be bold, aggressive, and ambitious. He could always go back to practicing law, but as a young entrepreneur, the sky was the limit. Nobody thought David was worried about not making partner. When he left the practice of law he was respected more than ever.

Ten years later when I quit my job as an attorney to stay at home with my three young children, people were shocked that I would give it all up. Other women cautioned me about becoming financially dependent on my husband. The perception of most was that I was making the biggest mistake of my life. Now that I had evolved, and no longer desired to be Miss America, or Cinderella, and was self-sufficient, why would I let any man ever cause me to be dependent again? The reality was that I had gained independence and self-confidence by achieving the status of Senior Partner. No matter the future, I would never be dependent on my husband. There is a difference between dependency and support. Having established myself as a competent attorney I could always return to the practice of law to make a living. While I wouldn't be able to step into the same position at the same firm, I would always be in a position to support myself and my children if the need should arise. Thus I was not dependent. After I quit, David's income simply paid the bills, as mine had when we were first married. I didn't opt to stay at home to clean the bathrooms, do the laundry, and sweep the floors. If that had been the tradeoff for quitting my job, I wouldn't have traded.

What I was trading was more professional success for personal success. I traded the fame and fortune of further success in the court room to increase the chance that my children would experience success in life, and that my husband and I would have success in our marriage. I knew that disappointment might still accompany the raising of children. Yet I also knew that spending more time with my children, and devoting the majority of my time to raising the next generation of Litmans, would give me the best chance of having healthy, happy, children. There was no guarantee that Prince Charming and I would celebrate our 50th anniversary, but I knew if my level of resentment continued, David would surely have become my First Husband. If our family was to survive, change was essential.

The Prince was happy with the arrangement. I was working, bringing home a significant six figure salary. Simultaneously, I was caring for the children. Most days I made dinner for the Prince. The nanny was my responsibility. The housekeeper was my responsibility. If the air conditioner broke, I'd take care of it. If one of the kids had an ear infection it was my job to take them to the doctor, get the medicine from the pharmacy, and ensure that the medicine was taken at the appropriate times during the day and night. If someone needed a Halloween costume, it was my job to identify the appropriate costume and either acquire it or sew it. If any of the kids had a birthday party to attend, it was my responsibility to ensure that they made it to the appropriate place, at the appropriate time, on the appropriate date, bringing an appropriate gift. If one of the kids had a birthday coming up, it was my job to plan the event, send out the invitations, arrange for the food, acquire the party favors, and teach the kids about thank you notes. If the child received an article of clothing from a well-meaning relative, it was my job to teach the child about the importance of gratitude, even when they were not grateful.

Each of the three kids played a musical instrument at some point during their formative years. It was my job to help them identify their chosen instrument, pick out the instrument, locate and hire someone to give lessons, harass the child about practicing, transport them to their lessons, and endure the wrath of the teacher when the child had not practiced as instructed. Fortunately for me, Katie was the only child that took dance lessons. She only had recitals twice each year. Katie also did gymnastics, played soccer, volleyball, basketball, softball, and swam on a swim team. Zach played basketball and soccer. Anna played soccer, volleyball, and basketball. It was my job to get each signed up on the team with their friends, make sure they had the appropriate uniforms and equipment, transport them to practices, keep up with game schedules and snack schedules, hire a coach, and acquire the coach's gift to be given at the end of the season party, …which we hosted.

Summer schedules for three kids were more complicated than college algebra. Not only did I have to prioritize their must-have-camps, but I had to arrange to get them signed up before each camp filled up. In planning the camps located around the Dallas Metroplex, I had to make sure that I could transport each child to their camp at the assigned time, and that the pickup times didn't conflict.

Schools always required check-ups before each year began. The dentist insisted on seeing each child twice every year. All three had braces which required monthly visits to the orthodontist. Swimming lessons were not optional for any child living in Texas. Zach worked five days a week during the summers for three years due to his severe dyslexia. Katie was only somewhat dyslexic, so she only had to work with a tutor three days a week during the summer. Each child had their tonsils and wisdom teeth removed. Each child worked with a tutor to better prepare for standardized college admissions tests. It always amazed me when people at cocktail parties asked what I did to fill my days as a mother. It was as if they imagined me wondering around the house hoping that a solicitor would call to brighten my day.

It was clear to me that Prince Charming was not the type of royalty that would ever make time to perform these mundane tasks of child rearing. If my choice had been to continue trying to do it all, I would have become more resentful, and more stressed. I would feel like a failure as an attorney and mother. I would have disappointed myself by not having enough time to do all that I perceived needed to be done for my children, and for my clients. Without doubt, my resentment directed toward the Prince would have become destructive to our marriage. Instead of living in the palace with the little Prince and Princesses, the kids would have had bedrooms in the castle and in my apartment. Instead of sharing a home-cooked meal at the end of the day with my kids and husband, it would have been a takeout meal the kids would eat with the nanny as I sat behind my overflowing desk at the office, getting ready for trial. I could do an acceptable job for my clients and an adequate job as a mother, but inevitably, I'd become an old bitter woman. My life expectancy would probably have been shortened by 10 years if I had continued on the path of self-destruction. The stress of doing in 20 years, what would normally have taken 40 years, was already taking its toll on my health and sanity.

I tried working part time. For me, "working part time" meant working full time, but receiving half the pay. I tried getting the Prince to accept more responsibility with the kids. However the demands on a Prince who was the CEO of a booming dot.com company were worse than those placed on the King during his coronation. After being out of town in a three week trial, leaving my 6 month old baby, 2 ½ year old daughter, and my 5 year old dyslexic son home with the nanny, I came perilously close to losing it all. It became clear that change was imperative for the future of my sanity, my children, and my marriage. I had to reach complete overload before being willing to give it all up. I told the Prince that either he had to help me more with the kids, and responsibilities of running the castle, or I had to quit my job. Initially the Prince perceived that I was just being overly dramatic. Whether it was the tears streaming down my cheeks, the shaking of my hands, or the tremor in my voice, the Prince finally realized that Cinderella's fairy god-mother had left the room. The glass slippers no longer fit. With each child, Cinderella's feet had grown longer and a bone spur was beginning to form from those pumps Cinderella had worn to work over the last 12 years. The handsome horsemen had all turned back to mice, and they were running around the castle scaring the kids. The Prince didn't know a song to sing to me to assuage my resentment, and he didn't have time to write a new one. The Prince knew he'd miss Cinderella's paycheck, but he also knew that the likelihood of his financial success was greater than that of Cinderella. The Prince was smart enough to realize that Cinderella must still love the Prince if she was willing to give up her professional success, for which she had worked so hard, in order to manage the affairs of the kingdom and the royal family.

Twenty years later the Prince is now the King, Cinderella his Queen. All the royal children are in, or graduated from, college and none of them have been thrown in the dungeon. Those out of college are no longer living in the castle and only visit at holiday time instead of when they need more treasure. The King and Queen are still married. The dances they share are slower now than on that magical night they met. Cinderella's M.S slows her down. However the King still holds his Queen close and doesn't mind the slow dances. He now realizes that Cinderella gave him a gift when she quit her job allowing him to pursue his dreams in business while his children were being loved and nurtured as only a parent would do. When the King talks to his kids about their day, they aren't describing their good friends in prison. Instead they share stories about their fellow associates in their offices and laboratories. The girls are each pursuing professional careers, knowing that if they never meet their Prince Charming, or if their fairy godmother develops Alzheimer's, they will still be all right. They know that the King and Queen achieved a balance between work and home life, by the King devoting himself to work, and the Queen devoting herself to the family. The Princesses may make different choices with their Princes, depending on their unique circumstances. Even Princesses and Princes have to sleep, eat, and find some time for each other, or they will be Ex-Princesses and Ex-Princes. Even the Queen of England has only 24 hours in each day.

Given the happiness that leaving my career brought to me, to my kids, and to my Prince, it is hard now to imagine why it was so hard to give it all up. As I reflect on the images of the stereotypical stay-at-home mom, it is no wonder that it was so hard to opt out of my career to stay at home. From the importance of douching with Lysol, to having our existence controlled by a man, like Barbara Eden in *I Dream of Jeanie*, we must understand our past to make strategic choices about the future.

C. Feminine Images

What is a successful woman? "What do you want to be when you grow up?" is the most common question asked of little girls. Perhaps the answers to these questions can best be answered by looking at what little girls were taught and the role models we had growing up. Creative play is something we all did as children. Our parents and teachers encouraged it. We cooked food in the pretend kitchen of our play house. We had tea parties. When mom had a baby we were given a baby doll to imitate what she did when she changed the baby's diaper, fed it a bottle, gave it a bath, or took it for a walk in the stroller.

My favorite doll was Chatty Cathy.[j] She was made of hard plastic, and was the first doll made with a string to pull to make her talk. The holes in her chest were designed to amplify the words she spoke. Those holes were also identical in size to the tip of the water-filled syringe that came with my nurse's kit. When Chatty Cathy got a shot, she must have been allergic to the medicine. From that day forward, when we pulled her string, all she said was "ARRRRGGG," which sounded remarkably similar to heaving. While my brother imitated the doctor, and I imitated the nurse, we ran Chatty Cathy down the hall to a proper receptacle for a person about to vomit. Steve became a doctor. I became a nurse. Chatty Cathy failed to evolve. She was discarded. Instead of limiting my role-playing to a mother feeding her baby, I was also imitating a professional treating a sick patient. My creative play included being a nurse and a mother. Perhaps I should have also pretended to represent Chatty Cathy in a medical malpractice claim, because her doctor and nurse negligently injected her with a toxic substance.

Charles Colton explained that: "Imitation is the sincerest form of flattery."[39] However imitation is much more than "flattery." Imitation is one of the most fundamental ways that humans learn. From babies imitating mom sticking out her tongue, to a child aspiring to follow in a parent's footsteps professionally, every parent watches their daughter imitate what she sees. Modern research shows that imitation is an innate mechanism for learning and communication.[40] It is therefore one of the most important considerations in developmental psychology. Some scientists have gone so far as to state that "all activities of men (and we therefore assume it applies to women too) in society… are in one way or another outcomes of the process of imitation."[41] Learning theorists emphasize that the role of observation, and imitation of role models, are highly significant.[42] Imitation has been identified to be "profoundly important" as a process of development of healthy children.[43]

Consequently, it was logical that I hoped to imitate Cinderella and Miss America as they were obviously successful women. The year of my birth was

------

[j] https://www.youtube.com/watch?v=f-sYQ8_2v_Q

1957. Looking back, the image of a successful woman conveyed in print, cartoons, and television in 1957, is more frightening than Linda Blair on her worst day.[k]

In the 1950's, few women had professions. Millions of women were working outside the home, but their collars were blue instead of white. If they worked outside the home they were relegated to low-paying, menial labor type of jobs. The only women who worked were either women who never married, or women who married a man perceived to be pathetic at supporting his family. Women were depicted as ignorant, uneducated, dependent, and subservient. No wonder it was so hard to opt out of my career! At best I'd only be perceived as ignorant, dependent, and foolish. At worst, I was afraid I might develop those characteristics.

a. Print

Consider the following images found in advertisements from the 1950's. These images conveyed social norms of the day. Women were valuable to society only to the extent they were desirable to men. If a couple was having marital problems, it was presumed that the problems were caused by the woman. Moreover, it was her responsibility to do something to fix her problem. Women were portrayed as being the only gender to have bad breath, body odor, or pungent private parts. If a man might have one of more of these maladies, women were expected not only to tolerate the condition, but be grateful for the companionship of any such odiferous male. The images below depict women as they were viewed by society in the first half of the 20th century. Fortunately women today no longer use Lysol for vaginal douching, and "projection" is associated with televisions, not breasts.

---

[k] https://www.youtube.com/watch?v=8QjrBjdb2T8

How to measure
your wife for
an
ironing table!

46

"PLEASE, DAVE..PLEASE DON'T LET ME BE LOCKED OUT FROM YOU!"

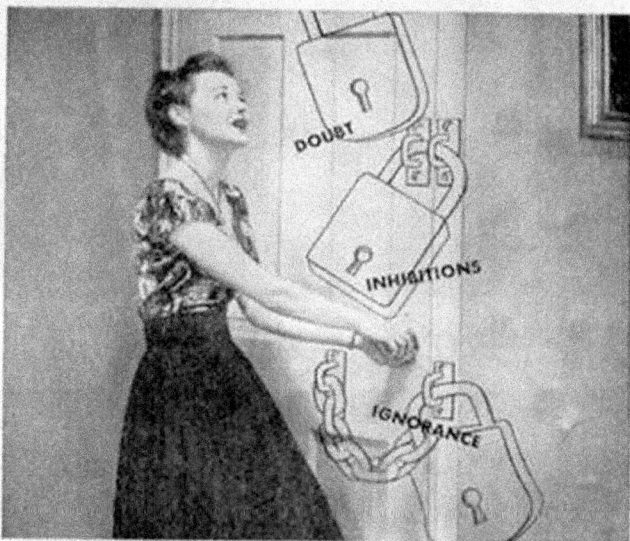

Often a wife fails to realize that doubts due to one intimate neglect shut her out from happy married love

A man marries a woman because he loves her. So instead of blaming him if married love begins to cool, she should question herself. Is she truly trying to keep her husband and herself eager, happy married lovers? One most effective way to safeguard her dainty *feminine allure* is by practicing *complete feminine hygiene* as provided by vaginal douches with a *scientifically correct* preparation like "Lysol." So easy a way to banish the misgivings that often keep married lovers *apart*.

Germs destroyed swiftly

"Lysol" has amazing, *proved* power to kill germ-life on contact . . . truly cleanses the vaginal canal even in the presence of mucous matter. Thus "Lysol" *acts* in a way that makeshifts

like soap, salt or soda *never can*.

Appealing daintiness is assured, because the very source of objectionable odors is eliminated.

Use whenever needed!

Yet gentle, non-caustic "Lysol" *will not harm* delicate tissue. Simple directions give correct douching solution. Many doctors advise their patients to douche regularly with "Lysol" brand disinfectant, just to insure feminine daintiness alone, and to use it as often as necessary. No greasy aftereffect.

For feminine hygiene, three times more women use "Lysol" than any other liquid preparation. No other is more reliable. You, too, can rely on "Lysol" to help protect *your* married happiness . . . keep you desirable!

For complete Feminine Hygiene rely on . . .

"Lysol"
Brand Disinfectant

A Concentrated Germ-Killer

Product of Lehn & Fink

NEW!...FEMININE HYGIENE FACTS!

FREE! New booklet of information by leading gynecological authority. Mail coupon to Lehn & Fink, 192 Bloomfield Avenue, Bloomfield, N. J.

Name_____

Street_____

City_____ State_____

48

Vitamins for pep! PEP for vitamins!*

Sabrina

DEMONSTRATES
THE WORLD'S
FINEST
PROJECTION
EQUIPMENT

.... HER
BELL & HOWELL
HEADLINER
COLOUR SLIDE
PROJECTOR

finer products through IMAGINATION

BELL & HOWELL Headliner Slide Projectors available at all leading Photographic Stores

Sole wholesale distributor: Sixteen Millimetre Australia Pty. Limited.

It's nice to have a girl around the house.

Dacron

Leggs

Sooner or later, your wife will drive home
one of the best reasons for owning a Volkswagen.

Women are soft and gentle, but they hit things.

If your wife hits something in a Volkswagen, it doesn't hurt you very much.

VW parts are easy to replace. And cheap. A fender comes off without dismantling half the car. A new one goes on with just ten bolts. For $24.95, plus labor.

And a VW dealer always has the kind of fender you need. Because that's the one kind he has.

Most other VW parts are interchangeable too. Inside and out. Which means your wife isn't limited to fender smashing. She can jab the hood. Graze the door. Or bump off the bumper.

It may make you furious, but it won't make you poor.

So when your wife goes window-shopping in a Volkswagen, don't worry.

You can conveniently replace anything she uses to stop the car.

Even the brakes.

52

A WIFE CAN BLAME HERSELF IF SHE LOSES LOVE BY GETTING "MIDDLE-AGE" SKIN!
SHE LEARNED HER LESSON
AND, MOTHER, HE NEVER TAKES ME OUT ANY MORE! SOMETIMES I THINK HE'S ASHAMED OF ME!
DO YOU THINK IT COULD BE YOUR COMPLEXION, NELL? YOU USED TO HAVE SUCH A LOVELY SKIN, AND NOW...
YOU MEAN IT'S GROWN SO DRY AND LIFELESS! I KNOW IT, MOTHER, BUT WHAT CAN I DO?
MAYBE YOU'RE USING THE WRONG SOAP! WHY DON'T YOU CHANGE TO PALMOLIVE?
YOU SEE, PALMOLIVE IS MADE WITH OLIVE AND PALM OILS, NATURE'S FINEST BEAUTY AIDS! THAT'S WHY IT'S SO GOOD FOR DRY, LIFELESS SKIN. ITS GENTLE, DIFFERENT LATHER CLEANSES SO THOROUGHLY, SOFTENS AND REFINES SKIN TEXTURE...LEAVES COMPLEXIONS RADIANT!
I'LL CERTAINLY TRY PALMOLIVE!
BOB'S SO PROUD OF ME AGAIN, SINCE I USE ONLY PALMOLIVE, THE SOAP MADE WITH OLIVE OIL TO KEEP SKIN SOFT, SMOOTH, YOUNG!
PALMOLIVE
DR. DAFOE SAYS, "ONLY GENTLE PALMOLIVE FOR THE QUINS!"

If your husband ever finds out

you're not "store-testing" for fresher coffee...

...if he discovers you're
still taking chances
on getting flat, stale coffee
...woe be unto you!
For today
there's a sure
and certain way
to test for freshness
before you buy

Chase &
Sanborn
COFFEE

The Harm · that
WOMEN DO
Themselves

Intimate use of harsh antiseptics *leads to untold damage.* Women now hail a gentle, *safe* means

The use of harsh, powerful antiseptics in connection with feminine hygiene often results in illness that may lead to an operation. Women suffering thus crowd the hospitals.

Will you sooner or later be one of them? Are you going to let half truths or ignorance of proper measure rob you of vitality, health, and peace of mind?

Do you realize that for ordinary hygienic purposes you should use only a gentle, mild antiseptic? One that will not harm delicate tissue. One that will not derange or impair important functions.

Literally thousands of well-informed women have rejected poisonous germicides in favor of Listerine, when a solution for cleansing only is desired. Their choice is based on these advantages of Listerine:

Listerine is first of all safe. It is neither poisonous nor irritating.

Its effect on tissue is soothing and healing.

It possesses great penetrating power.

Diluted with one part water it kills germs. Even when used with five parts of water it inhibits the growth of bacteria, and maintains cleanliness and freshness.

It deodorizes instantly.

Doubtless you have a bottle of Listerine in your medicine cabinet now. Why not try it this new way and see how superior it is! You will be simply delighted.

Send for our FREE BOOKLET OF HYGIENE—tells what to avoid, and do at social affairs. Address, Dept. F.W.2, Lambert Pharmacal Co., St. Louis, Mo.

Listerine for
Feminine Hygiene

b. Television and Movies

As a child, the shows I watched on television were magical. Television was a way to open my eyes to the world. I wasn't interested in watching the news. I much preferred movies and shows about women realizing their dreams of becoming Miss America, or being rescued by their Prince Charming. There was one other annual movie event that was shared by my entire family; the *Wizard of Oz*.

In 1939 Metro-Goldwyn-Mayer was run by men. The musical fantasy film released that year was the *Wizard of Oz*. It had it all…a dog, a witch, Munchkins, flying monkeys, a fairy godmother with a beautiful crown, sparkly red shoes, a beautiful young girl, and a man who could solve all the world's problems. The movie was nominated for six Academy Awards. *The Wizard of Oz* was written, directed, and produced by men. Its music was created by men. Once every year, for the entirety of my childhood, I went running down the hall to the safety of my bed as the wicked witch, snarled at Dorothy in her crackling voice, "I'll get you my pretty!"[1]

Looking back, what were my parents thinking? Did this annual event teach me about the role of women in society? Today I have more questions than answers about this classic.

1. Why was the villain an ugly, green pigmented, frightening woman?

2. Why did Dorothy think that a man would solve her problems?

3. Why were the men in her life in need of a brain, a heart, and courage?

4. Why didn't Dorothy just ask Glenda to send her home?

5. Why were beautiful shoes the secret to Dorothy's success? Was this foreshadowing of things to come in Cinderella?

6. Why did the wicked witch live in a big house? Was the message that only ugly green women could afford a big house without the help of a husband? If you didn't have a husband, did that mean you were like the wicked witch?

7. Why did Dorothy have to get her hair done before meeting the wizard?

---

[1] https://www.youtube.com/watch?v=WnXAl1ntt_4

8. Why did the wicked witch need men to guard her at the castle? Who would bother an ugly, green, frightening woman?

9. Dorothy killed one of the bad witches by smashing her with her house. Dorothy killed the other by hurling hot liquid on her. Why didn't Dorothy get credit for being a bad ass, and being clever enough to defeat her enemies?

10. How did Dorothy's dress stay freshly pressed throughout the tornado and her long road trip?

11. Who would eat the sandwiches in Dorothy's basket after Toto sat on them?

12. What do you do to bricks to make them turn yellow? Did some man think that would be the perfect color to compliment Dorothy's red hot shoes?

13. Did Dorothy have to show her companions the way to meet the Wizard, because the Scarecrow, the Tin Man, and the Lion were unwilling to ask for directions?

14. Why did Glenda wear a crown? Was it the outdated model from last year's pageant?

Television has been the primary mechanism for molding public opinion since the 1950's. Television brings the outside world into our homes. It has reinforced outdated roles for women. June Cleaver in *Leave It to Beaver* made her television debut in 1957, the year of my birth. If June read the *Feminine Mystique,* she never talked about it. Although I was too young to watch anything but re-runs of *Leave It to Beaver,* I did watch Aunt B in the *Andy Griffith Show*. If Aunt B ever worked outside the home, it would have been to volunteer at the church garage sale, or bake sale. Aunt B was much more appealing than the evil green witch in the *Wizard of Oz*. There was one thing the *Wizard of Oz* and the *Andy Griffith Show* had in common. Both lacked a mother figure. Dorothy lived with Auntie Em and Opie lived with Aunt B. No explanation was provided about what happened to the mother of either.

As television evolved, women became more voluptuous but still dependent on men. Television shows of the '60s portrayed women as attractive but not very bright, and certainly not professionals. Ellie in the 1962 *Beverly Hillbillies* was a stupid, beautiful blond. She had a "Grannie" but not a mother.[m]

---

[m] https://www.youtube.com/watch?v=-8jd-3qBi9g

The very next year, in 1963, *Petticoat Junction* joined the list of enlightened entertainment for young girls. This model for modern women depicted young beautiful women who, like Ellie, weren't very bright. The setting of this paragon of feminine virtues was **Hooterville,** in case the audience missed the fact that this town was identified by the Hooters of its occupants. The show opened every week with footage of three young women, apparently bathing in the nude. The opening theme song described the Petticoat Junction as "lots of curves, you bet, and even more when you get, to the Junction." The show had all the essential elements to appeal to men; nude women, breasts and a junction. June Cleaver and Aunt B were associated with apple pie. Ellie and the women of *Petticoat Junction* were associated with sexually desirable women; untouched, beautiful, and not too smart. Ellie, Dorothy, Opie, and the girls at the *Petticoat Junction* each lacked a mother.

I aspired to make pie like Aunt B, look like Ellie, have curves like the women of Petticoat Junction, and to have a cute little dog like Toto. I didn't notice the absence of a mother in any of these shows.

In case that was not sufficiently offensive, or obnoxious, the next in the series of embarrassing role models for women was Eva Gabor in the 1965 television series *Green Acres*. Eva played "Lisa," the ignorant, blond wife who didn't possess even the most basic of domestic skills. To illustrate her ignorance, she was portrayed as a beautiful woman who was incapable of cooking even the most basic of food. Her signature dishes included waterless coffee and inedible hotcakes, better used as gaskets for a truck, or shingles for the roof. The batter doubled as fireplace mortar. She was famous for her hot water soup.[n]

Lisa's idea of washing dishes was to throw them out the window. Even Lisa identified her only talent was imitating Zsa Zsa Gabor, her sister. She was a woman who embarrassed even the most recalcitrant of feminists. I couldn't identify with Lisa, as I already knew how to make pancakes that were fluffy and light. Lisa was a housewife who was too stupid to even cook. Implicit in this character was a complete lack of intelligence. She was portrayed as even stupider than the average woman who could at least perform the most basic of domestic chores. The message was clear: Women who perform cooking and cleaning around the house aren't very bright. Lisa wasn't bright enough to even do that. Because she was attractive, her husband was willing to overlook all other deficiencies. It was clear that intelligence was unnecessary if you were a pretty woman. The message was that the single most important characteristic for a successful woman was her appearance. Intelligence wasn't even a close second.

---

[n] https://www.youtube.com/watch?v=SzGdDqWJcFU

My favorite show of the 1960's was *I Dream of Jeanie*. The first episodes appeared in 1964 when I was an impressionable seven years old. It never occurred to me that Jeanie was symbolic of all women of the time who were dependent on men for their happiness, freedom, and success in life. Jeanie was dependent upon her master, Tony Nelson, for everything in her life outside of her bottle. If her master wanted to imprison Jeanie, he could simply leave the cork in her bottle. Her master was in total control of everything she did. Jeanie didn't wear a crown, but her harem suit resembled the swimsuits worn by the contestants in the Miss America pageants. It was equally believable that Jeanie's goal in life was to make her master happy. If she was lucky he might do her the favor of marrying her. Tony, being an astronaut, was representative of a successful, educated, man. Jeanie was just pretty.

In 1975 I graduated high school. That was also the year of the first season of *Saturday Night Live*. Not only did it provide the gift of comedy, but it was the first show to highlight ordinary looking women in roles equal to men. Laraine Newman, Jane Curtin, and Gilda Radner were just as funny as John Belushi, Dan Aykroyd, Garrett Morris, and Chevy Chase. Gilda Radner was my favorite, but not because she was a woman. She was the funniest of all the comedians. The show represented a breakthrough in the image of women as equal to their male counterparts. It was their talent, not their appearance. SNL was also significant because it aired on Saturday night, the night that most desirable women would be out on a date, rather than at home watching comedy.[o]

It wasn't until the appearance of Marlo Thomas in *That Girl,* and Mary Tyler Moore as Mary Richards, that I began realizing that women could be happy pursuing careers outside the home. When *Charlie's Angels* made its debut in 1976 I was a freshman in college. These women were clever, strong, intelligent, and unafraid of a fight. However it was clear that beauty was still essential to be a successful woman. These beautiful women still took orders from a man. As late as 1976, women in television were portrayed as dependent, unable to think for themselves, and incapable of directing their own affairs.[p]

I graduated college in 1979 and started Law School that fall. In 1980 a commercial appeared that defined the new image of the modern women. Enjoli was advertised as an "8 hour cologne for the 24 hour woman." [q] The sexy blonde woman flaunted her feminine curves as she sang:

> "*I can bring home the bacon, fry it up in a pan, and never let you forget you're a man...*"[44]

---

https://screen.yahoo.com/roseanne-rosannadanna-smoking-000000279.html
[p] https://www.youtube.com/watch?v=PcwPo37Q23w
[q] https://www.youtube.com/watch?v=_Q0P94wyBYk

The message was clear. If you were a real woman and wore the right cologne, you could have it all. If you were a 24 hour woman (i.e. the kind that didn't need sleep) you could have a booming profession, make lots of money, cook fabulous dinners, provide all the love your children needed, have a smokin-hot body, and have great sex with your husband.

The images of American women depicted on television have changed with the times. Thirty years later, nobody notices that some of our favorite comedians are women. We think of Ellen DeGeneres and Tina Fey as comedians rather than female entertainers.

By 2009, 78% of the world's households owned at least one television. In the United States, the numbers were even greater. Television networks in America are the largest and most syndicated in the world. Ninety-seven percent of households in the United States have at least one television, and the majority of houses have more than one. As of 2013 there were an estimated 115.6 million television homes in the United States.[45] Children ages 2-5 watch an estimated 32 hours of television each week. Children ages 6-11 watch an estimated 28 hours per week. Approximately 2/3 of American households have a television on during meals. Most households (51%) have a television on "most of the time." An estimated 71% of 8-18 year olds have their own private television in their room.[46] Entertainment experiences are both "powerful and consequential." People imitate what they see on television.[47]

Today the most powerful people in the television industry are women.[48] While men still work in the industry, there are many women in high places. We see them in programming, sales, executive suites, and often rising faster than men. Because women have gained a presence as television executives, the role of women in television shows is changing. Instead of being portrayed as a piece of ass, women are more often viewed as kicking ass.[49, r] The same is not true of the movie industry. In 2014, women accounted for only 16% of all directors, executive producers, producers, writers, cinematographers, and editors in the 250 top grossing films.[50]

---

[r] https://www.youtube.com/watch?v=HtOKlaXFxwk

c. Walt Disney

While television and movies have evolved, the same evolution is less pronounced in cartoons for young children. Many mothers rely on Walt Disney for wholesome entertainment for their toddlers. What are we teaching our kids? These cartoons portray women as passive, dependent, and submissive to men. Yet it's typically women who buy and play these movies for our little girls. Any woman who might be critical of cartoons like Snow White, Sleeping Beauty, and Cinderella would surely be labeled a radical feminist. Growing up, I didn't perceive these cartoons as offensive. I just thought the women depicted weren't too bright. Why wouldn't you want to look beautiful in your sleep, wear make-up to bed, and wake up to a handsome prince kissing you?

Two years before the creation of the *Wizard of Oz*, Walt Disney created the musical masterpiece *Snow White*. In 1937 *Snow White* was the magical portrayal of a beautiful young virgin who needed to be rescued by a Prince. The villain, a woman, was willing to kill Snow White, the minute Snow White's appearance was more pleasing than her own. The message was clear. Appearance for a woman is the most important attribute. Women are evil and jealous by nature. Men will protect and love women, if they are beautiful and are adept at cooking and cleaning. Men are royalty, handsome and virtuous. What was Disney thinking?

1. Why did it have to be a man who refused to obey the evil Queen's order to kill Snow White? Couldn't her maid-in-waiting have refused to poison Snow White's food?

2. Why was Snow White a peasant and the Prince royalty?

3. When Snow White arrived at the home of the dwarfs, why was she compelled to become their maid? She could have stayed at home all day and painted, sculpted, or run a small business out of her new home. She could have sold feminine hygiene items like Lysol to supplement the family's income.

4. Surely the dwarfs were happy with their level of cleanliness and the quality of their food before Snow White arrived. Wasn't Snow White concerned that she was insulting the dwarfs by suggesting that they weren't doing an adequate job cleaning their own house and cooking their own food?

5. Why was it acceptable for Snow White to live with single men? Was the message that Dopey or small men are not sexually active? Is the implication that a beautiful woman would never be romantically involved with a dwarf?

6. Snow White was portrayed as the helpless woman who was inept at locating food or shelter for herself. However, she was somehow able to find all the cleaning products necessary to make the dwarfs' house sparkle. The dwarfs went to work all day while Snow White stayed home, cooking and cleaning, in her beautiful dress, totally content with her role as a homemaker. The Feminine Mystique had not yet been written, so Snow White didn't even realize that she had a problem.

7. Snow White had no aspirations to work in the mine, or to find diamonds to ensure her financial security and independence. If Snow White had learned to surf the third wave of feminism she would have been able to support the dwarfs while they started a mining company of their own. She would not have been foolish enough to eat food given to her by a stranger. When Prince Charming arrived, she wouldn't have been asleep. Instead she would have arrived home after a long day at work. The Prince would have greeted her with dinner, featuring his new recipe for pot roast. She would have rewarded him with a kiss for being so supportive of her career. As things stood in 1937, if Snow White had taken a job outside the house she would have been paid half the salary of the dwarves even if she did the same job equally well.

8. Why would the Prince presume to kiss a woman asleep, who he'd never met? Why didn't the dwarves protect Sleeping Beauty from this strange man?

9. Was the name "Snow White" chosen to represent virginity?

10. Why would a poison apple make Snow White sleep, instead of killing her?

11. Why was the villain an ugly woman, again?

Fourteen years later in 1950 Disney produced its own animated version of Cinderella. This animated version told the same story as the Rogers and Hammerstein movie. There was a common theme in all animated Disney movies of the time. The protagonist was always a helpless and beautiful virgin. The antagonist was always an evil and vile woman. Cinderella's step mother and the step-sisters, were not just self-absorbed, spoiled, and vengeful. They were all ugly women. The evil step-mother represented the most hideous of villains because she was a mother figure. Cinderella had a magic female helper, her "fairy-god-mother." Her fairy-god-mother represented all that was good in mothers. She was beautiful. She was only interested in rescuing Cinderella. She was dressed in beautiful white clothes, suggestive of virginity. She wore the crown of a princess. Like Snow White, Cinderella was rescued by a handsome prince. This time the prince rescued his future wife, not with a kiss, but with a magical pair of shoes. How could any woman refrain from asking these questions:

1. Why did Cinderella tolerate the abusive step-mother and step-sisters? She should have had the courage to either demand equal treatment, or extricate herself from the abusive environment.

2. Why did the fairy-god-mother use her magical powers to give Cinderella pretty clothes, a fashionable updo, and those smoking-hot glass slippers, instead of a graduate degree and her own business?

3. Why couldn't the prince recognize Cinderella in her raggedy dress?

4. What if one of the step sisters had the same size foot as Cinderella?

5. Why didn't Cinderella drive herself to the ball?

6. Why was Cinderella's talent singing instead of playing the trumpet?

7. Why would Cinderella choose to hang out with rodents?

8. Why would Cinderella want to marry before getting a college degree?

9. Did the Prince have any attributes other than his appearance and the fact that he was royalty? Was he ambitious? Would he do his share around the castle? Did he simply want a wife who would look pretty?

10. After Cinderella gave birth to a couple of royal babies, would she still fit into her magical shoes?

11. Would the Prince still love her if Cinderella developed M.S. and had to walk with a walker? What if she had to trade in her glass slippers for a pair of Dr. Scholl's?

12. Are all ugly women evil? Are all pretty women good?

13. What is this obsession with shoes? Is the message that women care more about their shoes than anything else? How is it that shoes have the magical power to take you home, or transform you into a princess?

In 1959 Disney created another animated masterpiece, Sleeping Beauty. Once again the villain was an evil woman, a Witch by the name of Maleficent. Once again the main character was a beautiful virgin, who went to sleep, only to be awakened by the kiss of a prince. Instead of dwarfs to provide assistance, Sleeping Beauty had three fairy godmothers. Instead of giving her the gift of courage, cunning, and intelligence, they gave her the gifts of beauty, and song. Both characteristics were important for being crowned Miss America, but neither was of any benefit in avoiding the perils of that prickly spindle. The third fairy was about to bestow a gift equally superfluous to survival when the evil witch, Maleficent, appeared and imposed a curse of death. The third fairy godmother, Merryweather, wasn't powerful enough to break the spell. However, she altered the evil spell by transforming Sleeping Beauty's death into a deep sleep from which the beautiful princess could be awakened only by a kiss from her true love. As an adult, watching with my girls, this award-winning master piece of animation, I had to wonder:

1. Why were women always waiting in bed to be rescued by the man of their dreams?

2. If the fairy godmother could transform death into a deep sleep, why couldn't the thing that would trigger the awakening of Sleeping Beauty be a dream of scoring the winning basket in the Final Four, or winning the Nobel Prize for discovering a cure for cancer? Didn't Sleeping Beauty have an alarm feature to wake her on her cell phone?

3. Why didn't Merryweather give Sleeping Beauty the gift of intelligence to avoid spinning wheels altogether?

4. Sleeping Beauty's mother was a stay-at-home mom. What was she doing as Maleficent was casting deadly spells on her only child?

5. Why wasn't it a mother's hug that awakened the Sleeping princess instead of a sloppy kiss from a stranger?

6. Why did the Prince get the magic sword that cut down the thorns around the castle and kill the dragon that was the transformation of the evil Maleficent? Sleeping Beauty could have been a sleep walker; found the sword as women are good finders; killed the evil dragon in a demonstration of her skill and bravery with a sword, and carved up the carcass of the dragon to make Dragon Pot Pie for the Prince's dinner. Sleeping Beauty could have arranged the beautiful flowers that grew from the severed thorn bushes, and bandaged the fingers of any boy playing with the dangerous thorns.

7. Why was Sleeping Beauty sleeping with her clothes on? Shouldn't she have washed her face before bed? Sleeping with make-up on would surely cause her to have royal blemishes, and what prince would want to kiss a sleeping princess with zits?

8.   Why was the villain an ugly woman…again?

The Little Mermaid debuted in 1989. Fifty two years after the creation of *Snow White,* the creators of *The Little Mermaid* made a film that was marketed as a dream come true for a little mermaid named Ariel. In reality it was the wet dream of a young prince named Eric. Of course the villain was an ugly woman, Ursula, the sea witch. Once again the feminine heroine falls in love with a prince and her goal in life is to change her body so she can satisfy the prince. Ariel hopes to make her body worthy of marriage to a prince. Ariel, like Snow White, Sleeping Beauty, and Cinderella had a beautiful voice and a tiny waist. She was like Barbie with a flipper. Instead of waiting in bed for her handsome prince to find her beautiful enough to inspire a kiss, Disney portrayed Ariel as more resourceful. She saved Eric from drowning. But that wasn't the only difference between Ariel and her predecessor female protagonists.

Ariel is more voluptuous than Snow White, Sleeping Beauty, or Cinderella. Ariel's hair is longer, more sensuous, and fire-engine red. Her breasts are bigger and more exposed. Ariel is still dependent on her father, the King of the Ocean. Eric is a prince. Ariel's happiness is totally dependent on being asked by Eric for her hand in marriage. It is clear that it wouldn't be sufficient to love Eric, but she must marry him to be satisfied. She loves the treasures of the humans that include silver and jewels, but Eric is the real prize she seeks. The message is clear: women love royalty and jewels.

Liberated women everywhere were aghast when Ariel transformed from a mermaid into a human. Her tail splits in half. Pieces of her tail become legs which are splayed far apart. What was a fish's tail becomes a woman's naked legs and torso. While Ariel has a swim suit covering her bust there is no covering of her lower half. Instead of simply showing her feet and lower legs, the animators provide a complete side view of the woman Ariel has become. The only thing left to the imagination was whether her pubic hair is the same color as the hair on her head.[s] Questions that seem obvious include:

1.   Why couldn't Eric have turned into a merman and lived happily ever after with Ariel?

2.   Where was Ariel's mother?

3.   Once Ariel becomes a woman why can't she swim to the surface alone? Why does she need the help of a male character?

4.   Why couldn't Eric have loved Ariel for the person she was, instead of needing her to become more like him?

---

[s] https://www.youtube.com/watch?v=HOFZaW92nhA

5. Why did Eric only recognize Ariel by her voice? Why didn't he love Ariel for her character and integrity instead of something as fleeting as a voice? If one day she developed laryngitis would Eric want a divorce?

6. If Eric's dog recognized Ariel why couldn't Eric?

7. Why didn't Ariel get an education before she married? She was only qualified to be a lifeguard. Ariel certainly wouldn't be able to support a family on a lifeguard's salary.

8. Wasn't Ursula sufficiently ugly? Did they have to make her fat too?

In 1991 Disney released *Beauty and the Beast*. Once again the villain is an old ugly woman who cursed the handsome prince, turning him into a beast. The beast was unattractive and enormous. Even when he turned back into a prince he was still jacked. Logical questions arising from this animated love story include:

1. Why would a woman as beautiful as Belle love the Beast? Is the message that a woman will love any man regardless of his appearance? Is the message that even a beautiful woman is lucky to have a big, ugly, abusive, man in her life?

2. Was the name of the protagonist chosen because "Belle" in French means beautiful? Was beauty the most important characteristic for a young woman?

3. When the Beast was abusive to Belle why did she tolerate the abuse?

4. Where was Belle's mother? Why did she fail to teach Belle to leave any man who would be abusive to her?

5. Why did Belle wait to tell the Beast that she loved him until he was dying? The implication is that she was only willing to confess her love when she thought there was no way that she would have to marry the Beast?

6. Why did Belle need a magic mirror to tell her the Beast was dying? Didn't she know that the Beast would be devastated if Belle broke her promise?

7. Since Belle's father had fallen on hard times, how would Belle support herself? Was her only hope of financial security tied to marriage to a beast?

8. Why didn't the Beast fall asleep in a bed and awaken to the kiss of Belle? It was Belle's tears, not her kiss, which transformed the Beast. If we compare this tale to previous Disney movies, Belle should have given the Beast a kiss instead of shedding a tear for him. Is the message that women cry but are not interested in sexual gratification?

The impact of these movies on women and young girls is unmistakable. Some might suggest that Disney became more sensitive to women's issues as time passed. While the characters seemed to adopt a more modern image, the lessons taught were still prehistoric. The lesson of *Beauty and the Beast* was that beautiful women will love the ugliest, abusive man. The lesson of *Aladdin* was that the beautiful women who are royalty will love the poorest of men. When Disney sought to be socially correct with *Mulan* they stopped characterizing women as helpless females. Disney demonstrated that its animators knew that women were capable of kicking ass. However, in order to fight, Mulan had to dress like a man. In case her clothing wasn't sufficiently clear the message expressly conveyed in the lyrics of the movie's theme was "I'll make a man out of you." Why couldn't the message have been "I'll make a strong woman out of you?"[t] Why wasn't Mulan beautiful? Is the image of a beautiful woman necessarily inconsistent with an independent woman who could take care of herself? Why did she end up alone without a prince to marry because she was willing to defend her homeland?

After becoming victorious in war, Mulan was not recognized by her community as a hero. She returned home to her father's house where she was dependent upon him. The war hero was still single when the movie ended. The lesson was obvious. Strong, independent, heroic, women will end up alone, dependent, and burdened with the care of their old sick fathers.

Even in 2015, Disney returned to the old story of Cinderella. Times have changed, both in animation and technology. However the role of the female protagonist and her male champion remains unchanged. Ugly women are portrayed as evil. Beautiful women are the ones who live happily ever after. Skills associated with women who are virtuous continue to be cooking, cleaning, and being kind.[u]

Women born in the 1950's and '60's grew-up with advertisements in magazines and newspapers that depicted women as ignorant, unable to provide for their own support, and completely to blame for rejection by any man. *The Wizard of Oz* and the Disney animated cartoons reinforced the image of a man as the person who could solve all of a woman's problems. Women were identified as

---

[t] https://www.youtube.com/watch?v=ZSS5dEeMX64
[u] https://www.youtube.com/watch?v=20DF6U1HcGQ

either ugly villains, or chaste beautiful girls who could only find happiness through marriage to a handsome prince. The marriage decision was totally dependent upon the prince. If the prince didn't rescue the helpless woman, she was destined to either sleep for the rest of her life, or cook and clean for others. As young girls we played dress up, wearing the clothes of one of the princesses. Even my daughters asked for costumes of Snow White, Cinderella, Sleeping Beauty, or Belle, but not Mulan. I don't even remember Disney selling a Mulan outfit. The image of Miss America and the Disney Princesses directly clashed with a feminist's notion of what a woman could or should be.

Bold, aggressive, insolent, and audacious are all words that describe feminists of the 60's. Those same descriptions would also have been appropriate to describe Betty Friedan. However none of these adjectives would ever be used to describe Dorothy, Snow White, Cinderella, Sleeping Beauty, or the Little Mermaid. As women were fighting for equality, young girls were being taught to be complacent. Women of the 50's and 60's were struggling to break free of these stereotypes which were being marketed as "wholesome family entertainment." Not much has changed in entertainment for young girls.

When women emerged in the 70's and 80's as professionals it was necessary to defy the traditional roles for women. If a woman married a Prince, the woman was perceived to be dependent and weak. If women dressed in colorful clothes, we were perceived as attractive but not serious. If our hair was long, people perceived we were exploiting our sexuality. If we liked to cook or had children, but didn't work outside the home, we were inevitably compared to Elle of the Beverly Hillbillies or Lisa of Green Acres. In order to gain respect women found it necessary to distance themselves from the images of Miss America, Cinderella, and Elle.

Snow White, Cinderella, Sleeping Beauty, and the Little Mermaid had a single goal in life; to marry. The message was unmistakable. If a woman had a job, and planned to continue working, she must not have planned to marry. Either she was uninterested in men, or they were uninterested in her. Marriage was always the preferred path. Was the absence of mothers in all these fantasy worlds, an indication that mothers were not important or that they would abandon their children? Was the fact that the antagonist was always female an indication that evil will always come from women? The stories always ended upon marriage, suggesting that a woman's life was over when she married. There was never an animated feature with a mother protecting her children. There was never a cartoon about a powerful professional woman doing good things for her family or country. There was never a cartoon made where the female character ended up happy who didn't find her true love, marry him, and devote the rest of her life to making him happy.

No wonder feminists disrespected stay-at-home mothers. Women struggled to be viewed as equal to men. The public's image of women was outdated. We were fighting the image of being uneducated, capable of only cooking, cleaning, and raising children. In order for women to become independent, we had to become autonomous and almost defiant. I shouldn't have been surprised that it was so hard in 1994 to discard my profession. Perhaps the difference is that in 1994 when I opted out of my career I was choosing to be a wife and mother. I was not choosing to become a dependent sleeping female or an ugly villain. My motivation was to dedicate myself to raising children, not to be the perfect homemaker. When I cooked I did so because I enjoyed it. I didn't do it because it was my job. I didn't make cookies because I wasn't smart enough to do anything else. I did it because the people for whom I baked were smart enough to realize that I had chosen to bake for them. They appreciated the fact that I could make money spending my time doing something other than baking. That made their cookies taste even sweeter.

In spite of progress in the professional and educational advancement of women, it is astonishing that the stereotypes of women as ignorant, dependent, and weak still exist. Toy stores still carry toys designed to imitate housecleaning that are marked "Girls Only". [51]

d. Toys

All toys teach. The question is, what are they teaching? Children play to learn. Toys can teach desired behavior or reinforce unhealthy images of women.[52] Toys are marketed specifically for boys or girls. Toy stores are organized into boy-toy aisles and girl-toy aisles. The girl aisles are almost exclusively pink. Toys include dress-up clothes to simulate princesses and whores.[53] The toys available on the pink aisle that don't relate to clothing, are focused on care for a baby or the home. The blue aisle will include a variety of action toys, science toys, and toys associated with building.

As women began to realize that toy selection might be limiting future expectations for our daughters, mothers began demanding more gender neutral toys. In 2011 Lego introduced its Lego Friends line. It was heavily "pinkified." These politically correct building blocks for girls allowed the girls to construct scenes at beauty parlors and cupcake bakeries. "All the girls did was sit at home, go to the beach, and shop, and they had no jobs. …The boys went on adventures, worked, saved people, had jobs, and even swam with sharks."[54]

Dolls are another classic example of unhealthy images of girls and women. The two leaders in this category are Barbie and Bratz dolls. Barbie was first marketed in 1959, two years after my birth.[55] Barbie has received a lot of criticism over the years for disproportionate body parts. She is too skinny. Her breasts look more like cantaloupes than oranges. She has been accused of causing eating disorders in children who try to match the image of a perfect woman.[56] When compared to a life-size person, Barbie would have a 39" bust, and an 18" waist.[v]

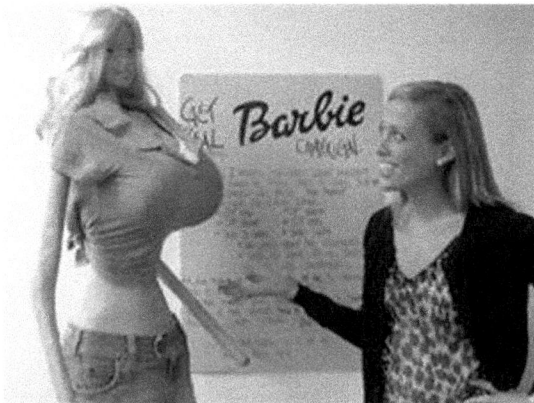

---

[v] http://www.nbcnews.com/id/21134540/vp/42643430#42643430

Here are other toys that can be found on the pink aisle:

My Cleaning Trolley Set,

Pole Dancing Dolly,

Hello Kitty Hooters Plush,

and The Stylin' Studio?

The Stylin Studio teaches little girls how to change their anatomy through plastic surgery to make themselves more appealing to men.

There are clothes marketed for girls, which expressly convey the message that intelligence is unnecessary for pretty girls. Surely these are the type of clothes worn by girls who later became Miss America.

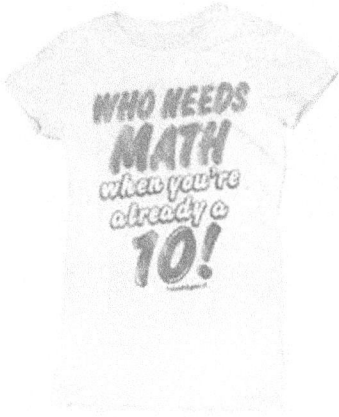

Men, their rights,
And nothing more.
Women, their rights,
And nothing less.

- Susan B. Anthony [57]

CHAPTER III. THE WAVES OF FEMINISM

Sometimes when we play in the surf we fail to appreciate the treacherous nature of that monster wave approaching. When that wave hits, it's like an explosion. You find yourself lying in the gritty sand, gasping for air, and choking on salt water. Hopefully Prince Charming didn't see what just happened. The salt in your eyes burns. The sand in your crotch is annoying. You were at the ocean. You knew there were waves in the ocean. You knew the waves were bigger than you and that they could knock you over if you weren't paying attention. Yet you still got knocked off your feet. Maybe the beauty, the power, and the potential danger of the ocean were the inspiration for describing feminism in waves.

A. The First Wave

Lucretia Mott, Susan Anthony, and Elizabeth Cady Stanton were the leaders of the first wave of feminism.[58] The first wave began in the mid-nineteenth century with the fight to gain the right to vote for women. The goals of these three women were the same, but their lives were diverse. Susan Anthony was a professional; a teacher and writer. She never married and never had children. Stanton and Mott were both married with children. Mr. Stanton traveled a great deal, so Elizabeth had responsibility for the vast majority of the child rearing in her family. Lucretia Mott had 6 children and was happily married. However, Mott's husband was around much more than Stanton's. Mr. Mott was not a stay-at-home dad, but he was much more involved in raising the children than Mr. Stanton.[59] Thus Lucretia Mott had more time than Elizabeth Stanton to pursue professional endeavors. In addition to raising 6 children, Lucretia Mott was an author and founder of Swarthmore College. Hence even the three most prominent leaders in the First Wave of Feminism represented a complex mix of life-styles.

Anthony was a professional only. Stanton was a stay-at-home mom. Mott was a combination of the two. She was a professional woman attempting to balance a professional and personal life. The three rode the first wave of feminism until their deaths; Mott in 1880, Stanton in 1902, and Anthony in 1906. None lived to see the passage of the 19th Amendment giving women the right to vote in 1920.[60] It was their common spirit that inspired other women to join the battle to fight for equal rights. They weren't riding the first wave of feminism in an attempt to have it all. They simply wanted to be represented by officials who would recognize their rights as citizens. Women couldn't consider having a voice about abortion, contraception, or equal pay if they didn't have the right to vote. They weren't concerned about how to gain the respect of men at work. They were focused on being treated as a "person" under the Constitution. These women understood that as long as women were not allowed to vote, only men would be treated as people.

Ida Wells (1862-1931) is less well known. However, she played a significant part in the quest for suffrage. Ida was an African American woman who was a journalist, a newspaper editor, and a sociologist.[61] When she married during the late 1800's, she retained her maiden name which was an unprecedented commentary on the independence of a woman at the time. In 1884 Ms. Wells refused to give up her seat on a crowded train car which was reserved for only white passengers. The conductor and two men dragged Wells out of the car.[62] That was twelve years prior to the landmark case argued before the United States Supreme Court in 1896, of <u>Plessy v. Ferguson</u>.[63] Plessy is the case which established the rule of law that *separate but equal* was constitutional.

Like Rosa Parks, Ida Wells was committed to fighting for equal rights for Blacks and for women. However, Wells had four children. She struggled with the challenge of balancing the demands of her family with those of the civil rights movement. She found it hard to feed her babies while addressing a crowd about the importance of the vote for women. Ms. Wells explained in her autobiography that she struggled with this balancing act and was unable to combine the two.[64] After the birth of her first child, Ms. Wells continued to work, bringing the baby with her when traveling. However, after the birth of the second child, speaking engagements and travel obligations became overwhelming. Ultimately, Ida withdrew from being a public spokesperson for the civil rights movement. Her passion for the cause had not changed, but her responsibilities at home had. Susan Anthony, a single woman, described Ida as "being distracted" after her second child was born.[65]

In 1920, when the 19th Amendment passed, women involved in the first wave of feminism felt they had survived. Their perception was that there was no further need for women to organize or fight for their rights. Many women thought that if they earned the right to vote they had achieved equality.[w]

They were wrong. Ten years after earning the right to vote, 26 of 48 states still had laws prohibiting the employment of married women.[66] Virtually all states had laws which limited the type of jobs women were allowed to hold. For example women were prohibited from working more than eight hours, working at night, or working in jobs that required lifting more than 15 lbs. (the estimated weight of a toddler). Women in America faced discrimination in virtually every aspect of life. Credit was only available to women if their husband co-signed. Single women were often not allowed to purchase a house or car. Laws were blatantly biased against women including regulations concerning welfare, crime, prostitution, and abortion. Even criminal laws were different for men and women. A woman who killed her husband would be charged with homicide. A man who killed his wife was guilty of a crime of passion. Some states even required that a woman convicted of a felony receive the maximum sentence. Women were arrested and charged with the crime of prostitution but their male customers were not.[67]

---

[w] https://www.youtube.com/watch?v=lqf6d4ImqvU

In the past, it wouldn't be unusual for a woman to be fired simply because she was pregnant. Even the federal government participated in active discrimination against women. In 1932 Congress passed the Federal Economy Act which excluded employment of a married woman in a government job if her husband already worked for the government. Twenty-six state governments enacted similar laws which prohibited employment of married women.[68] Thus the first wave of feminism was associated with earning the right to vote but not the right to be treated equally under the law.

Not all women felt that discrimination persisted after the passage of the 19th Amendment. The President of the League of Women Voters explained that "nearly all discriminations have been removed."[69] Her statement was more of a commentary on the end of women's enthusiasm to fight for equality than the end of discrimination. It was particularly bad for women of color. In spite of the ratification of the 19th amendment, Black women were not allowed to vote until the Civil Rights Movement of the '60's.[70] Black women in the 1960's were relegated to jobs serving white families as in *The Help.*[x]

Even after Caucasian women won the right to vote, many failed to exercise that right. Some women were indifferent to voting. These women remained uninformed and unconcerned with politics. Worse yet, some women voted as instructed by their husbands. Thus, ten years after ratification of the 19th amendment, women had virtually no effect on politics in America.[71]

The Great Depression lasted from 1930 until the beginning of WWII.[72] Before Pearl Harbor, more than 80% of all Americans thought it was WRONG for wives to work outside the home if the husband was employed. Schools refused to hire female teachers if they were married. If a woman married after being employed as a teacher, she was fired. Unemployment in 1933 reached 25% and didn't fall below 14.3% until 1941. The Great Depression had a dramatic effect on women. Society realized that women not only could work outside the home, but they performed their jobs as well as their male counterparts. Because women were paid less than men for doing the same job, hiring a woman was a guaranteed way to reduce overhead while producing the same quality of goods and services. Couples were so strapped for money during the Great Depression that many people delayed marriage. Divorce rates dropped sharply. Birth rates dropped. The economic reality of the Depression mandated a dramatic change in the traditional role of women. It was not a case of women rebelling against societal norms. Instead it was a demonstration of the resilience of women. Everything changed when the war began. Now employment of women was not only acceptable, but necessary.[73]

---

[x] https://www.youtube.com/watch?v=5h_-Nu7tiag

Expectations for women changed in an instant. At the beginning of WWII there were only 43 women employed in seven airplane factories. Eighteen months later those same seven plants employed 65,000 women. Similarly, in 1939, only thirty-six women were employed in the construction of ships. Three years later, 160,000 women were working in the construction of ships. From 1941 to 1945, the number of women working outside the home increased by 55%. Six million women were added to the labor force over a period of four years during WWII. That translates into an average of 1.5 million women per year, who were transformed from happy homemakers, into the essential labor force in America.

The transformation was not limited to the sheer number of women working outside the home. Typical jobs for women in the 1930's were sewing, toy making, and cleaning. An average salary for a woman during the 1930's was around $5 per week, for a grand total of $20 per month. That translated into a whopping 12 cents per hour. There was also a dramatic change in the type of jobs women began performing. For the first time in history women were operating overhead cranes and blast furnaces. Women worked as lumberjacks, pilots, steelmakers, and taxi drivers. Industries that had previously been run by only men were now dependent on women's participation. The munitions industry was one example. Rosie the Riveter, although based on a real-life munitions worker, was a fictitious character used by the government to recruit women. The bandanna-clad image of Rosie was one of the most successful recruitment tools in American history. The iconic image of a strong, patriotic, independent woman forever changed the perception of women in America.[74]

Women also became an essential part of the military. The military excluded women only from participation in direct combat. Women worked in the motor pool, as radio operators, repairwomen, gunnery instructors, mechanics, flight instructors, and in other advanced technical and scientific fields.[75]

By 1942 60% of Americans reported that women should be employed outside the home. Seventy-one percent believed that more married women should work outside the home.[76] In the span of four years the majority of Americans experienced a total reversal in their perception of the proper role for women. The impetus for change was the war. Once the war was over, it was hard to ignore the reality that women had proved themselves capable of much more than dusting, mopping floors, and cooking meals.

In addition, there was a dramatic change in perception of the type of women who would work outside the home. Employment outside the home was no longer limited to young single women, or married women whose husbands didn't make enough to support the family. Four million, of the 6.5 million women who joined the labor force during the war, listed themselves as former housewives.[77]

For some wealthy women, the war was of little consequence to their every-day lives. However, at least 60% of men and women had their lives forever changed by WWII.[78] Just as men went to war to demonstrate their patriotism, women demonstrated their patriotism and skills by going to work outside the home. Women satisfied the crucial demand in the labor force to keep American businesses operating, and simultaneously demonstrated their support for the military. Without women, the American military would not have had the arms necessary to win the war. Without the nursing care provided by women, wounded soldiers might not have survived. Yet even though women were essential to the economy and to the recovery of injured soldiers, women were still treated as second-class citizens.

In 1939 the median salary for a male teacher was $1,953. Women teaching in an identical situation earned only $1,394.[79] Because employers paid women less than men for the same job, women often remained employed while their male counter-parts were fired. Instead of helping out at home many men felt so impotent that they simply walked out on their families. A 1940 survey indicated that 1.5 million married men had abandoned their families.[80] Instead of leaning in to their jobs women learned to live lean.[81] Women didn't work to achieve professional recognition. They weren't trying to have it all. They worked to survive. Unfortunately, the importance of women in the work force did not equate to better treatment of women. The hardships women faced during the Depression and during WWII led to the women organizing to protect and secure their rights.

By 1940, a total of 800,000 women had unionized. That was triple the number from ten years before. During WWII the United Auto Workers had 250,000 female members. An estimated 350,000 women served in the U.S. Armed Forces.[82] Due to a severe shortage of pilots in 1942 the military leaders gambled and trained women to fly military aircraft. The women were called Women Air Force Service Pilots (WASP). These women were trained to fly military aircraft so that male pilots could be released for combat duty overseas. Even though the women were quite successful pilots they were not granted military status until the 1970's. In 2010 President Obama recognized these women for their service.[83, y]

By 1945 nearly one out of every four married women worked outside the home.[84] My paternal grandmother was one of those women. She left five children, ranging in age from 5 to 16, on a farm in Broken Arrow, Oklahoma. Grandma became a worker in a bomber plant in Tulsa. Annabelle had an 8th grade education. She didn't work because she wanted to have it all. She worked because, without her income, the family could not eat.[85] The participation of women in the building and servicing of aircraft was critical. More than 310,000 women were employed in the aircraft industry. During the war those women

---

y https://www.youtube.com/watch?v=jdzI5vEb9yM

represented 65 percent of the industry's total workforce (compared to just 1 percent in the pre-war years).[86]

Annabelle's husband, my grandfather, contracted tuberculosis from the gas that filled his lungs during WWI. My dad's father was an invalid by the time my dad was 7 years old, and before the commencement of WWII. My grandmother had to work to support her five children. She didn't have the ability to demand equal wages for performing the same work as a man. She didn't worry about making a choice to give up her job to spend more time with her five children. She was focused on survival. She didn't have to decide upon the best nanny or day care center for her children. She couldn't afford ANY child care. The children were left alone on the farm to care for themselves.

When the war ended men returned home to contribute to the financial support of the family. However many families remained dependent on the income of the mother. In 1950, women comprised an estimated 34% of the work force. [89] The war left some women widows. Some women had husbands who were unable to provide sufficient support for the family. Some women realized the difference they could make in the standard of living for their family if they worked outside the home. Whatever the reason, one-third of women in America worked outside the home by 1950.

In 1950, most women and men lacked a college degree.[90] However, the majority of college graduates were men.[91] The disparity in 1950 between men and women who had earned Master's and PhD's was even greater.

Many perceived that the vast majority of women of the 1950's, who were married, were primarily stay-at-home mothers. That perception was wrong. Women over the age of 35 comprised half of the female work force. Forty percent of married women with small children were employed outside the home. Unfortunately due to lack of education, and discrimination, 70% of all employed women during the period of 1955-1960 were working in clerical positions, assembly lines, or the service industries. In the late 1950's, less than 15% of women were professionals. Women in management represented an even smaller percentage. Minority women had even fewer choices because they were only permitted to work in low paying, physically taxing domestic service jobs.[92]

The ideal job for a woman in the 1940s and 50's was working as an airline stewardess. The credentials for these women related to virginity, age, and appearance. In 1936 the New York Times listed the requirements for a job as a stewardess.[93]

1.   Petite

2.   Between 100-118 lbs.

3.   Between 5'0" and 5'4"

4. 20-26 years old

5. Single, with no children (Even a widow with children would not qualify.)

The stewardess was idolized by girls everywhere. She was like the happy homemaker, beautiful and happily waiting on men. Simultaneously she was a professional, working outside the home. Flight attendants appeared on magazine covers, lectured in schools, and hosted White House functions.[94] The interview for a job consisted of the applicant lifting her skirt so the man interviewing her could evaluate the applicant's legs. The appearance of the applicant's legs seemed to be the most important criterion for the job. In the 1950's I was too young to be a stewardess. The only thing I needed from the stewardess would have been a bottle of formula.

Grandma died in 1969. She never considered working as a flight attendant. She was too tall, too heavy, too old, and the mother of five children. She worked outside the home for virtually all of her adult life. Annabelle supported her five children on her sole income for over 10 years. If she felt stress, it was due to worry that her children would go to bed hungry, rather than concern that she was devoting too much time to her profession and not enough to her children. She never wondered *is this all*? She might have wondered *is this enough*?

Grandma was unconcerned with her image as a woman who made things. I remember the nose warmers she crocheted for me and the afghan draped on the back of our couch. I remember the sweet rolls she served our family every Sunday, steaming hot with real butter melting on the top. I remember her laugh, her smile, and the unlimited hugs she gave to every grandchild. I remember her simple house that seemed like a palace to her. She missed countless moments with her children because she had to work to support them. However I never saw my grandma when she wasn't smiling. I never heard her say a harsh word about anyone. I always think of Grandma when I see the sign on my desk:

> "People in life who are the happiest
> don't have the best of everything…
> They make the best of everything they have."

Annabelle was typical of women of her time. She did the necessary without complaining, and with no hope of ever being treated as equal to men. She never had the option of pursuing success as a professional. She never had the option of staying home to raise her five children. She was strong, resilient, courageous, and self-sufficient. She did the necessary for her children, even though it was harder for her than for a man.

I crochet now. Perhaps it is a way to relate to Grandma. When I was the first of her female grandchildren to graduate from college my aunt gave me Annabelle's wedding ring. The worn edges on that band of gold remind me of her life. When

I look at the ring I imagine the struggle she experienced every day, trying to support her five children at a time when women were treated so badly. Her commitment to her children was unmistakable. She took a job outside the home to provide necessities for her children. I quit my job to provide for my children. Our motivations were the same. Neither of us wondered at the time *is this all?* Both of us did the necessary. Annabelle leaned in to her job. I leaned out. Annabelle sacrificed being with her children for the sake of her children. I sacrificed my career for the sake of my children. Annabelle was riding the first wave. I was riding the second. My struggle to master the second was made easier because of women like my grandmother. I hope that my struggle to master the second wave will make it easier for my girls to master the third. Maybe their journey to find their happily ever after won't be so long or treacherous.

B. The Second Wave

The reality of discrimination against women in the 40's and 50's set the stage for the second wave of feminism.[z] WWII ended in 1945.[95] By that time women had proved themselves competent to work outside the home. Social mores had evolved. Once people changed their perception of the proper role for women it was hard to justify a reversion to an antiquated image of the happy homemaker. Betty Friedan was born in 1921, one year after women won the right to vote. Betty was 24 years old when the war ended. As a young woman she witnessed the transformation of society's expectations for women and the fulfillment of those expectations. Yet having satisfied the demand for women to step up during the war, Friedan watched as women returned to their pre-war dependency. It was like watching fish evolve to grow legs and then asking them to return to the water. Having experienced life outside the pond, it was difficult to return to a life of struggling for air. Women had evolved. Society had changed. It took another 20 years for women to stand and fight for their rights, but it was inevitable that they would. Perhaps it was no coincidence that women who had children shortly after the war ended, were ready to return to the work force 20 years later, when their children were grown.

In 1963, when Betty was 42 years old, she published the *Feminine Mystique*. That book has been regarded as the impetus for the Second Wave of Feminism.[96] The "Feminine Mystique" became synonymous with the question *is this all*. Friedan explained:

> **"The problem lay buried, unspoken, for many years in the minds of American women. It was a strange stirring, a sense of dissatisfaction, a yearning that women suffered in the middle of the twentieth century in the United States. Each suburban wife struggled with it alone. As she made the beds, shopped for groceries, matched slipcover material, ate peanut butter sandwiches with her children, chauffeured Cub Scouts and Brownies, lay beside her husband at night -she was afraid to ask even of herself the silent question- 'Is this all?'"[97]**

I was six years old in 1963. I wasn't focused on women's issues or the feminist movement of the '60s. I wasn't focused on the dreams of a man speaking in the nation's capital. I was focused on my dream to one day have a sister. I wasn't concerned with an unnamed problem. I had two problems. First, I had three obnoxious brothers. Second, I had to find a way to keep the cafeteria-lady from discovering that I hadn't eaten all the food on my plate lunch. My problems had names: Frank, Steve, Phil, and grits.

---

[z] https://www.youtube.com/watch?v=XcH2ppft2Gw

It was during the 1960's that America was focused on the importance of protecting the civil rights of every citizen. Congress passed the Equal Pay Act in 1963 because women were paid a fraction of the wages paid to men who performed the same job. Women made $.59 for every dollar made by a man.[98] The same year the *Feminine Mystique* was published, 200,000 people stood in the National Mall and listened to MLK's "I Have a Dream" speech.[aa]

That speech was made as part of the March on Washington to combat racial discrimination and to emphasize the urgency of passage of the Civil Rights Act. The Civil Rights Act that was passed in 1964 was a law that prohibited, not only discrimination on the basis of color, but also on the basis of sex. [99]

The Feminine Mystique created a sensation and sold over 3 million copies. At the time of publication, Betty was already a mother of three children, Emily, Daniel, and Jonathan, ages 15, 11, and 7. The book inspired a revolution. Women were given permission to want more than cooking, cleaning, and child rearing as their mission in life. Readers were quoted as saying:[100]

> "The Feminine Mystique left me breathless. I finally realized I wasn't crazy. It literally changed (and perhaps saved) my life."

> "Something clicked."

> "It slammed me in the face."

> "A bolt of lightning."

> "A revelation."

> "A bombshell."

Women related to Betty's observation that women were smart, ambitious, and often underestimated. More importantly, Betty gave voice to the realization by many women that they were dissatisfied with the limitations placed on them by society. Those limitations are best illustrated by statistics from the 1960's:

1. In 1960, 60% of women who entered college didn't graduate. The high drop-out rate for women was directly associated with becoming engaged.[101] Immediately after becoming engaged it was clear that the future Mrs. would have no need for an education.

2. In 1960, the 38% of women who worked outside the home were teachers, nurses, or secretaries [102]

[aa] https://www.youtube.com/watch?v=HRIF4_WzU1w

3. In 1960, women accounted for only 6% of doctors, 3% of lawyers, and less than 1% of engineers.[103]

4. Working women in the 1960's were routinely paid lower salaries than men. Most employers assumed women would become pregnant and quit. Unlike their male counterparts, women weren't perceived to be the primary breadwinners.[104]

In 1960, the FDA approved the sale of birth control pills. Women were suddenly able to determine when and if they would have a child.[105] That was excellent timing as the 60's was also the decade of hippies. The notions of peace, love, and personal freedom, promoted by hippies, were particularly significant for women. Women were encouraged to experience sexual freedom like their male counterparts.[106] The availability of contraception meant women could embrace their sexuality like never before. Without fear of pregnancy, women had more latitude to choose partners and determine the timing and frequency of sex. That kind of female autonomy was unprecedented.[107] The availability of birth control pills and the resulting control over all aspects of pregnancy had significant implications regarding the professional career paths of women.

Politicians were also focused in the early 1960's on the challenges faced by women. Before the publication of the *Feminine Mystique,* JFK appointed a Commission on the Status of Women. Eleanor Roosevelt agreed to spearhead the commission.[108] That Commission gave the federal government incentive to evaluate women's rights and to determine whether laws were being interpreted discriminately. President Kennedy's Commission on the Status of Women report revealed:[109]

1. The American population in 1963 was estimated to be 189 million. Over half (an estimated 96 million) were female.

2. Americans were marrying at younger ages than in previous decades.

3. Couples in the 1950's and 1960's were having more children than their parents.

4. "The current lack of fuller employment bears specifically on many women in low-income families unable to offer their children opportunities that better-off citizens take for granted...."

5. "Higher quality in American life was a specific concern of this Commission both because of the potential contribution of outstanding women to it and because women in their families are transmitters of the central values of the culture."

6. "We note with satisfaction that even while the Commission was engaged in its inquiry a number of its recommendations were put

into effect. Employment opportunities for women in Federal public service were notably widened by changes in policy and procedure following a directive to executive agencies of July of 1962. Among administration measures submitted to Congress, several have contained provisions which we had endorsed or recommended, outstandingly the bill that became the Equal Pay Act of 1963."

7.   "We believe that one of the greatest freedoms of the individual in a democratic society is the freedom to choose among different life patterns. Innumerable private solutions found by different individuals in search of the good life provide society with basic strength far beyond the possibilities of a dictated plan."

That report contained a picture of Eleanor Roosevelt, and a quote from her in June of 1962:

"Because I anticipate success in achieving full employment and full use of American's magnificent potential, I feel confident that in the years ahead many of the remaining outmoded barriers to women's aspirations will disappear. Within a rapidly growing economy, with appropriate manpower planning, all Americans will have a better chance to develop their individual capacities, to earn a good livelihood, and to strengthen family life."[110]

The "invitation to action" of the Commission declared that:

"The 96 million American women and girls include a range from infant to octogenarian, from migrant farm mother to suburban homemaker, from file clerk to research scientist, from Olympic athlete to college president. Greater development of women's potential and fuller use of their present abilities can greatly enhance the quality of American life."[111]

The Commission noted in its findings:

"Economic expansion is of particular significance to women. One of the ironies of history is that war has brought American women their greatest economic opportunities. In establishing this Commission the President noted:

'In every period of national emergency, women have served with distinction in widely varied capacities but thereafter have been subject to treatment as a marginal group whose skills have been inadequately utilized.'"[112]

In the early 1960's women were underrepresented in institutions of higher learning and in professions. Seventy-eight percent of college faculty were men. A whopping 95% of physicians were men. Ninety-seven percent of lawyers, senators, members of Congress, and ambassadors were men. Yale and Harvard were still male-only institutions. The National Press Club invited female reporters. Yet, those women had to sit in the balcony. They were not allowed to ask questions.[113] Thus the very reason the *Feminine Mystique* created such a sensation was that while women knew that they wanted more, they now realized that they were not alone. Millions of women knew that they were individually capable of more. Now women realized that collectively they wanted more. Women demanded more.[bb]

It was not a revolution of women wanting to have a job outside the home. It was the realization of women that they wanted more professionally, without intending to minimize the importance of a woman's role in raising children. The book failed to address the great balancing act of raising children while pursuing an education and professional success. The importance of raising children was presumed. It was not addressed because there was never any intention of abandoning that job. Instead women were interested in adding more professional responsibilities, not eliminating personal responsibilities. The problem was that there was no concurrent attempt to encourage men to take on a more significant role domestically. It seemed unnecessary at the time to recognize the importance of the parent who would stay at home to raise children. Betty Friedan had her first child when she was 20 years old. By the time her child was 15 years old Betty had completed the most time consuming part of her job as a mother. There was little concern about balancing home and professional life, as her obligations at home were dwindling every year. As their children became self-sufficient, the mothers began to realize that they wanted the next 15-30 years to be meaningful. Professional success seemed the obvious next-step. The women who were frustrated wanted the satisfaction and financial rewards of a profession, rather than the meager salary they earned on assembly lines. If they were already working outside the home, they wanted a chance for a better job. If younger women stayed at home raising their children, they hoped that when the kids were grown that they could find fulfillment in a professional position.

In June 1966, Betty Friedan attended the third annual conference of the Commission on the Status of Women. There she met Dorothy Haener from the United Automobile Workers' Union and Pauli Murray, the Black lawyer who had helped draft civil rights legislation. Friedan invited both women to meet in her hotel room with about 20 other professional women. Those women created the National Organization for Women, which was dedicated to protecting the rights of all women.[114] NOW became a critical organization over the next several decades for unifying women in their quest for equal rights. The quest for equal rights necessarily focused on the legislative efforts to infuse more women into the work force. There was no contemporaneous legislative effort to make the work place more accommodating to parents and their children.

---

bb https://www.youtube.com/watch?v=xO304aoUAWE

As American women became more focused on barriers to success professionally, change was inevitable. Women quickly identified the need for more education if they were to be prepared to compete with men. By 1970, 22% of women in the civilian labor force had either attended some college, or graduated with a degree. Forty years later that figure had increased over three-fold, to 66.7%. The percentage of women in the civilian labor force with less than a high school diploma decreased from 33.5% in 1970, to 6.8% in 2010.[115] By 2009, 59% of women in the U.S. were in the labor force.[116] Thus by 2009 a majority of women in America were working outside the home, and the vast majority of those had attended college.

On the fiftieth anniversary of the Feminine Mystique, some critiqued Friedan and her book. It was reported that "by all accounts Betty Friedan was not a particularly likable woman."[117] She graduated from the prestigious Smith College for women in 1942. Betty herself explained that most women at Smith were not "geared (toward) having careers". The goal of most women graduating from Smith was to get married and have children.[118] Implicit in the expectations of women who were bright enough to gain admission to Smith, was the notion that they were bright enough to attract husbands who could provide for the financial needs of a wife and family. Thus the men that would be attractive to Smith college graduates would make enough money so that their wives could stay at home. Working outside the home would not be necessary.

Betty Friedan was criticized as an elitist. Some felt the focus of the *Feminine Mystique* was upper-class white women. The complaint was that Betty had ignored working-class, nonwhite women.[119] However Betty was not writing the book for the woman who worked out of necessity to provide financial support for her family. That woman was already working and didn't have time to read a book about feminism. She might not have had a college education. She was focused on putting food on the table rather than pursuing a fulfilling professional career which would maximize her education and leadership skills.

Betty Friedan was far from the typical woman in the 1960's. Ms. Friedan described the typical stay-at-home American woman of 1963 this way:

> "In the fifteen years after World War II this mystique of feminine fulfillment became the cherished and self-perpetuating core of contemporary American culture. Millions of women lived their lives in the image of those pretty pictures of the American suburban housewife, kissing their husbands goodbye in front of the picture window, depositing their station-wagonsful of children at school, and smiling as they ran the new electric waxer over the spotless kitchen floor. They baked their own bread, sewed their own clothes, and kept their new washing machines and dryers running all day. They changed the sheets on the beds twice a week, took rug-hooking class, and pitied their poor frustrated mothers who had dreamed of having a career. Their only dream was to be perfect wives and mothers. Their highest ambition was

to have five children and a beautiful house, Their only struggle was to get and keep their husbands. They had no thought for the unfeminine problems of the world outside the home. They wanted the men to make the major decisions. They gloried in their role as women, and wrote proudly on the census blank: 'Occupation: housewife.'"[120]

The Feminine Mystique

Betty was writing for women like herself, who had a college education. She wrote for those women who were prepared to pursue a professional career, but found themselves without executive and professional options. Clearly Betty could have gotten a job on an assembly line, but she wanted more. The problem wasn't that women couldn't find work outside the home. The problem was that women were relegated to low paying jobs that offered no future, no promotions, and in which their boss would always be a man. Betty was interested in addressing disparate treatment of women in compensation, promotions, and placement in executive positions. Her book lifted the spirits of millions of American women because they were given permission to aspire for more.

Friedan's book was based upon her own experience and that of other women who attended the prestigious Smith College. Smith College was founded as a women's college. Sophia Smith founded the college 140 years ago. In her will she left a fortune for the establishment of facilities for the higher education of women. Those facilities were to be "equal to those afforded now in our colleges for men." To this day Smith is still recognized as a women's school, committed to responding to the "intellectual needs of today's women."[121] While Smith purports to be open to male applicants, the class of 2019 is comprised of 2604 women and 2 men.[122] In addition to Betty Friedan, Smith College touts famous alumnae including Gloria Steinem (1956), Nancy Reagan (1943), and Barbara Bush (1947).[123] Each was far different from the average woman.

Betty Friedan graduated summa-cum-laude from Smith College. When she published the *Feminine Mystique* she was 42 years old. At that time she had been working for more than ten years as a successful freelance magazine writer. The Friedans had household help three or four days a week, which allowed Betty to travel for her research. Her husband provided financially for Betty and her children. She was not expected to assist in the financial support of the family. She was Caucasian, well educated, and Jewish by birth. Betty Friedan enjoyed her ability to write and express her opinions irrespective of the financial consequences. She lived in a big house in a crime-free neighborhood. "By any material measure, and relative to the aspirations of most people, she was one of the most privileged human beings on the planet."[124]

The New York Times described Ms. Friedan in her obituary as "famously abrasive" and "subject to screaming fits of temperament."[125] A feminist writer, Germaine Greer, described Friedan as "pompous and egotistic." Betty perceived that it was essential to the struggle for equality for every woman to stand up and express outrage if ever treated with a lack of respect.

Betty even described herself as a "bad-tempered bitch."[126] If she was to insist on being treated equally with men, she perceived that it was essential to be famously abrasive. Friedan's children described her as less than the perfect mother. T.V. dinners were the norm. Her daughter Emily described her as a "mass of contradictions."

> **"She made so many connections and yet was exquisitely lonely," she said. "Maybe the ultimate contradiction was that Betty just didn't fit into this world. That was her curse, and yet she started a revolution."**[127]

Like Betty Friedan, I graduated at the top of my class in college. However, I graduated with a Law Degree. Had Betty been given the opportunity to attend Law School, she more than likely would have thrived. At the time she would have considered Law School, she would not have been admitted simply because she was a woman. Like Friedan, I established myself in college as intelligent and committed to higher education. I live in a big house, have household help, and enjoy financial security provided by my husband. Instead of being a free-lance writer of articles in magazines, I write on the internet on my own blog, with over 4.5 million views. I enjoy the freedom of writing with none of the typical restraints of most writers who have to rely on financial support of their readers and advertisers. Like Betty, I am accountable to no one. I consider myself to be one of the most privileged human beings on the planet. While Betty was born into a Jewish family, I married into one. Betty was 26 years old when she married her husband, and so was I. Her son obtained a PhD. in science from Berkeley. My son currently attends Berkeley, pursuing a PhD. in science. Friedan's daughter, Emily is a medical doctor. One of my daughters is still in college on a pre-med track. At the time Betty wrote the *Feminine Mystique,* Betty was a stay-at-home mother, even though she was writing. I too am a stay-at-home mother, even though I write daily. The similarities between us are amazing.

However there are significant differences between myself and Betty Friedan. First, Betty was 36 years older than me. She was born 13 years before my mother. Second, Betty and her husband divorced after 22 years of marriage when Betty was 48 years old. I am happily married to my first husband of 30 years. Before they divorced, Betty had never supported her husband and his partner while they started a new business. I did. I was never fired from my job because I was pregnant. Betty was. From the time I reached maturity, birth control was always available to women. For Betty, birth control was not available until after her children were born. This book is being published when I am 57 years old. Betty was 42 when her book was published. In 1963, when Betty's book was published, all three of Betty's children were still at home. All three of my children are adults. Each is in, or graduated from, college. None live at home.

The most significant difference between Betty Friedan and me is that I have the benefit of women that came before me that taught me to surf the second wave of feminism. Betty had to teach herself. If she was allowed to surf with men, she had to fight for that privilege. I was given that privilege as soon as I was old enough to surf. Betty was described as "not a particularly cooperative spouse or attentive mother." After the divorce, her husband Carl told a reporter that "She hates men."[128] My husband might describe me as being opinionated, confrontational, emphatic, and tenacious. However he would admit that I have his back and have provided an assist to him on multiple occasions. My Prince Charming would also describe me as an attentive mother who committed 20 years to enriching the lives of her children, and thereby enriching his. I like men and find them to be some of our best advocates. There are times that I might call myself a "bad tempered bitch." However, they'd be limited to those times that someone, man or woman, treated me or my children inappropriately. The phrase "kicking ass and taking names" comes to mind. Occasionally, in the practice of law, the only appropriate response I could have had was fury, ferocity, and rage. When an older male attorney hit me during a deposition, he learned the definition of a bad tempered bitch. When an opposing attorney lied to a judge in Court, I became famously abrasive. A stranger might have described me as subject to screaming fits of temperament when she observed my encounter with a working mother. That working mother made the mistake of informing me that I had failed in my job as the soccer team mother. That woman, who happened to be a medical doctor, thought it was my job to inform her, and her husband, separately, of the soccer game schedule for our kindergarten daughters. She and her husband weren't divorced. They still lived in the same home. The husband brought their daughter to practice. He was given a printed schedule. The schedule was available to all parents on the internet. I mistakenly assumed that if I found the soccer field for practice, found and hired a coach, signed the team up at the Y, passed out a printed schedule of games and snack schedule to each parent at practice, designed, picked-up and delivered uniforms to each girl at practice, and brought popsicles to every practice, that I had done my share for the girls and their parents. Some might have thought that my resting bitch face would have sufficiently conveyed my receptivity to her criticism. However my screaming fit of temperament served two important purposes. The volume of my response underscored the passion of my retort. The added benefit to my famously abrasive commentary was a release of years of pent-up rage towards medical doctors who failed to appreciate the extent of my effort to do a good job. I wasn't responding to a man disparaging me. If a man had belittled my efforts, I might have anticipated his attitude. However because this was a woman, I expected her to be more aware of the extent of my efforts to provide a meaningful experience for our children. I would not tolerate being treated as her subordinate. A professional mother learned that day, as she reclined on the bench at the soccer field, that women are only famously abrasive when we are treated with a lack of respect. It is not the gender of the person demonstrating a lack of respect for the contribution of stay-at-home mothers that is particularly bothersome. It is instead, the total lack of respect and appreciation for the efforts of the stay at home mother, to do that which a professional thinks he/she is too busy to do.

If I had been born in 1921 and fired when I became pregnant, I expect that I might also have been described as famously abrasive. I am indebted to Betty Friedan for fighting to give women equal opportunities. Because of her efforts, and other like her, I had the option of attending Law School in 1979. When I was pregnant during my employment as an attorney, I wasn't fired. Instead, I was given a three-month, paid, maternity leave after the birth of each of my three children. Because of the difference in the ages of Betty and me, we have struggled to master different waves of feminism. Betty initiated the Second Wave, encouraging women to fight for the right to pursue a profession. I am fighting for the right of women not to pursue a profession. Women capable of achieving great things professionally may now opt to dedicate themselves to their children. We should be able to do so without facing criticism or being disrespected.

We have answered the question *is this all*? No, it's not. We are capable of achieving great things professionally. Instead, the question that we face today is: "Is this my happily ever after?" Women today are plagued by determining *what is the right balance* for us and for our families. The challenge for men and women today is to be bold and daring. We must make the choices that best suit our particular circumstances, regardless of what we perceive to be the popular choice. Our challenge is to continually find the right balance between personal and professional happiness, given our unique circumstances.

In Betty Friedan's **Feminine Mystique** she explained that in many ways women were worse off in 1963 than they had been in 1945, or before. In 1920, 15% of Ph.D.'s were awarded to women. In 1963 it was only 11%. In 1920, 47% of college students were women. In 1963 it was only 38%. In 1963, the median age for marriage was dropping; so much so, that almost half of all women who married in 1963 were teenagers. The birth rate for third and fourth children was rising in 1963. By way of example the birth rate for fourth children tripled between 1940 and 1960.[129] Thus the second wave of feminism was not about discarding the notion that women wanted to find a husband and have children. Betty Friedan was simply pointing out that many women wanted more professionally. When Friedan identified the nagging question, "Is this all?", she was not intending to limit or modify the importance of marriage and children. Instead she was pointing out that *all* for most women would include something in addition to marriage and children, not instead of marriage and children.

Betty Friedan explained in an interview that she would never give up the experience of having children. The interview went like this:

Question: "As you look at your life, what are you most profoundly pleased with: your family or your professional activity?"

Answer: "It's not really either/or. I mean, you say, "Well, do you get more thrill out of the books you've written, or your kids?" You can't compare, can't compare. I wouldn't give up at all, ever, the experience of having my kids and the joy they've given me and now the grandkids. That's a great part of life, very satisfying. But so is the fact that I have written several books that had an impact on my life and times, you know, the life of my time, as you might say. And there's a great satisfaction in whenever I take time to think about it, which is almost never. To have used my life in a way that opened up possibilities of life for those that came after me. So I feel good about that."** [130]

Today women seem to be finding that there are many reasons to focus on children when they are young. Married stay-at-home mothers are more likely than single or cohabiting stay-at-home mothers to say they are not employed because they are caring for their families (85% said this in 2012). Unmarried women are more likely than married stay-at-home mothers to say they are ill or disabled, unable to find a job, or enrolled in school. The recent rise in stay-at-home motherhood is the flip side of a dip in female labor force participation after decades of growth.[131] While the reason for the increase in stay-at-home mothers is unclear, survey data does not indicate that this slight elevation will result in an ongoing trend. Most mothers say they would like to work.

Other significant changes in the nation's demographics since 1970 have reshaped the profile of stay-at-home mothers. As women's education levels have risen, 25% of 2012's stay-at-home mothers were college graduates, compared with 7% in 1970. Perhaps because 19% of stay at home mothers in 2012 had less than a high school diploma, those mothers with a college education may be worried about being compared to the uneducated mothers. In spite of educational gains made by mothers, the share of stay-at-home mothers living in poverty has more than doubled since 1970.

Analysis of time-use diaries indicates that mothers at home spend more hours per week than working mothers on child care and housework.[132] Stay at home mothers report having more time for leisure and sleep. Time use also varies among different groups of mothers at home: Married stay-at-home mothers put more time into child care and less into leisure than their single counterparts.

Predictably mothers at home spend more time with their children than professional mothers (18 hours a week on child care, compared with 11 hours for working mothers).[133] The child-care time gap between mothers who work outside the home and those who do not is largest among married mothers with working husbands. There is a nine-hour disparity in weekly child-care hours of stay-at-home married mothers with employed husbands (20 hours) compared with working married mothers with unemployed husbands (11 hours).

Americans continue to think that having a parent at home is best for a child. In a recent Pew Research survey, 60% of respondents said children are better off when a parent stays home to focus on the family, compared with 35% who said children are just as well off with working parents.[134]

C. The Third Wave

Scholars seem to agree that there are three waves of Feminism. The first and second waves are easily identifiable. We know when each began. The goals of each are clear. There is no agreement about the description of, or goal sought by, women trying to master the third wave of feminism. Even Wikipedia struggles to define it.[135] Every discussion of the "third wave" has a common thread; some group of women is struggling to be treated equally and fairly. The reason there has been no agreement on the definition of the Third Wave is that there are too many different groups of women struggling for acceptance and respect.

In the First Wave we struggled as a group to gain the right to vote. Once women as a group earned that right, women disagreed about how an individual woman should vote. In the Second Wave we struggled to gain the right to be treated equally by men with regard to higher education and professional success. Now that we have the right and ability to pursue higher education and professional achievement, there is disagreement about how any individual woman should use her education and professional accomplishments. Stay-at-home-mothers attack women who pursue professional success, arguing that the professional woman is neglecting her children. Professional women disparage women who devote themselves exclusively to their families, implying that those women aren't smart enough to do more professionally. Women who try to do both simultaneously are susceptible to criticism from both stay-at-home-mothers and professionals. The women who try to balance both at the same time can't achieve the same level of success as the women who devote themselves exclusively to one pursuit. Thus the third, and final wave of feminism, is the fight of women to gain acceptance and respect from other women. We fought for the right to be treated equally by men in the first and second waves. Now women fight to be treated equally by other women.

In some ways women are superior to men. Women are biologically healthier. Admittedly, men are typically the stronger of the sexes.[136] However, women demonstrate a strength associated with child-birth that is unrivaled by anything a man is expected to experience as part of his normal life cycle. Studies show women have a more accurate sense of smell, are better drivers, are better at describing a person, perform better in timed tests, and communicate better than men.[137] Men feel more sorry for themselves when they are ill.[138] Women outnumber men.[139] We live longer.[140] We vote more often.[141] Women volunteer at a higher rate.[142] Since 2011 women have earned more advanced college degrees than men.[143]

Women are becoming the nation's job-creation engine. We will be responsible for creating 1/3 of the 15.3 million jobs that economists project will be created over the next five years.[144] In 2012 there were 84 million women in the country and 72.6 million were employed outside the home.[145] Women entrepreneurs are the fastest growing segment in the small business community. There are more than 8.9 million women-owned businesses in the U.S. that employ 7.8 million people.[146]

Yet, in spite of advances, we have a long way to go. Discrimination persists, in spite of our strength, resilience, tenacity, and intellect.[147]

Young women today have grown up during a time when people have been trained to be very careful about what they say that might be perceived as discriminatory. Some people still think that men are smarter and more capable than women. They have just learned to be more careful not to reveal their true feelings publically. Specific examples of discrimination illustrate the point:

1. Female prostitutes are arrested by policemen much more often than their male Johns or pimps. Of the total arrests made associated with prostitution, 70% are the female prostitutes, and only 10% are the male johns or pimps.[148] In essence police, who are predominately male, arrest women for prostitution, but not their male customers. This is particularly troublesome when the crime of prostitution is compared to the crime of using illegal drugs. Enforcement efforts in the drug trade are focused not on the users, but on the drug dealers. Like the drug dealers, pimps promote the illegal activity. Yet it isn't the pimps, usually men, who are typically arrested. It is the prostitutes, usually women, who are arrested. The pimps are free to stay in business and recruit more women.

2. Rick Brittan, a State Representative in Kansas, proposed a law preventing an abortion unless the woman obtained notarized, written permission from the father of the baby.[149] If that law had passed, a woman getting pregnant from a rape, would not be able to get an abortion unless she knew her rapist, could find him, and could get his notarized consent. Wouldn't a man be admitting his crime by signing such a notarized consent form? If a rape is a crime of power, violence, and control, why wouldn't a rapist want to continue to exert power, and control over his victim by making her have his baby? Wouldn't the law maker become an accessory to the crime by promoting the continuation of that power and control?

3. A Missouri Republican, Todd Akin, advocated giving a man the ability to prevent a woman from having an abortion unless she was the victim of a "legitimate rape."[150] Mr. Akin indicated that if the rape was legitimate, the female body has ways to "shut that whole thing down." [151] The implication was that if a woman was pregnant, that pregnancy could not be the result of a rape. The truth is that an estimated 50,000 pregnancies every year are the result of rape.[152]

4. Richard Murdock, Senate Candidate in Indiana, claimed that women should be forced to carry their rapist's baby to term because their pregnancy resulting from rape was a "gift from God."[153]

5. Mike Huckabee is the former Governor of Arkansas.[154] He was a presidential contender in 2008 and is again in 2016. He explained that:

    > *"I think it's time for Republicans to no longer accept listening to Democrats talk about a war on women. Because the fact is, the Republicans don't have a war on women. They have a war FOR women. For them to be empowered; to be something other than victims of their gender. Women I know are outraged that Democrats think that women are nothing more than helpless and hopeless creatures, whose only goal in life is to have a government provide for them birth control medication. Women I know are smart, educated, intelligent, and capable of doing anything anyone else can do. Our party stands for the recognition of the equality of women and the capacity of women. That's not a war ON them, it's a war FOR them. And if the Democrats want to insult the women of America by making them believe that they are helpless without Uncle Sugar coming in and providing for them a prescription each month for birth control because they cannot control their libido or their reproductive system without the help of the government, then so be it, let's take that discussion all across America because women are far more than Democrats have made them to be. And women across America have to stand up and say, enough of that nonsense."[155]*

    The fundamental flaw in the logic of this presidential contender is that it is always a woman who needs birth control. It's like saying that the government should not pay for mammograms for women, because that would unfairly impact men who don't need mammograms. In the case of birth control, the argument is even less persuasive since women wouldn't need birth control if men could control their libidos.

6. In January of 2015, it was reported that women performing the same job as men, who performed it equally well, were paid less. Debate relates to the extent of the difference. It has been reported that women earn as little as 77 cents to the male dollar, and as much as 93 cents per male dollar. Yet all sources agree that women still earn less for the same job, performed equally well.[156]

7. Gender discrimination claims have declined in recent years. Yet it isn't clear that the work place has come to require equal treatment of men and women. Perhaps women are still treated unfairly but men are just more careful about how they discriminate. In March of 2015, a case of gender discrimination went to trial in Silicon Valley against a venture capital firm.[157] The women in the case asserted that they were excluded from a ski trip and a dinner party because of their gender. The suit included allegations of a nude photo book and a bathrobe-clad man who showed up at a female colleague's hotel room. This is just one example of many instances of inappropriate conduct that persists.

8. Women in law enforcement still report discrimination. It may be more subtle but "it's still there."[158]

9. In February of 2015 the elite military academies including West Point, the Naval Academy, and the Air Force Academy all disproportionately benefit men. Women at West Point have represented a mere 14-20% of each class for the last 25 years. The Naval Academy has reached the 25% mark for women. The Air Force Academy still has less than 25% women in its graduating classes.[159]

10. Once women enter the military, they are viewed as sexual prey rather than contributing members of the military. One woman described women in the military as either a bitch, ho, or dyke. Women in the military are discriminated against by undermining women's authority, denying promotions, denigrating their work, sexual harassment, sexual assault and rape.[160]

    Rape of women in the military is horrific and prolific. It has been described as "epidemic."

    - In 2004 study of women veterans from all wars who were seeking help for post-traumatic stress disorder (PTSD), revealed that 71% of those women had been sexually assaulted or raped while serving.

    - A VA study found that 30% of women veterans reported they had been raped while serving.

    - Thirty seven percent of the attempted raped and raped women in the VA study also reported being raped more than once. Gang rape was reported by 14% of the women in the study.

- The study also discovered that 75% of raped women in the military failed to report it.[161]

- Female soldiers in Iraq died from dehydration due to fear of rape. Some of the female members of the military deployed to Iraq were so fearful of rape committed by fellow soldiers, that they would stop drinking liquids after 3:00 to 4:00 in the afternoon to ensure that they would not need to use the latrine at night. They were fearful because the latrine late at night was a prime target for rape.[162]

11. The FBI reports that women and children are bought, sold, and smuggled into this country like modern-day slaves. These "slaves" are often beaten, starved, and forced to work as prostitutes.[163] In 2005 the Department of Justice reported that 14,500-17,500 women and children were being trafficked to the U.S. annually.[164] Human trafficking is a multi-billion dollar industry. It has been associated with the Super Bowl, motorcycle rallies in South Dakota, fields in Florida, gangs in California, and brothels in Washington D.C. In 2014 the National Human Trafficking Resource Center (NHTRC) hotline received reports of human trafficking in every state in the country.[165] While it has been shown that actual estimates of victims may be dramatically understated the Department of Homeland Security reports that as many as 100,000 to 300,000 American children are "at risk" of being trafficked for commercial sex in the United States.[166]

12. An estimated 19% of women in America have been raped. Another 44% of women have experienced other forms of sexual violence. The pattern of sexual abuse of women indicates that women are heavily impacted over their lifetime as a result of sexual violence.[167]

13. Women are victims of nonfatal violent crimes almost four times as often as men. Nonfatal violent crime includes rape, sexual assault, and stalking. In 2008 females age 12 or older experienced about 552,000 nonfatal violent victimizations by an intimate partner. Men were five times less likely to be victims. In the same year men experienced 101,000 nonfatal violent victimizations by an intimate partner.[168]

14. Women are underrepresented in elected office. Congress is dominated by men. Even though the majority of voters are women, there is a disproportionately low number of women in Congress. In 2015, only 20 of the 100 Senators were women. Of the 435 Members of the House of Representatives, only 84 are women.

15. In spite of the requirement under Title IX that men and women are supposed to be treated equally in any schools receiving federal funds, discrimination persists. Women have been forced to file lawsuits rather than the government policing the schools and withdrawing funding when discrimination occurs.[169] Every year male athletes get $179 million dollars more than women in scholarships. Colleges spend 76% of their athletic operating budgets on male sports. A mere 16% of their recruiting budgets is devoted to finding the best female athletes.[170]

16. Women in the clergy may be discriminated against more than in almost any other profession. Denominations that are the most likely to discriminate against women are Roman Catholics, Eastern Orthodox, Church of Jesus Christ of Latter-day Saints, and Southern Baptists. The justification for this disparate treatment of women is a book written by men, the Bible.[171] An estimated ten to twelve percent of clergy across America are women.[172]

17. Women are profoundly underrepresented in the Executive Offices of major corporations, including those who market their products to women.[173]

18. Women are also underrepresented on college boards. The numbers are increasing, but not fast enough. In 1981 20% of college boards were women. By 2007 the percentage had increased to 31%. During that same period, female Board Chairs increased from 10% to 18%.[174] This disparity is especially troubling when contrasted to the gender gap in college. For the last 35 years women have outnumbered men as students in college.[175] Yet 70% of college boards are men.

19. Some laws and law-making bodies in the United States are blatantly discriminatory towards women. Here are just a few examples:

    a. In Florida it is illegal for a single woman to parachute or skydive on a Sunday.

    b. In Montana a legislator explained that he was serious about wanting to outlaw yoga pants.[176]

    c. In 2012 a California Appeals Court overturned a rapist's conviction after a judge cited a standing 1872 law stating only married women could legally be raped.

d. In 2012 a legislator in Missouri proposed a bill reading, "No abortion shall be performed or induced unless and until the father of the unborn child provides written, notarized consent to the abortion." It is still legal in more than 30 states in the United States for a rapist to sue his rape victim for child visitation and custody if his forcible insemination resulted in a pregnancy.

e. In 2011 the Texas Legislature, known to be a predominantly large group of misogynistic men, circulated a picture of a child breast feeding with the words printed "Don't Expand the Nanny State." Female legislators were outraged and spoke out. One of the female law makers reported that some male lawmakers had pornography on the House floor.[177]

As women have come closer to achieving equality, discrimination has become harder to prove. In the 1970's, if a law firm had no female associates it was obvious that they were in need of some serious sensitivity training. In 2015, if 85% of the same firm's partners are male, it may be much harder to prove that the Senior Partners are unfairly promoting men over women. Any woman who might complain that she was unfairly denied a partnership position would be subject to intense scrutiny. Promotions are even more subjective. A person intent on discrimination knows to create a file documenting reasons for their failure to promote a woman.

The reality is that discrimination women faced in the 1960's related to women being excluded from many professions. Today the discrimination women face is in promotion and advancement into leadership positions after initial hiring. Even though women hold almost 52% of all professional-level jobs, we remain substantially underrepresented in executive and leadership positions. For example:

➢   Women hold only 14.6% of executive office positions.

➢   Women hold only 16.9% of Fortune 500 board seats.

➢   In the financial services industry women make up 54.2% of the labor force. However, only 12.4% of executive officers and 18.3% of board directors are women. There are no female CEOs.

➢   Women account for 78.4% of the labor force in the health care industry. Only 14.6% of executive officers and 12.4% of board directors are women. There are no female CEOs.

➤ Since 1973, women have consistently outscored men on Law School admission tests.[178] Yet women only represented 19% of students in Law Schools. In 2011the numbers of women in Law School had increased. However, of the top 25 schools, only two had more women than men.[179]

➤ In 2014, women accounted for 45% of associates in law firms. However women only represented 25% of non-equity partners, and 15% of equity partners.

➤ In 2014 women comprised 34.3% of all medical doctors. However only 15.9% of medical school deans were women.[180]

The evolution of Feminism has brought us to this third wave. Mastery of the third wave is dependent upon personal mastery of the first two. One Hundred years ago when women fought for the right to vote, they weren't riding the First Wave so that women wouldn't need to vote. They assumed that if women had the right, they would vote. Today, every woman must appreciate the importance of her vote. By going to the ballot box each woman learns to surf the first wave of feminism. It is easier to surf that wave because women before us led the way. Yet it still requires a conscious decision and dedication of time to learn about the issues, the candidates, and then to cast a vote.

Personal mastery of the second wave is also essential for every woman. The second wave was characterized by women fighting for the right of women to seek higher education and professional success. Women today must take advantage of the educational and professional opportunities available to them in order to master the second wave. While the opportunities for women vary, both educationally and professionally, each woman must take advantage of what is available to her. Pursuit of educational and professional achievement is not easy, but it is essential to mastering the second wave of feminism. Through education and professional achievement women gain the confidence and independence that allows them to move on to the third wave. Without that accomplishment, women remain dependent and subservient.

Personal mastery of the third wave of feminism is the most elusive. Mastery of the third wave depends on searching for your personal *happily ever after* and respecting other women for reaching a different destination on their journey. Just as men desire different life styles, so do women. Some men choose to stay single. The same is true of some women. Some fathers find happiness staying home to raise their children and some mothers do too. Some men and women do both simultaneously, but they have to apportion their time accordingly. Learning to surf the Third Wave of Feminism is the personal search for the right balance between home and professional life. The Third Wave is characterized by women fighting for respect from other women who have made choices different than their own. Until we respect each other we will never achieve respect from men. It is a prerequisite to making a "choice" that women attain an education. Until we have earned the ability to have a profession, there is really no choice to be made. We may make many choices during our lives, as circumstances in our lives change.

Women of color may have fewer choices available to them than their white counterparts. Ethnicity is just one factor in determining what choices may be available to a woman.

D. Double Discrimination

On January 1, 1863, President Abraham Lincoln signed the Emancipation Proclamation declaring that slavery had come to an end.[181] One Hundred Fifty Eight years later Blacks in America continue to be treated as second-class citizens. It is no secret that discrimination against all minorities is the norm. Twenty-four years ago, 82% of college students perceived that discrimination was a problem. In 2014, 75% of students reported that racism still exists in America. Over a period of 24 years, only 7% of Americans changed their perception regarding discrimination.[182]

Unfortunately we see the effects of discrimination in every aspect of life. Minorities have higher rates of unemployment. When they are hired, employers pay them less than Whites. However, disparate treatment in employment is of little concern when compared to violence directed toward minorities. In 2014 at least 238 Blacks were killed by police. That represents more people than all Blacks killed on 9 -11. [183] Nobody keeps track of the number of unarmed Black men who are killed by the police. However in August of 2014, Mother Jones reported that Michael Brown was one of at least four unarmed black men who had been killed by police in the last month. [184] A typical example of the outrageous conduct of police is seen in the video of the killing of Walter Scott. Mr. Scott was stopped for a broken tail light. Within minutes of the stop, he was executed. The video records the police officer firing his gun 8 times at the back of the unarmed black man, as he ran, fearful of the policeman about to kill him.[cc]

People of color are disproportionately represented at every stage of the criminal justice system. The Innocence Project is credited with exoneration of 297 prisoners through DNA analysis. The frightening thing is that 70% of the people exonerated by the efforts of the Innocence Project were minorities. Of those minorities, 63% were African-Americans.[185]

Discrimination in the United States has been identified as the cause of political, economic, and social inequality for over a century. Even though 1 in 8 New Yorkers are Asian-American, only one serves in the state legislature. Unemployment rates are higher among minorities. Unemployment of Black youth is 4.5 times the national average. In June of 2011, the median wealth of White households was 20 times that of Black households, and 18 times that of Hispanic homes. Ethnic minorities are denied equal educational opportunities. The Washington Post reported in 2000, that even in large U. S. cities, few residential areas are actually racially integrated. In 1998, 72.2 percent of the White families owned their own homes while the proportions for African American and Latin American families were only 46.4% and 44.9% respectively. [186] An investigation in 1996 indicated that 90 percent of the chief

---

[cc] https://www.youtube.com/watch?v=8nrqFaSRclc

executives or managers of U.S. companies have never given any Blacks the same status and responsibilities as Whites.[187]

Thus, women who are minorities face double discrimination. They fight discrimination due to their gender and color. Women of color may fail to be considered for a job simply because of their names.[188] Minority women are more than twice as likely to be unemployed as their White counterparts. Moreover, the unemployment rate for minority women has not substantially changed over the last 30 years.[189] Pakistani and Bangladeshi women are particularly affected. The following unemployment rates are quite revealing.[190]

Unemployed:

- Pakistani and Bangladeshi women - 20.5%

- Black women - 17.7%

- White women - 6.8%

Women of color make up 36.3% of America's female population. They constitute 33% of the female workforce. Yet women of color hold:[191]

- 11.9% of managerial and professional positions

- 3.2% of board seats on Fortune 500 companies

- 0 seats on the board of directors at more than 66% of Fortune 500 companies

Education is also significantly different for women of color. Caucasian women achieve significantly higher levels of education than African American women.[192]

- In 2010, 21% of African American women obtained a college degree, while thirty percent of White women did.

- Twenty four percent of science, technology, engineering, and math majors were women. However only 2% of the 24% were Blacks.

- White women earn more than Black women among full-time, year-round workers, regardless of what degrees they held.

Black women continue to have higher rates of unemployment. Those who are employed earn less than their White counterparts. In 2010 White women earned 78.1 cents for every dollar earned by White men. Black women earned 64 cents.[193]

Women of color are more likely than White women to be pushed into the lowest-earning occupations in the service sector, in sales, and in office jobs. Among working women in 2014, 62% of Hispanics, 57% of Blacks, 51% of Whites, and 44% of Asians, worked in service occupations. In 2014, only 35 percent of Black women and 26 percent of Hispanic women were employed in higher-paying management, professional, and related jobs—compared with 48 percent of Asian women and 43 percent of White women.[194]

It is never fair to generalize about racism. Blacks can be racist, and Whites can be strong advocates for the minority community. Men may be feminists, and women may not be. For example, Barack Obama is a feminist. Sarah Palin is not.[195, z] It was Barack Obama who signed the Lilly Ledbetter Fair Pay Act into law, on his first day in office. That law required employers to pay women and men the same salary for a job done equally well.[196] Sarah Palin opposed the Lilly Ledbetter Fair Pay Act. She is a woman who promoted herself as being in favor of equal pay for women, but opposed a law that would require it.[197]

In 2008, it was gratifying that the majority of women in America recognized that the person committed to representing the interests of women was not the ticket with the woman. If gender alone had been the basis for women voting, the GOP would have won the election in 2008 with Sarah Palin as McCain's Vice Presidential choice. Instead the majority of women in America voted for Obama. The gender gap was critical to Obama's success in 2008. Fifty-six percent of women voted for Obama, while only 43% voted for McCain. Men only favored Obama by 1%.[198]

In 2012 the gender gap was even greater. Obama won the female vote by 12 points, but lost the male vote by an 8 point margin. Thus there was a 20 point gender gap in the 2012 election. That gender gap represents the largest Gallup measured gender gap since Gallup began compiling statistics in 1952.[199] The 2012 election was described as an historic moment for women. Not only was Obama re-elected, but more women were sent to Congress than ever before.[200]

The impact of women voting in America is powerful and unequivocal. Women represent the majority of the electorate in the United States. The majority of votes cast in the 2012 election were female votes (53%).[201] Women represent the majority of the population in America. Women are more likely to vote than men. In the 2012 elections, it was estimated that women out-voted men by 5.5 million votes.[202] Susan Anthony, Elizabeth Stanton, and Lucretia Mott would have been proud.

Because of the discrimination faced by women throughout the last century, women should be more understanding of the challenges faced by women of color. If White women were unenthusiastic about voting for a misogynistic white man, women of color were even less inclined to vote for him. If White women felt a sense of defeat when applying for admission to college, women of color felt worse. When a potential employer refused to hire Elizabeth O'Connor because she was a woman, women across the country might be outraged. When a potential employer refused to interview Ayesha Umar because of her name, women across the country should cry out even louder.

E. A Stalled Revolution

In recent years the feminist revolution has stalled. During the 20th century the gender wage gap narrowed, sex segregation in most professions declined, and the rate of women climbing into management roles steadily increased. However, the rapid rate of change that I experienced during the 70's and 80's, became stagnant in the last two decades. For example in 1980 there were no women in top executive positions in Fortune 100 companies. By 2001 those same companies employed 11% women in those top positions. Today only 9% of those positions are held by women. Simultaneously, the percentage of women on corporate boards has stagnated over the last decade at 12%. The percentage of women on Fortune 500 boards has remained at 17% for the last 8 years.[203]

The legal field also provides a clear view of the stalemate women have faced in the last 10 years. In 2012, Harvard Law Professor, Nancy Gertner, confirmed that the feminist movement had stalled. She explained that the Second Wave needs a second wind.[204] As evidence to support her conclusion, she explained that half of all new lawyers are women. However, only 16% of equity partners are women. Of the attorneys who leave the profession, most are women. Most who leave do so for family and social reasons.[205]

Between 1994 and 2000's the equality revolution was viewed as stuck in neutral. Those Americans preferring a home with a male breadwinner and female homemaker, rose from 34% to 40%. During that period working women who preferred to work part time rose from 48% to 60%. While other countries continued to realize an increase in their female labor-force participation, the number of women in the United States' labor force was leveling off.[206]

To complicate matters, the cost of child care has skyrocketed in recent years. The cost of child care has increased at almost twice the rate of other goods and services. By 2012 the cost of child care in 31 states was more expensive than college tuition. This cost is especially critical for first-time mothers who are unmarried. Today more than 40% of first-time mothers are unmarried. More than half of those will separate from their mate by the time the child is five years old.[207]

Considering the cost of child care alone, we understand why so many women live in poverty in America. In 2012 the poverty rate for women stabilized after three years of increases. Poverty rates for women and children remain at historically high levels. In 2011, 18 million women lived in poverty. Over half of poor children in the United States live in a household headed by a woman.[208]

Some have suggested that the way to jumpstart the gender revolution is to change gender pressures on men.[209] Another alternative is the institution of a federal program for child care. In the history of the United States, the only time we had a comprehensive, universal system of child care, was during WWII. The Lanham Act of 1942 created a system of government-subsidized childcare that enabled women to go to work. More than 500,000 children were participants in that type of childcare between 1943 and 1946. While women were working in factories supporting the war effort, the children were being cared for through government-subsidized day care. When the war ended, women and children returned home.[210]

Another factor contributing to the suspension of the feminist revolution seems to be the rejection of young women of the "feminist" label. Modern women would like to avoid being associated with the image of feminists as being "famously abrasive." Women don't want to be categorized as bra-burners, or anti-men. Young women today are embarrassed that there was ever a group of women known as SCUM, the Society to Cut Up Men, or a group known as WITCH (the Women's International Feminist Conspiracy from Hell). Women today want to distance themselves from women who described pregnancy as barbaric, and those who compared marriage to cancer.[211] Some media personalities have made significant contributions to the idea that being a "feminist" is something negative. Rush Limbaugh, the radio personality with the most listeners in America, refers to feminists as "Feminine-nazis."[212] Limbaugh explains that "Feminism was established so as to allow unattractive women easier access to the mainstream." Rush Limbaugh has made a name for himself by attacking women.[dd] He has even gone so far as to say that in his opinion feminism is the reason that the average size of a man's penis is getting smaller.[ee] Unfortunately, Mr. Limbaugh is only one outspoken man who demeans women every chance he gets.[ff]

Women, sensitive to the label feminist, started a Twitter group, with a hashtag campaign on Tumblr: #womenagainstfeminism. The goal was to disassociate themselves from women who seemed too strident and angry. The attempt was to divide women who perceived themselves to be attractive to men, and attracted to men, from those who were uninterested in men, or unable to attract men. The proponents of this heterosexual attractive group delineated women as either feminists, or not. Attractive, heterosexual, women were standing in defiance of unattractive, homosexual women. The implication, promoted by the likes of Rush Limbaugh, was that if you were not involved in a relationship with a man, you were either too ugly or too lesbian. Instead of objecting to this characterization regarding the value of women being determined by their attractiveness to men, some women choose to attempt to make themselves more sexually attractive to men. Instead of working to improve their intellect and independence, they worked to improve their appearance. Their efforts resulted in being dependent on men, rather than becoming more independent. Instead of

---

[dd] https://www.youtube.com/watch?v=CRUKCEj7qqA
[ee] https://www.youtube.com/watch?v=jCFySez-4tw
[ff] https://www.youtube.com/watch?v=asUrboJyc78

trying to educate other women about their values, women became antagonistic and aggressive towards each other.

Yahoo's CEO Marissa Mayer said she didn't consider herself to be a feminist because even though she believed in equal rights, she didn't have the "militant drive and the sort of ...chip on the shoulder" that she associated with the label.[213] She isn't alone. Many famous women have declared that they are not feminists: [214]

1. Madonna says she is a humanist, not a feminist.

2. Katy Perry thinks feminist is too strong a label, even though she sings songs about female empowerment.

3. Carrie Underwood feels that the term feminist is too strong a term to describe herself. She admits that she is a strong female.

4. Lady Gaga doesn't like the label feminist because she likes men.

5. Gwyneth Paltrow has strong feminine beliefs, but has no interest is being labeled a feminist.

6. Taylor Swift sings about finding your own strength and independence but doesn't identify herself as a feminist.

7. Susan Sarandon articulated the problem. She explained that the term feminist is antiquated. She doesn't want to be associated with the negative connotations of feminism. She simply believes in equality.

Most women agree that being treated equally to men is critically important. Women want to be viewed as part of the team rather than a torch-bearer for women. A woman won't be viewed as one-of-the-guys if she sues the guys for treating her differently. Instead of working to defend the company in a suit by an adversary, women claiming discrimination become the adversary.

It is often assumed that if you are a woman, you are necessarily committed to protecting women. However that assumption is dangerously wrong. A woman can do more damage to other women than a man can. As an example, it was a female principal in April of 2015 who authorized the photo-shopping of a class photo to remove the word "feminist" from the shirt of an eighth grade girl in the photo.[215] It was a woman who said that women are being raped in college because too many women go to college.[216] Ann Coulter said: "I think all real females are right-wingers...and I can tell you that based on experience — and my bodyguard will back me up on this — all pretty girls are right-wingers."[217] She also explained that:

"...rape isn't really rape unless the victim has been hit on the head with a brick."[218]

Ms. Coulter explained that women allege rape to try to get attention.[219] Joni Ernst, the hog castrating Iowa Senator, voted for a personhood amendment, giving rights under the constitution to a fertilized egg, before implantation in the uterus.[220] The law she supported would have prevented all abortions, and the use of the pill.[221,] Christine O'Donnell is a woman who condemned women who masturbate.[gg] Sharon Angle proudly proclaimed that if a woman was raped by her father, the solution was to make lemonade.[222] Each of these women are, by definition, not feminists. Each of these women would limit the fundamental rights of women to control their bodies and their futures.

Over 75% of American women believe that the woman's movement has had the effect of making life better for them. The dictionary defines feminism as a "person who supports political, economic, and social equality for women." The majority of men and women in America consider themselves to be "feminists," by that definition. When no definition is provided, less than half of women surveyed considered themselves to be feminist. A majority of voters feel women are not treated equally in the workplace (63 percent), in politics (63 percent), in the armed forces (55 percent), and in the press (54 percent). But only 14 percent considered themselves to be a feminist. Only 17% would want their daughter to be a feminist.[223] Thus there is a significant disconnect between the fundamental principal of equal treatment of men and women, and the willingness of women to be associated with the label feminist.[224] If women were treated equally to men, the importance of being an advocate for equal rights would be of little concern. The reality is that there remains a need for men and women to stand up to those who view women as inferior to men.

Hillary Clinton is likely to be the Democratic nominee for President of the United States in 2016. If she were to be elected as the President of the United States, many women would consider her election to be the final crack in the glass ceiling.[225] Hillary has already identified pay equity for women as a central message in her campaign. She singled out Patricia Arquette's comments, from the actress' Oscar-winning speech, to emphasize the need for women to demand equal treatment.[hh]

However, even if Hillary Clinton should be the first female President of the United States, we are fooling ourselves to believe that discrimination against women will magically go away.[226] It seems likely that when the glass ceiling is shattered, women will find that the glass was actually a mirror. Beyond the

---

[gg] https://www.youtube.com/watch?v=RzHcqcXo_NA
[hh] https://www.youtube.com/watch?v=L-EmDy3w1X8

mirror is an attic, and a roof. Both must be demolished before women will enjoy true equality.

Consider the impact of having our first African-American President. It is undisputed that our country took a monumental step forward in race relations, when a majority of voters cast their ballots for our first black President. However, some feel that race relations is worse now than when Obama took office. James Peterson, the director of African Studies at Lehigh University in Pennsylvania said: "We are more racially fractured and fragmented" since the 2008 election. Blacks earn less money and graduate from college at lower rates than Whites. Blacks are disproportionately represented in prisons than Whites. Unemployment rate for Blacks is 11.1% which is more than double the national rate for all races. The unemployment rate for Whites is 4.9%.[227]

In fact 4 in 10 people surveyed believe that race relations have actually gotten worse during Obama's term.[228] It seems likely that discrimination against Blacks isn't worse. We are just seeing people who have always been bigots feel a greater need to speak out because now they feel threatened. Women should be prepared. If Hillary should be elected the first female President, people who view women as inferior to men may feel threatened. They may feel a need to assert their dominance more publically. People who hold discriminatory attitudes toward women may feel threatened if the majority of Americans view a woman as competent to lead our nation.

"Over my lifetime, women have demonstrated repeatedly that they can do anything that men can do, while still managing traditional women's work at the same time. But the same expansion of roles has not been available to men."

-Anne-Marie Slaughter [229]

CHAPTER IV. EVOLUTION

A. The Transformation of Mothers

The perception of mothers has changed over time. Mothers were once demonized as "freeloaders who were destroying America."[230] In the early 1900's, as theories of Freud became popular, mothers were blamed for many of the problems of their children. The decades of mom-hate continued into the 1940's and 1950's.

One author summarized the disrespect for mothers when he wrote in 1955:

> *"[L]et us look at mom. She is a middle-aged puffin with an eye like a hawk that has just seen a rabbit twitch far below. She is about twenty-five pounds overweight, with no sprint, but sharp heels and a hard backhand which she does not regard as a foul, but a womanly defense. In a thousand of her there is not sex appeal enough to budge a hermit ten paces off a rock ledge. She none the less spends several hundred dollars a year on permanents and transformations, pomades, cleansers, rouges, lipsticks, and the like — and fools nobody except herself."*[231]

Images of mothers, and especially stay-at-home mothers, are better today than in 1955. Yet there remains some lingering disrespect. Not surprisingly, mothers still feel some insecurity as a result. Mothers who don't work outside the home are easily intimidated. The first and last question asked of a mother at a social gathering is "What do you do?" The person asking the question isn't really interested in a stay-at-home mother's answer. The real focus of the question is to determine if the woman is a professional. The only person to ask the next question, once a mother has identified herself as a stay-at-home mother, is another stay-at-home mother. A professional man isn't interested in what a stay-at-home mother thinks about the newest brand of disposable diaper. He doesn't really care what that mother might be making for dinner. It probably never occurred to him that a stay-at-home mother might have an interesting perspective on the conflict in the Middle East, or a strong opinion about the national debt. A professional mother may be interested in what the stay-at-home mother has been doing for her children. Yet, the professional mother doesn't really want to hear about it. It might make her feel guilty since the professional had not had time to do the same for her kids. Moms have been described as their own worst enemy. Guilt and motherhood are almost expected to go together. Stay-at-home moms feel guilty that they aren't contributing financially to the family. They worry their kids won't respect them as much as if they had a real job. When some mothers leave for work, they fret over neglecting their children."[232]

Those who appreciate mothers have said:

1. "All that I am or ever hope to be, I owe to my angel mother." — Abraham Lincoln

2. "My mother was the most beautiful woman I ever saw. All I am I owe to my mother. I attribute my success in life to the moral, intellectual and physical education I received from her." —George Washington

3. "A mother is the truest friend we have, when trials heavy and sudden fall upon us; when adversity takes the place of prosperity; when friends desert us; when trouble thickens around us, still will she cling to us, and endeavor by her kind precepts and counsels to dissipate the clouds of darkness, and cause peace to return to our hearts." —Washington Irving

4. "Kids don't stay with you if you do it right. It's the one job where, the better you are, the more surely you won't be needed in the long run." —Barbara Kingsolver

5. "Mothers and their children are in a category all their own. There's no bond so strong in the entire world. No love so instantaneous and forgiving." —Gail Tsukiyama

6. "The best place to cry is on a mother's arms." —Jodi Picoult

7. "If I have done anything in life worth attention, I feel sure that I inherited the disposition from my mother." —Booker T. Washington

8. "I realized when you look at your mother, you are looking at the purest love you will ever know." —Mitch Albom

Even though so many women are working outside the home, the time spent by mothers with their children has actually increased. In 1965 mothers spent an average of 10 hours a week on child care. As of 2011, moms, including mothers who worked outside the home, were spending an average of 14 hours a week on childcare.[233] Previously, mothers turned to the government for advice about the appropriate way to care for children. Now mothers seem to rely more on their individual ideas about childcare, and less on advice from the government.[234]

Mothers and their children would never put a dollar value on the importance of mom being at home. However, it is an interesting exercise to consider the financial contribution of a mother to the family's budget. When the contributions of a mother are considered for only their economic value, the results are surprising. The financial contribution of a stay-at-home mother, who doesn't generate any revenue, has been valued from as little as $30,000 per year.[235]

Some mothers find that the solution to the great balancing act is to work out of their homes. Mothers have been very creative in their options for employment where their desk is located in their home. As an in-house counsel to Prince Charming's business, I use the same desk and computer as I use when writing my blog. Other women, working out of their homes, have held a variety of positions including: Bilingual Senior Technical Advisor, CEO-Executive Director, Community Gardens Director, Company Chef, County Transportation Planner, Director of Global Advertising, Director of Strategic Accounts, Grant Writer & Manager, Human Resource & Recruiting Coordinator, K-12 Teachers, Online Fitness Coach, Project manager, RN nurse coach, and Vacation Planning Counselor.[236]

Some women have started businesses that operate out of their homes.[237] There are 10.1 million women-owned businesses in the United States. Over 90% of moms interviewed in one study said the desire for family flexibility is the number-one reason they work from home.[238]

There are an estimated 85.4 million mothers in America. Thus being a mother didn't make me unusual or special. With so many women achieving such amazing success in the professional world, it is harder than ever to be just a mom. Perhaps it is the ease of becoming a mother that minimizes its importance. Any 13 year old girl with less than a high school education can figure out how to become a mother. There is no public recognition for the mothers who do a good job with their kids, and no public humiliation for those who ignore their children. Even a special-needs teen could become a mother. How many men or women born in the '50's could achieve the status of Senior Partner at a major firm, in a major city, within 7 years of starting their career?

An increasing number of women are choosing not to have children. In 1976, 90% of women were mothers by the age of 44. By 2012 that percentage had dropped nine points, to 81%.[239] The majority of mothers in America were in the labor force when they became a mother.[240] In 2011 five million women stayed at home with their children. They only represented 23% of married couples with children under 15 years old.[241] Four in ten women with children are the primary breadwinners in their homes.[242] Even though almost half of all Americans report that children are better served if their mother is a stay-at-home mom, nobody was encouraging me to quit my job.[243]

When the wife earns more than the husband, the couple is more likely to report dissatisfaction with their marriage. Those couples have a higher rate of divorce and are more likely to revert to stereotypical sex roles regarding domestic chores and child care.[24] According to the Pew Research Center: [245]

- Most people in America (73%) feel the trend toward more women in the workforce has been a change for the better.

- Most Americans (62%) believe it is preferable for the husband and wife to each work outside the home, and to each participate in both domestic chores and child rearing.

- A minority of Americans (21%) believe that the trend of mothers who have young children, and work outside the home, has been a good thing for society.

- More working mothers (40%) than working fathers (25%) report feeling "rushed." Mothers who stay at home feel "rushed" less often (26%) than mothers working outside the home.

- Most working mothers (62%) would prefer to work part-time as compared to 21% of fathers.

- Few mothers (12%) feel that having a mother who works full time is the ideal situation for the child.

- The majority of mothers in America work outside the home. The number of single mothers supporting children is increasing.[246] Today, twenty years after I quit my job, there is an increase in the number of women who opt to stay at home with their children. Fifteen years ago, 23% of mothers chose to stay at home. Today, for the first time in decades that number has risen to 29%. Even the number of stay-at-home-fathers has risen.

The impact of women choosing to have fewer children has resulted in an unprecedented change in demographics in America. White women are more likely than Hispanic or African American women to remain childless.[247] For the first time in the history of the United States, deaths of Caucasian people in 2012, outnumbered the birth rate of Caucasians. No other racial group experienced a similar decline.[248]

I did not contribute to the decline of the Caucasian population in America. I had three children. I had a choice due to the financial security my husband provided. While financial security provided by a spouse is desirable, it is the reason that I had to make a choice. If we were dependent on my financial contribution, I wouldn't have struggled to make a choice. I would still have had children, but perhaps not three. Instead of waiting to be a Junior Partner before having children, I might have waited to become a Senior Partner.

Never have I taken my financial security for granted. Nobody wishes to be restrained by financial considerations. More money is always better. Yet it was our financial security that put me in a position to feel as if I needed to choose whether to devote myself to my children, or to my career. I worked quite hard to distinguish myself professionally. It was hard to imagine a life without my professional status. I felt vulnerable and uncertain of the path ahead. It was unimaginable that I would simply give up everything I had worked so hard to achieve. How could I give up a great job, great salary, and all the professional accolades that came with being a Senior Partner at a big Dallas firm? Didn't I realize that if I successfully raised smart, independent children, that they would reward my commitment and sacrifice by leaving me to pursue their dreams? My dream was to build a loving and nurturing home for them. If I accomplished that goal they would grow up to be strong, independent, adults... and leave home. Every mother faces the same problem.

B. The Transformation of Fathers

Fifty years ago Betty Friedan gave birth to the *Feminine Mystique*. The question she identified for women was "Is this all?" Betty wasn't focused on identifying everything that could be part of *all* for a woman. There was no consideration of whether women could have, or even wanted to have, *all*. Rather, Betty was simply highlighting the desire of women to have more than what they had. The *more* that women wanted was a chance to excel professionally. Women wanted a chance to be treated equally to men in the realm of their professions.

In 1963 there was no simultaneous movement among men to become better fathers or participants in household tasks. Men who were successful professionally weren't lying awake at night feeling dissatisfied. They weren't thinking that they needed to be more involved in the care of their children. Fathers were feeling that they had fulfilled their fatherly obligations if they were good providers. What more could a father be expected to do for his children than provide for their financial security? The expectation for fathers was clear. A father's job was to provide financially for the family. The mother's job was to do everything else; including keeping her husband happy.

After women began finding success professionally, two things happened. First, women had less time for child rearing and domestic chores. Women were spending more hours of every day in professional pursuits. Secondly, men faced the reality that they were required to do more domestically. Fathers had no choice. They had to be more involved with the care of their children. Because women were contributing more to the financial security of the family, women had less time for domestic chores and child rearing. The presumption was that domestic chores and child rearing was still the responsibility of the mother. However, because mothers were helping fathers meet the father's obligation to provide financial security for the family, fathers began to help mothers meet their obligations to raise the children. This was not the result of male enlightenment. Men did not wake up one morning and appreciate the importance of spending more time with their children. It was only after spending more time with their children that men began to appreciate the difference they could make in the lives of their children. Men were not motivated by a commitment to correct the years of oppression of women. They simply realized that if they wanted to continue to enjoy the financial contribution of their wives, men had to help their wives find more time to make more money. In a way, the man was doing his job to provide for the financial security of the family, because he facilitated his wife being able to continue to work.

The attitude of courts in custody disputes reflects a similar evolution of thought. In the 1940's Judges (who were typically male) ruled that mothers were better suited to raise children. That presumption favoring mothers continued until the 1960's. During the 1960's divorce rates were rising. More women than ever were pursuing professions. In the event of a divorce, men challenged the presumption that the mother was the preferred parent to raise a child. By the mid-70's, most states had abandoned the maternal presumption. In its place they adopted gender-neutral laws.[249] In 1970 the National Conference of Commissioners on Uniform State Laws adopted the Uniform Marriage and Divorce Act. It was ultimately adopted by a majority of states.[250] For the first time in history, custody decisions were based on the best interest of the child, rather than on gender or rights of the parents. Now custody decisions were based on the psychological parent and the need for continuity in parenting. When appropriate, the child's own wishes could be considered. The concept of joint custody originated in the early 1970's. It was the logical next-step in recognizing the interest of fathers and the desire of a father to take a more active role in the life of his child. The concept of shared custody was enhanced by several other developments that occurred in the 1970's. The child development field began during the decade of the '70's. The research and publications of experts in the field indicated that the contributions of the father to his child's development had been undervalued. Simultaneously, there was recognition of the importance of the child's attachment to their father. As families have increasingly become dependent on the financial contribution of the mother, families have increasing become dependent on the domestic contribution of the father. In divorced couples, fathers have increasingly experienced a sense of loss and alienation if they are not awarded joint custody.[251]

The father's sense of loss and alienation experienced in a divorce was the subject of the 1979 movie *Kramer vs. Kramer*. The five Academy Awards received by the movie illustrated the excellence of the actors and actresses who starred in the movie. However the award of "Best Picture" was, at least, partially motivated by the relevance of the subject-matter to moral dilemmas of the time. Audiences across the country were moved by the testimony of Dustin Huffman as he described the plight of fathers who became a part of their child's life, and then faced the possibility of losing custody. He explained: [ii]

"If I understand it correctly, what means the most here is what's best for our son. What's best for Billy. My wife used to always say to me: 'Why can't a woman have the same ambitions as a man?' I think you're right. And maybe I've learned that much. But by the same token, I'd like to know, what law is it that says that a woman is a better parent simply by virtue of her sex? You know, I've had a lot of time to think about what it is that makes somebody a good parent? You know, it has to do with constancy, it has to do with patience, it has to do with listening to him. It has to do with pretending to listen to him when you can't even listen anymore. It has to do with love, like, like, like she was saying. And I don't know where it's written that it says that a woman has a corner on

---

[ii] https://www.youtube.com/watch?v=re0xt6hDdqE

that market, that, that a man has any less of those emotions than a woman does." [252]

In 36 years since the release of *Kramer vs. Kramer*, more fathers are winning custody of their children. In 1979 fathers were awarded sole custody in only 5% of cases. In 2014 fathers were awarded sole custody in roughly 15% of cases. In November of 2014 the **National At-Home Dad Network** met in New York for its annual retreat.[253] One Hundred men from across the country traded recipes, attended workshops on seatbelt safety, exchanged e-mail addresses, and listened to a panel of women discuss feelings when a husband buys a gift for her with her money.[254]

No longer is it unusual to see a family in which the father accepts a significant responsibility in both household chores and child care. Even though mothers continue to carry the "lion's share" of responsibilities at home, dads are doing more.[255] Mothers still spend almost twice as much time on childcare as fathers. Yet, fathers have almost tripled the time they spend on child care. In 1965 fathers spent 2.4 hours per week on child care. Fifty-six years later, in 2011 fathers spent an average of 7.3 hours a week on child care. At the time of the publication of the Feminine Mystique the typical father spent an average of 4 hours per week doing household chores. Today that number has more than doubled to 10 hours per week. During that same period mom's time doing housework declined from 32 hours per week to 18.[256] These numbers don't add up. Today couples are spending 8 hours less per week on domestic chores. Either couples are hiring more domestic help, or we are changing our sheets less often. Either way, couples seem to be realizing that having clean sheets more often doesn't really make us happier. Perhaps the increasing involvement of fathers in domestic chores has had an unanticipated benefit. Men have taught women that spending more time cleaning the house, doesn't really result in greater happiness. If we clean too often, we spend more money on cleaning products and devices, and have less time to search for our happily ever after. Most men would happily trade more free time for a little more dust on the furniture. If a multiple choice question were asked of anyone regarding whether a man would choose to attend a sporting event or scrub the bathroom floor, everyone would get that answer correct. [jj, kk]

A majority (63%) of fathers feel it is harder to be a dad today than a generation ago. Perhaps that is because the general public is relatively critical of the job men do as fathers. Only one in four adults think fathers today are actually doing a better job than their father did. One third of adults surveyed indicated that

---

[jj] http://sports.yahoo.com/blogs/mlb-big-league-stew/hero-dad-makes-one-handed-catch-while-holding-baby-181701279.html
[kk] https://www.youtube.com/watch?v=s5XPD5zWcUY

fathers today are doing a worse job than their father did. Among fathers, 47% feel they are doing a better job with child care than their father.

A strong majority of the public feels that children need a father in the home. Sixty-nine percent of adults surveyed feel that having a father in the home is essential to a child's happiness. Those statistics are consistent with the changes that have taken place over the last four decades with regard to the amount of time that dads spend with their children. In 1965, married fathers with children under 18 years of age, spent an average of 2.6 hours per week caring for their children. Over the next 20 years, the time fathers spent providing care for their children gradually increased to 2.7 hours in 1975, and 3 hours per week in 1985. From 1985 to 2000 time spent by dad with his kids more than doubled to 6.5 hours per week. Thus as women were working more outside the home, and their time with the children was on the decline, fathers were spending more time with their children.[257] As women have increased their contribution to the economic security of the family, fathers have increased their contribution to the domestic tranquility of the family. While the majority of fathers still earn more than their wives, the number of mothers who are the primary breadwinners is on the rise. In 1960 the wife only surpassed her husband's income in 4% of families. In 2011 23% of women earned more than their husbands.

More importantly, the norm for families in America has changed. The model of dad as a provider and mom as a homemaker, no longer represents the typical family. Two-income families are now the norm in America. Nearly 60 percent of married couples with children under the age of 18 were dual-income families in 2011, up from about 25 percent in 1960.[258]

In June of 2014 the White House, for the first time in history, hosted a Summit on Working Families.[259] The focus of the Summit was to consider the "state of working dads." The focus of the summit was the number of fathers who are taking a more "hands on" approach to raising children. Finding a work-life balance for fathers may be even more difficult for dad, than for mom. If women who stay at home to raise their children feel marginalized, imagine the disrespect a father feels. If professional women minimize the importance of a stay-at-home mother's contribution, imagine the lack of respect realized by stay-at-home fathers from professional fathers.

One in five kids at daycare have a dad identified as the primary caregiver. Most of these dads are employed. Modern dads are spending more time on both childcare and housework while balancing a career. More dads today change diapers, do school pick-up, help with homework, and have to be able to pick up a sick kid from preschool. With more time spent on childcare and housework and little reduction in time spent in the workplace, fathers are increasingly reporting work-life conflict. In the last 30 years the number of father only families has more than tripled.[260]

In April of 2015 a new study on the health of children in divorced families reported that children fare better when they spend time living with both of their parents.[261] Thus, joint custody may be the optimal situation for both dad and his kids.

The search for happily ever after is no longer limited to women. The critical importance of child care is no longer a woman's issue. As fathers have evolved to take a more significant role in child care, men have begun to truly respect and value the contribution of any parent, male or female, in raising the next generation. As more men accept a more active role in parenting, men are beginning to respect parents more. It is not because they are trying to be politically correct. Fathers actually appreciate the level of difficulty and challenge of being a good parent because they are doing it. It's like telling a person that it's really hard to be confined to a wheelchair. The average person thinks they are sympathetic. However, it is not until being confined to a wheelchair them self, that their perception actually changes.[ll] Likewise, it is not until actually caring for a child that people, men and women, appreciate the importance of parenting.

[ll] https://www.youtube.com/watch?v=0Vxjh6KJi8E

"My philosophy is that not
only are you responsible
for your life,
but doing the best at this moment
puts you in the best place
for the next moment."

-Oprah Winfrey [262]

CHAPTER V. ADAPTATION

Charles Darwin's theory of evolution has been condensed into a simple doctrine:

"It is not the strongest of the species that survives, nor the most intelligent, but rather the one most adaptable to change."[263]

Adapting to changes that inevitably occur in our lives is essential for every woman if she is to achieve success. Even characters in nursery rhymes teach us a valuable lesson about the importance of adaptation for both men and women. When Humpty Dumpty fell off the wall, the mistake all of the king's horses and all of the king's men made was trying to put the broken pieces of Humpty back together. They were unable to adapt to the notion that Humpty had permanently fallen on hard times. Instead they should have gathered up the egg shells, deposited them in the compost heap, and made scrambled eggs for the king.

As Miss Muffett was minding her own business trying to eat her breakfast, she didn't feel defeated when she had to abandon those high calorie curds and whey. She knew that she still had a granola bar in her purse. The granola was a much healthier choice and would promote bowel health. When she successfully escaped that venomous spider, she didn't feel she had been a coward by running away. Instead, Muffett prided herself on thwarting the attack of the spider. Her escape was not characterized by screams of horror precipitated by the hairy arachnid. She did not complain that she had been victimized by the spider. She didn't file suit alleging intentional infliction of emotional distress. She was not afraid that somebody might call her a sissy for removing herself from the threat. Instead we applauded her intelligence and ability to correctly identify the deadly nature of the fiddle back. We marveled at her athleticism as she extricated herself with agility and speed from the potentially fatal encounter.

Jack was nimble and quick when he jumped over the candlestick. However, Jill didn't see the point. She didn't play with fire. Jill put out the candle before it burned somebody. When she and Jack needed to go up the hill to get water Jack injured himself when he fell. Jack went running to the local doctor, who happened to be a woman. Jill fell down but she protected her head as she rolled down the hill. With no assistance or sympathy from anyone Jill got back up, retrieved the heavy pail, and brought back the water all by herself. By the time Jack got home, Jill had already made soup with the water, bathed the children, and washed their sheets. Jack woke the children when he slammed the door upon his arrival home. Jill quickly quieted the children and helped them return to their state of slumber, so as not to disturb their ailing father. Jack complained all night that his head hurt. Jill comforted her ailing husband by giving him a back rub with her right hand. Jill adapted to her limitations as she couldn't raise her left hand due to the re-injury of the herniated disc in her back from carrying that damn pail of water.

All the king's horses were stallions and all the king's attendants were men. Being unable to recognize the futility of repairing a broken egg, the horses and men continued to work until the egg began to stink and the shell began to decompose. They were unable to adapt.

Miss Muffett and Jill were each resilient women who adapted to their circumstances. Each modified their definitions of success based on the challenges before them. Each woman adapted to the obstacles presented without complaining and resolved to make the most of their situations. Instead of lamenting that they had been victimized by a dangerous assailant or a slippery slope, each met their challenges head-on. Pride didn't prevent Muffett from running. Instead of standing her ground when faced with a dangerous enemy she took action. She removed herself from the potentially fatal encounter. Jill had to limp through town due to the pain in her back. She didn't complain about the pain. She simply walked slower and allowed more time to compensate for her sluggish gait. Each woman adapted to her circumstances. Survival is a powerful instinct of women. In order to survive, we must, and do, adapt.

The implicit message is that if we adapt to our circumstances we will be happy. The very notion of adapting suggests that we have considered all significant factors and modified our approach to maximize success. As a nurse and as an attorney I was repeatedly reminded of the importance of adapting. As my circumstances changed with clients and patients, adaptation was essential for success. Women are resilient, capable, and determined. It is our ability to adapt that makes us powerful executives, formidable adversaries, and resilient mothers. It is our ability to adapt that will allow us to conquer the third wave of feminism.

A. Boobs

As a strategic young woman I knew that the secret to becoming the Florence Nightingale of the 1980's was to gain experience meeting the needs of patients even before graduating from Nursing School. Florence wouldn't mind changing a bed pan and neither did I. Some nurse's-aides were unenthusiastic about bed baths, catheter care, and wound care. I was the exception. I didn't mind helping a patient onto a bed pan or changing the dressing of a wound oozing with pus. If a patient was congested I was glad to open his airway by suctioning thick green mucus through his tracheotomy. I prided myself on my skill at giving a bed bath to the most obese of patients. Finding dirt under a fold of skin was like finding treasure. I took pride in being the best nurse's-aide that I could be. When the other aides called me "gung-whore" I paid no attention.

It was with this same commitment to excellence that I entered the room of Mr. Williams. He was an elderly man who gave new meaning to the moniker "dirty old man." His skin was leathery and wrinkled like an elephant. He smelled like the port-a-potty at the soccer field. When he flashed a smile at me it was hard to ignore his yellowing teeth, highlighted with black spots of decay. I couldn't tell if his bad breath was caused by his rotting teeth or the white film across his tongue.

The diagnosis on Mr. Williams' chart was uncontrolled diabetes. It was not clear if one of Mr. Williams' rotting teeth was the result of a sweet tooth or whether he consumed so much alcohol that he forgot to take his insulin. It was clear that he, and his diabetes, were out of control. Because I was a committed professional I viewed Mr. Williams, not as a dirty old man, but as a patient in desperate need of care. Being educated about the risks of diabetes, it was obvious that a thorough evaluation of Mr. Williams would not be complete without checking his pedal (foot) pulses. Diabetics often have problems with circulation in the lower extremities. As I entered his room, it appeared that this sly old man was sound asleep. I mistook his lethargy for sleeping. Being the compassionate aide that I was, my goal was to assess Mr. Williams' pedal pulses without disturbing him. Somehow I thought that if I didn't pull back his covers, he would sleep through my examination of his lower extremities. I quietly and inconspicuously slipped my hand under the blankets at the end of his bed. Mr. Williams appeared to be unaffected by my examination of his left foot as my cold hand felt the pulsation of the pedal artery in his dry, cracking, old left foot. It was as if he was unaware of my presence. It didn't occur to me that Mr. Williams might be pretending to be asleep or that this dirty old man might be anticipating a good laugh at my expense.

After determining that Mr. Williams' left pedal pulse was strong and regular I patted the bed, feeling everywhere for the right foot. Where could that sucker be? I patted all around. Moving my hand under the covers to the right and the left, up and down, his other foot was nowhere to be found. Had he flexed his knee, moving his foot up to his crotch, hoping that I would move my hand up to his hip? I wasn't that stupid. Realizing that he was hiding his right foot from me I was overcome with a sense of indignation. I jerked the covers back, probably more than was completely necessary, as a way of expressing my displeasure with the joke being made at my expense. This old man deserved to be cold if he purposely hid his right foot from me. As I lifted the covers to locate the missing limb my keen powers of observation kicked in.

The old man had only one foot. Only one artery pulsated with that elusive pedal pulse. Mr. Williams had dirt under only five of his toe nails instead of the expected ten. Mr. Williams flashed every yellow tooth in his head at me. He saw the terror in my eyes as I realized he was an amputee. I was his entertainment for the day.

Because Mr. Williams was an amputee it was obvious, even to an uneducated aide, that Mr. Williams would need help when it was time for his daily activity. His activity for the day was moving from his bed to a chair located next to his bed. Perhaps he could hop. Given his age and frail appearance it seemed much more likely that he would be unable to support his own weight or move himself to the chair without assistance. It was my job to move Mr. Williams from his bed to the plastic covered chair next to his bed. Fortunately for Mr. Williams, I had been trained in proper body mechanics, so the technique of moving an elderly patient from the bed to the chair was second nature to me. I should have been easily able to accomplish this move.

Placing my feet apart in an effort to create a wide base of support, as I had been taught, I placed Mr. Williams' arms around my neck and shoulder blades. I wrapped my arms around his waist. The first step in the transfer process was to pull Mr. Williams upright onto his left leg. Next I'd utilize a pivoting motion of my feet and his single leg. The final step was to slowly, and gently lower Mr. Williams into the chair.

I completed the first step in the process with ease. I was an experienced nurse's aide, committed to high standards of care. The second phase of the transfer did not go as smoothly. As Mr. Williams stood up on his single leg, his arms moved with unanticipated speed from my back to my breasts. It wasn't as if my breasts were so pendulous that they were the obvious place for a patient to grasp if he was fearful of falling. If he'd been afraid of falling grabbing my arms would have provided more support. My arms were certainly more accessible. It was as if all the strength of his amputated right leg had miraculously moved into his upper extremities. He was like a pit bull refusing to open his vise-like grip. Suddenly my goal for this patient transformed from gently moving him to the bedside chair to refraining from screaming and dropping him on the floor. I didn't scream. I didn't drop him. Instead I fell with him into the chair as he pulled me onto him. As I pried his claws loose from my breasts, hateful remarks filled my head. Never before had I wanted to call a patient a "perverted old man" but the words were on the tip of my tongue. Suddenly the image of myself as a dedicated health care provider evaporated. Instead I pictured myself as a roller-derby champion, ready to eviscerate the enemy with colorful expletives and titanic blows to his head, body, and groin. If he touched me one more time, I surely would have become a famously abrasive nurse's aide.

I said nothing. No words were exchanged. No charges for assault were filed. I left the room, quietly muttering the most appropriate description of Mr. Williams that came to mind. Mr. Williams remained sitting motionlessly in the chair with every yellow tooth peering out of the smile on his ugly face. Nobody ever knew about the incident as I was too embarrassed to share the events of the day with anyone. Mr. Williams was still sitting in the chair when I finished my shift. Every time I passed his room he extended his arms and flexed his bony fingers, as if re-living our encounter. Then he flashed those spotted yellow teeth at me as if to ensure that I hadn't forgotten just how happy he was to have been the one doing the examination that day.

Adapting to the circumstances of having a dirty old man as a patient was challenging but essential for the successful completion of my shift. I avoided any criticism from my supervising nurse by not dropping Mr. Williams. By avoiding Mr. Williams for the remainder of my shift I was able to eliminate the possibility that I would become victimized once again. It was only a result of my commitment to patient care that I was able to keep Mr. Williams vertical. Because of my commitment to preserving my self-esteem I avoided further humiliation while preserving my good standing as a competent and compassionate nurse aide. Never again would I be assigned to provide care, or entertainment, for Mr. Williams. I survived because I adapted.

B. Boots

The same summer I encountered Mr. Williams I was also assigned to care for Mr. Tucker. Mr. Tucker was a mentally ill patient with an unknown physical malady. Mr. Tucker was unconcerned with any health considerations. His only concern was the retrieval of his most prized possession, his filthy footwear. On the counter across from his bed sat an old pair of army boots. The dried flakes of mud on the floor were only a fraction of the dried mud and rotting plant life that had covered his footwear. The laces of the boots were so brittle that if Mr. Tucker had tried to tie the laces they would surely have broken in his hands. The boots emitted a stench that could only have been earned from years of wear. The soles were so old and worn that they could not have been repaired. Yet Mr. Tucker's sole goal in life was to be re-united with his boots. It was as if he was unaware of the I.V. line taped to his arm, the Foley catheter terminating in his bladder, or his recumbent position in bed, which for most sane patients would indicate that footwear of any kind was unnecessary. He seemed to be oblivious to the restraints which secured his arms and legs to the bedrails. Mr. Tucker was a filthy mess. The grime on his hands was only surpassed by the filth on his feet. My goal for the day was to give him a bed bath, washing him from head to toe, cutting those fingernails and toenails that harbored that black film, and changing his gray bed linen.

Fortunately because our patient census was low that day, the 90 minutes it took to wash Mr. Tucker didn't interfere with care of my other patients. When I exited his room Mr. Tucker was completely clean, with his arms and legs still restrained. The bed linen was sparkling and white. His hospital gown wasn't soiled. His hair no longer appeared to have nits… although I might have missed a few. I was careful to tie the restraints tightly as Mr. Tucker spoke of nothing during the entire 90 minutes of cleansing except the retrieval of his boots. As a committed nurse aide I remembered to raise both bed rails, ensured that his IV was running without obstruction, emptied the Foley catheter bag of all urine, and secured it to the bed rail.

Thirty minutes later I was walking the main hallway just peeking in on my patients. In room 34, Ms. Anderson was sleeping soundly. In room 35, Bertha was eating her pureed dinner of liquid peas and blended meat loaf. In room 36, Mr. Cooper was looking at his wife as she explained what he should be doing. In room 37, Mr. Tucker was sitting on a broken bed rail. He didn't seem to notice, or care, that his I.V. was disconnected. The open I.V. line allowed blood to run directly from his vein onto the linoleum floor. His catheter was pulled taut, causing his penis to remain suspended parallel to the floor. His hospital gown hung off his shoulder, descending between his bony legs. The army boots on his feet rested in a three foot circle of blood made by the dripping of blood from the I.V. tubing. The laces of his boots remained untouched and had found their resting place in the pool of blood. Socks were an unnecessary part of this ensemble. Drops of blood marked the path of Mr. Tucker's penis on its journey from lying in the middle of the bed to its taut position at the end of the bed. The smile on his face must have been related to the attainment of the Army boots rather than the loss of blood from pulling out his I.V. tubing or the pressure on his bladder. To my surprise, I learned that those catheter balloons, inflated with 100 cc of fluid to secure their position in the bladder, really worked in spite of significant tension. Never before had I considered the possibility that boots could cause a patient to remain oblivious to the pain associated with the forceful removal of an I.V., and the unimaginable pressure from the tug of a catheter.

After re-connecting the I.V., mopping up the blood, repositioning the catheter, changing the bed sheets again, retying the restraints, and repositioning the broken bed rail, I neatly arranged Mr. Tucker's hospital gown. I made sure the bed linen wasn't too tight over his army boots. While I had never seen a nursing care plan that illustrated the proper technique for making a bed, with hospital corners big enough to accommodate army boots, I improvised. Mr. Tucker was content. I adapted.

C. Pizza

"Joey" was the name of my 7 year old, blond-haired, blue-eyed, adorable little patient in ICU. Joey was fighting for his life after being hit by a drunk driver who came barreling over a hill as Joey's mom, Linda, watched. Joey had crossed the street to get the mail as his mom stood watching on the front porch of their modest rural Oklahoma home. Linda witnessed the brutal impact of the speeding auto as it lifted her only son off his feet and deposited his apparently lifeless body in a ditch. It was as if Joey was a pebble, kicked up by a race car, shooting down that deserted country road. Linda sat in the old wooden chair in Joey's room where she had been from the moment her son had arrived in ICU days ago. Linda clasped her hands around a Bible, as if she thought that squeezing it tighter would somehow save her son. She looked up at me as I entered the room at the beginning of the 3-11shift. I was the Registered Nurse assigned to care for Joey that night. Linda smiled ever so slightly. The circles of gray around her eyes were a testament to her lack of sleep during the last five horrific days.

The neck brace around Joey's neck was secured tightly so that his broken neck remained immobile. The bandages on his right leg hid the shattered bones. The bandages protected the family from seeing the grotesque injury of their son's leg, but they were unable to mask the putrid smell of gangrene. If Joey survived the unspoken assumption was that amputation was inevitable. The respirator had been turned off but Joey was still breathing. In an effort to ensure continuity of care I had been assigned to be the nurse for Joey every day since he had arrived at the hospital. The number of IV medicines and dressing changes for this little boy filled an entire nursing care plan. While I worked for eight hours providing physical care for Joey, I knew that even with the best of nursing care, his hospital bed would probably be the last bed he'd occupy.

Until I was assigned to care for Joey I believed that I could save any patient entrusted to my care. If I just worked hard enough and knew enough about the trauma or disease of my patients, I knew that I could facilitate their recovery. How could I be a successful nurse if one of my patients died? Watching Joey deteriorate every day following the accident, in spite of the best care I could give, was devastating. Joey was unconscious so there was no indication he could hear me as I talked to him throughout the 8 hour shift. Most of my remarks to Joey were actually intended to help Linda remain hopeful. With all the psychology courses I'd taken and books I'd read to educate myself on the grieving process I never-the-less felt helpless to have any positive impact on Linda or Joey. What could I say to a 7 year old child to explain why he would never have to worry about what he wanted for his 8th birthday? How could I justify the death of an innocent boy? How could I begin to understand the unimaginable pain of this young mother as her only son lay dying before her? Why wasn't there something I could do? I'd seen a baby born and the magical bond between a mother and child that immediately formed. Even though I was single, without children at the time, I knew that watching your child die was a parent's very worst nightmare.

On this, the fifth day of Joey's demise, something miraculous happened. Joey opened his eyes. Linda came rushing to the side of the bed opposite me. Joey was smiling. He was a boy at peace. There was no grimace or sign of pain. It was as if he was oblivious to his condition. He had no recognition of the devastating trauma to his spine and leg. He spoke. He asked us to pray with him. Joining hands Linda and I held Joey's hands and together we said the Lord's Prayer. Each word of that prayer echoes in my mind 30 years later. We came to the end of the prayer. Joey remembered every word: "…For Thine is the kingdom, the power, and the glory forever. Amen." As soon as the prayer was over Joey asked for pizza. Linda and I laughed together, elated that Joey was hungry. Then as quickly and abruptly as Joey awoke he fell back into his state of unconsciousness. Joey died that night.

Linda and I never spoke again. Yet I knew that if there was ever a chance of Linda being able to deal with the untold anguish of losing a child, that our moment of prayer with Joey made all the difference. I was unable to save Joey's life. Perhaps I was able to help Linda save her own. I thought Joey was my patient that week. Now I realize that Linda was the real patient. The nursing care I provided to Linda might have made a real difference at a critical juncture in her life. Adaptation was essential to surviving an unbearable waste of human life. By adapting I was able to help at least one patient, Linda. Maybe my goals were unrealistic. Saving Joey's life was not possible. Linda was the only patient I could help. Nothing I learned in school prepared me, or taught me the skills necessary, to provide the understanding and support that Linda so desperately needed. In the solitude of the Lord's Prayer each of us found a reason to hope; not for Joey's life, but for our own. It was only because of adapting to these intolerable circumstances that I was able to feel that my presence made a difference. I may never see Joey's mom again but I bet she'll always remember the time we shared together on the last day of Joey's life. I adapted because I wanted to help this young mother. She adapted because she had no choice.

Ultimately I adapted by leaving nursing. I loved nursing but I hated always being in a subordinate role. I went back to school to earn a degree that would transform me from the one needing advice to the one giving advice. Instead of fighting with the boss, I became the boss. I didn't give it all up. Everything I learned in nursing became extremely helpful representing doctors as a litigation medical malpractice specialist.

D. Whores

Having graduated in the top 10% of my Law School class, and being the Moot Court Champion, it was clear that I was destined for greatness in the Courtroom. I expected to win all my cases. Opposing attorneys would feel remorse upon learning that they had drawn me as an opponent. I wouldn't just beat my adversary. I'd humiliate him. "Rip him a new one" was the phrase that came to mind when I fantasized about the discomfort I planned to inflict on any opponent in the courtroom. Yet my demeanor was disarmingly innocent. Men often underestimated me in the court room.

The first case that I would try to a jury was accepted by the firm for the purpose of giving me trial experience, rather than to make money. Because the firm was so grateful for cases like this one, the insurance company who sent us the case was not charged a fee. Any time a young attorney spent on such a case would be part of training, but not time that would generate revenue for the firm. Any expenses incurred in preparing the case for trial would be borne by the firm. Thus we were to be keep expenses to a minimum. If I were to defeat my opponent by ripping him a new one, I would have to do it with resources available to me personally.

In anticipation of decimating my opponent, I took my personal instamatic camera to the scene of the fender-bender. Without accounting for my time, I took pictures of the road and path traveled by my client. My client was actually a victim. My client had been rear-ended by the Plaintiff. Any person who hit an innocent driver from behind, and then had the nerve to sue the driver of the car he rear-ended, deserved all the vengeance I could inflict. Of course the Plaintiff asserted that Michael, my client, had stopped in the middle of the road just beyond the crest of a hill. The Plaintiff said he didn't have enough time to avoid the accident. The road was a four-lane, one way road! The Plaintiff must have been speeding or not paying attention if he was unable to avoid the accident even if my client had slowed or stopped in the road. This was the perfect case to prove my proficiency in the court room. Just to be on the safe side I asserted a claim of comparative fault, suggesting that even if my client shared some miniscule portion of blame, the jury could apportion a percentage of fault that was appropriate for each party.

Because the case only involved minor property damage to the Plaintiff's car I couldn't justify the typical discovery that might include depositions and designation of experts. I waited until the day before trial to meet with my client, the driver of the car that was hit from behind. To my delight when I called my client to set up our meeting, I learned that he had an independent witness. James, a friend of Michael's, had been a passenger in the car. James could provide independent corroboration of Michael's story. I asked Michael to bring James for the meeting in my office.

The day before trial I was pleasantly surprised when James and Michael both came for our meeting and arrived on time. Being the clever trial attorney that I was, I realized that the testimony of James might have more impact on the jury than the testimony of Michael, since Michael was an interested party. Thus, before asking Michael any questions, I asked James to tell me in his own words what happened that day. James offered his crystal clear recollection of the accident:

> "We wuz drivin alung, an we wint ovr this hill and as we cum ovr the hill I sez to Michael...LOOK AT THEM ASSES ON THEM WHORES! ...Then BAM! THIS ASSHOLE SLAMS INTUH US!"

As if suddenly hit by a tsunami I found myself breathless and struggling to reach the surface. Time stood still. In the span of 5 seconds my perception of myself as a promising trial attorney morphed into an unemployed attorney working as a janitor at the Court House. With just seven words, and a mere 27 characters, James erased any chance I had of becoming a world-renown trial attorney. How could I survive as a trial attorney if I couldn't win a simple case where somebody hit my client's car from behind? Who would ever believe that it was those whores who caused this accident instead of my unsuspecting client? Didn't those women know that they created a road hazard? Didn't they realize that advertising their buttocks along a busy street could cause risk to life, limb, and to my career? ... "Look at them asses on them whores!" It was like something from a Far Side Cartoon but I was the character in the cartoon...and I wasn't laughing.

I knew I was supposed to ask the next question but my voice had left the room. In its place was a faint sucking sound. Fighting to compose myself, I did what any good trial attorney would do and considered alternative explanations for the accident. I realized that the impetus for stopping abruptly and without warning, in the middle of the road, after passing over a hill, was actually irrelevant. If the driver of the car that hit my client had the opportunity to avoid the collision, then the reason for my client's momentary distraction was irrelevant. After all the jury would be applying a reasonable man standard. What reasonable man would not have stopped the car? What virile young man, overcome by his hormonal instincts, could remain unaffected by these tantalizing women? It was like an Act of God. Acts of God typically include hurricanes, tornadoes, and lightning. However, there was no logical reason Acts of God couldn't have also included "asses on whores." Surely the Plaintiff was following too closely, driving too fast, or failing to take precautionary measures to avoid hitting Michael's car. Perhaps the Plaintiff was also distracted by the whores! I would adapt. I would modify my strategy but would still be victorious!

Relying on my quick wit, I determined that if I was able to identify the exact location of the collision I could prove that the Plaintiff had plenty of time to avoid the car stopped in the middle of the road. The jury should still blame the

Plaintiff for the collision. If I could establish that the impact occurred far enough down the hill then Michael should have been able to check out the whores on the side of the road without being victimized by an oncoming car. After all prostitutes on the side of the street is a well-known phenomenon and one that should always be anticipated by a reasonable man using ordinary care.

Fortunately I had my instamatic photos easily accessible to assist in locating the exact point of the impact. Again relying on James' memory, I showed him the photos. I was devastated to learn that James was unequivocal about the exact location of the impact. Surely James was not able to precisely locate the point of impact just beyond the crest of the hill? He only thought he could. Surely I would be able to convince him that his memory was not as accurate as he thought? It seemed impossible that James could remember the exact location of the impact. The road was long and there were no distinguishing characteristics about any particular stretch of the long sloping hill. Upon suggesting that James might not have a clear memory of the precise location of the collision, James explained that he was 100% sure of the location of the collision because of the street light on the side of the road that was clearly visible in my picture. I questioned James about why the street light helped him pinpoint the exact location of the accident. James explained that he remembered after the accident where the car came to rest at the curb. He remembered because he had to place the floor mats on the sidewalk, next to that street light, to dry. Unclear about the reason James had to dry out the floor mats immediately following the accident, I asked James the last question of our interview. "Why did you have to dry out the floor mats?" As if the answer was obvious, James explained with a little disdain in his voice, "It was the beer of course! It spilled all over those damn floor mats!"

As politely as possible I explained to my client that we would not need James at trial so he could stay home tomorrow. I asked Michael to come to court but explained that he would not be called to testify. When the jury determined that Michael was only 70% at fault I felt victorious. Although I originally expected to win this case, the reality of the situation changed. Adaptation was essential. No longer could I hope to win. I had to be content with the apportionment of any amount of fault on the opposing party. It was only because I adapted to the challenge of having a beer-drinking, hooker-gazing, client that I was able to achieve success. By not putting my client on the stand to testify about what really happened that day the jury thought Michael was only 70% at fault instead of 100%. Adapting is an essential characteristic for every successful professional woman, trial attorney, and mother.

E. Successful Women are Adaptable

Success is a fluid concept. Like Miss Muffett and Jill I have learned through trial and error. Goals which were originally well conceived might have to change to fit the circumstances. Adaptability is essential. Instead of trying to give Mr. Williams the maximum amount of exercise, the more appropriate goal instantaneously became not to drop him. For Mr. Tucker my objective changed from keeping him in a clean bed, free of footwear, to allowing him to wear boots in bed to ensure his safety. I couldn't save Joey's life but I could make the tragic loss of his life a little more bearable for his mother. As an attorney I learned that winning is a relative term. Sometimes in order to "win" you can't tell anyone you won. What may seem like a loss to others may in fact be a victory for you. Set your own goals. Modify them as the circumstances change. Adapt. Victory is personal and sometimes can never be shared with others. Satisfaction may come from an unlikely place, but embrace that sense of accomplishment, regardless of its source. Be strategic like Miss Muffett and resourceful like Jill. Adaptability is essential for women if we are to achieve our goals. As circumstances change, both professionally and personally, we must adapt.

Marriage, the birth of a healthy child, the birth of a child with special needs, the illness of a parent, or an unpredicted divorce, might each have a dramatic impact on a woman's life. We may be successful only if we adapt to the new circumstances of our lives. The new goals may be equally fulfilling or perhaps even more rewarding than the previous goals. However the failure to adapt will predictably result in disappointment. If my original goals had stayed the same, I would have dropped Mr. Williams on the floor. He'd have probably broken his left hip, thereby leaving him unable to stand on his remaining leg. Mr. Tucker might have needed a blood transfusion if he'd continued to attempt retrieval of his precious boots. If I had put Michael on the witness stand, the jury would have surely found my client to be 100% responsible for the accident. Juries in Texas tend to appreciate the dangerous conditions caused by men drinking beer and checking out prostitutes while driving an automobile.

If Miss Muffett had continued on her course without adapting she would have been bitten by the venomous spider and died a slow and painful death. If Jill hadn't adapted the kids wouldn't have been fed or bathed, she probably would have been so disgusted with Jack that she'd have given him another blow to the head, and the kids would forever think of their father as a klutz. By relying on herself Jill saved her marriage, ensured that her children would grow up thinking only good things about their dad. The family would have enjoyed financial security when Jack invented a system of pipes to transport water to the town at the bottom of the hill.

While we set goals for our professional and personal lives, circumstances may change. Prince Charming might lose the glass slipper, his GPS might be broken, or he might get lost trying to find Cinderella's house. What if he becomes an alcoholic or has an affair with one of the ugly step sisters? Suddenly the goal of being married to Prince Charming might change. If the children in the Royal family are in desperate need of parenting, the Prince may be so tied up with dealing with other problems within the kingdom that he may be unable to see the problems at home. Even if Cinderella identifies the problem, the Prince may not share her concern. Even if Cinderella loves her job, she may love her children more. If we overlook a problem at work, somebody else may step in and fix it. However if there's a problem at home, there may not be anyone else to fix it. While Cinderella may fill an important position within the kingdom, the position she holds as a wife and mother is unique. There is no other person in the kingdom that can do for her children, that which she alone can do. While others may provide for the physical needs of our children, nobody can provide the emotional support, the discipline, and the inspiration of a parent for his/her child. Whatever satisfaction we derive from our professional success, deep inside we know that if we have made the choice to marry and have children, we have necessarily made those people our top priority. Adapting to their needs may require modification of professional goals. Even if the mean step-mother perceives that everything at home is fine, Cinderella must rely on her own perception of the needs of her family and act accordingly. No other solution will be satisfactory to Cinderella.

If Cinderella determines that the Prince is not being supportive of her career, she may choose to divorce the Prince and move to another kingdom in search of another Prince. However, the moment Cinderella chooses to have children she has forever changed her circumstances. It will now be her responsibility to ensure that the children are thriving. Cinderella may blame the Prince for not doing his share of the child rearing, but ultimately it is the responsibility of both parents to ensure that kids have their needs met. Failure of the Prince to do his share for the kids doesn't excuse Cinderella from her obligation to ensure that her children receive proper care. In fact the failure of the Prince to provide the necessary parenting makes Cinderella's contribution even more important. The more children Cinderella has, the more likely she will need to make a change in her professional life. Even if someone in the kingdom stops by for dinner and perceives that everything in the castle is fine, Cinderella may be in a position to know that it is magical thinking. People who evaluate the family dynamics from the outside often have an inaccurate perception. They may think Cinderella simply lost her glass slippers, when in fact the kids threw them at each other, breaking the slippers and requiring stitches in the youngest one's head. Outsiders might think that the Prince had gone to voice lessons when in fact he was having a rendezvous with Cinderella's lady-in-waiting. Cinderella must chart her own course, regardless of the perceptions of others.

"I'm not interested in trying to
Work on people's perceptions.
I am who I am, and if you
Don't take the time to learn about
That, then your perception
Is going to be your problem."

-Jim Brown [264]

CHAPTER VI. PERCEPTIONS

"Perception," unlike truth or fact, implies that a person uses their senses to become aware of another person or situation. A perception is only as accurate as the person's ability to perceive the truth. We perceive people and experiences through our senses but we interpret the truth only as accurately as our senses allow. The majority of people are hesitant to reveal their true selves to the public. Instead we attempt to promote the most favorable images of ourselves as possible, regardless of how unrealistic it is. If you see any woman who purports to have it all, beware. She is probably about to have a nervous breakdown. Her children are about to be arrested. Her husband is about to ask for a divorce. She may be about lose her job. When any of these traumatic events occur, all other aspects of her life will likely be affected. We can't live to satisfy the perception of others. We must establish our own criteria for a happy and fulfilling life. Beware of the false perception of yourself by others, and your misguided perception of others.

Remember the story of Little Red Riding Hood. She knew her grandma's ears, eyes, and teeth were smaller than those of the wolf. Yet, Riding Hood was fooled by the perception created by the wolf wearing granny's clothes. Had she perceived the truth, she would have known that grandma was not in bed, but rather inside the wolf's stomach. Had Little Red Riding Hood's mother been perceptive, she would have known that the forest was a dangerous place for her little girl. An astute mother would never have let her daughter walk alone. The woodcutter saved the little girl and her grandmother. Even though the woodcutter had been perceived as a nice guy, in reality he might have saved grandma and Riding Hood only to make them his prisoners so that he could eat their homemade cakes? Little Red Riding Hood teaches little girls that they aren't expected to make good choices about their safety. There will always be a man around to rescue them. We wrongly perceived that a woman could be eaten by a vicious animal and remain intact as if simply held in a prison. When the woodcutter disemboweled the wolf, grandma emerged unscathed. How was it that she was unaffected by the wolf's sharp teeth, the acidic juices of the wolf's stomach, or the lack of oxygen in the wolf's digestive tract. Our perception that the granny was a goner was wrong. Things are often not what they seem.

A. Sex

My goal throughout high school, college, and law school was to be a straight-A student. With hard work and determination I was usually able to achieve success in academic endeavors. In Nursing School making A's required not only success on written exams, but we were also evaluated in the hospital setting as well. The hospital experience was called the practicum, suggesting that our experiences reflected the practical, real world. We were required in the classroom to demonstrate competence in knowledge of anatomy, physiology, and pharmacology. Our instructors expected us to demonstrate competency in inserting a catheter, starting an I.V., and passing an N-G tube (inserting a tube through a patient's nose, down to the stomach). In the hospital practicum, students convinced patients that we knew what we were doing.

In our practicum we prepared a nursing care plan for each patient to whom we were assigned. To enable the preparation of such a plan it was the responsibility of every committed nursing student to fully assess the needs of her patients. Being shy, or easily intimidated, were not attributes that facilitated a thorough assessment of many different types of patients. You have to hold onto a man's penis in order to catheterize him. You have to touch a woman's breasts to show her how to help her baby latch on when demonstrating the proper technique for breast feeding. We were expected to talk to patients about the most private of matters. Conversation over lunch or at a cocktail party doesn't typically include questions about sexual gratification following surgery on the prostate, medications available for urine leakage, or the proper technique for removal of vaginal packing following treatment for a fistula. However all of these topics might be the subject of a dedicated nurse's conversation with her patients.

According to my nursing instructor, every thorough assessment of every patient would include a detailed analysis of the specific ways a patient's sexuality might be affected by a medical disease or condition. She wasn't only considering the patients who had diseases or disorders that obviously affected their sexuality, such as a mastectomy or prostate surgery. My nursing instructor wanted us to assess how every patient might be affected sexually by their ailment. This nursing instructor seemed to feel that even a bunion on your toe, or a splinter in a finger, might affect a patient's sex life. If a nurse didn't ask the question, the patient wouldn't volunteer to talk about something so private as impotence resulting from an ingrown toenail. My nursing instructor was including patients like Mrs. Gibson, an 87 year old patient, who suffered with long-term, debilitating, arthritis. Some less experienced nurses might perceive that the elderly were more concerned with the possibility of dying than the possibility that their disease might affect their degree of sexual arousal. My instructor knew better.

Mrs. Gibson was my first patient, in my first year, of nursing school. For some strange reason it seemed that all nursing students started nursing school treating elderly patients, who'd been sick a long time, weren't expected to live much longer, and had poor memories. When I met Mrs. Gibson she had suffered from the pain and crippling effects of rheumatoid arthritis for almost 60 years. The contractures of her fingers made it difficult for her to hold silverware. She was able to walk, but her gait was painfully slow. Mr. Gibson was still alive, but in a wheelchair. The fact that he was still alive was the good news for Mr. Gibson. However, it was the bad news for me. The fact that there was a man in Mrs. Gibson's life, regardless of his age or disabled state, and regardless of my patient's disabled state, meant that I would have to assess the impact of Mrs. Gibson's arthritis on her sexual relations with Mr. Gibson.

I was a 20 year-old-virgin trying to figure out how to ask an 87 year old married woman if her disease had adversely affected her sexuality. God forbid that she would answer in the affirmative. Then I'd have to ask for details. What clueless nurse would inquire about how an 87 year old arthritic woman could pleasure her 90 year-old-wheelchair-bound husband? I was too honest. I should have just lied to my instructor. She would have believed me if I told her that in place of sex, this elderly couple each preferred a good bowel movement.

Being the committed and honest student that I was, I felt compelled to ask the most private of questions to Mrs. Gibson. Unable to look her in the eye, I waited until I couldn't see her face, hidden by a bathroom stall, during a visit to the ladies room. Shielded by the swinging door of her stall, I popped the question. "So…Mrs. Gibson…how has your arthritis affected your sex life?" Whether Mrs. Gibson was hard of hearing, or simply in a state of shock, she responded with a booming "WHAT?!"

After repeating the question at a volume that could be more easily heard through the stall door, I anxiously awaited the answer, hoping it would come before the opening of the door. Mrs. Gibson chuckled; then laughed out loud. Mortified, I wondered how I'd face Mrs. Gibson as she emerged from the privacy of her stall. Was she laughing because I implied she was having sex at 87, or because I was so obviously uncomfortable talking about sex? As Mrs. Gibson opened the stall door she was shaking her head, side to side. With a slight wave of her arthritic hand she said, "Honey, I haven't had sex since I was 27, when I had that hysterectomy!"

It was my good fortune that there were no flies in the restroom, as I would surely have caught one in my mouth. Perhaps it was a blessing that I was unable to speak. In my state of stupor, I tried to decide if I should tell her that she unnecessarily missed the opportunity to have sex for the last 60 years of her life. Maintaining my silence, I decided that the correct response was no response at all.

Both of our perceptions were wrong. Mrs. Gibson had the false perception that she could not have sex. I was under the false perception that she had been having sex with Mr. Gibson, until he was confined to his wheelchair. Realizing that perceptions may be false, I also came to realize that some misperceptions are best left intact. Because we often lack a complete appreciation for the unique circumstances in the lives of others, we tend to perceive most people as normal, average, or typical. It is however the variable circumstances of our lives that make every person different, and every family unique.

The truth is that the only thing we have in common is that we are all different. Thus what works in one woman's life in achieving a balance between personal and professional life, may be completely wrong for another woman. Once we realize that our perceptions may not accurately reflect reality, we are much more accepting of the different choices that others make.

B. Soccer Moms

Soccer moms spend hours watching their children compete on the playing field. When Anna was 5, she didn't know that she was the worst player on her team. She didn't perceive that she was any different than the other kids on the team. They all had on purple jerseys, black shorts, soccer shoes, and shin guards. Anna didn't realize or care that she was one of the only players never to score a goal or to even touch the ball except in practice. Anna ran at the back of the pack of kids chasing the ball. At age 5 all soccer players run in a pack. Anna was chasing the kids who were chasing the ball. What could be better than having a uniform to wear, a water bottle to hold her favorite beverage, and to eat a fruit roll-up at the end of the game? Some parents would have been humiliated to watch their daughter demonstrate her total lack of understanding of the game, or even a desire to learn. I realized that the perceptions of the other parents and players was unimportant to Anna, or to her parents.

The highlight of Anna's first year playing soccer came on the day she proved that she did understand the concept of dribbling. She proved that she understood it was something you did with your foot and a soccer ball, instead of what happened when you laughed while drinking out of your water bottle. Anna spent the first half of the game demonstrating her commitment to her team by religiously following behind the group of kids in purple. In the second half one of the kids in a green shirt kicked the ball out of bounds, beyond the end zone. All the kids in the green and purple shirts stopped chasing the ball. Being oblivious to the notion of an out of bounds line, Anna immediately realized that this was a unique opportunity to feel what it was like to touch a soccer ball during a game. She shifted into high gear, as if she had morphed into the Pink Power Ranger. Anna dribbled the ball as fast as she could go. Of course it helped that nobody was running after her, except her coach. Anna never heard the laughter of the parents as she ran the length of the practice field next to our game field. When her coach caught up to her at the playground, beyond the practice field, she was too far away to see the other kids in purple shirts, rolling their eyes. Anna left the game that day proud of her athleticism. She had finally proven her mastery of dribbling a soccer ball. The parents' perception of Anna was that she was a failure. It was not until high school that the parents of all the kids in purple shirts saw that same perseverance and determination in Anna as she became a nationally ranked debater. At 5 and 17, Anna set her own goals and she fought to achieve them. She was happy as a youngster, and as a young woman.

Zach was only slightly more athletic than Anna. What he lacked in finesse, he made up with his lightning fast speed. Disliking competition, he preferred to play on defense, always protecting his team rather than scoring goals. As a scientist working on his PhD, Zach sets his own goals. When he expressed frustration because he didn't get a perfect score on a graduate exam, at one of the top schools in the country, I made the mistake of asking him how the other graduate students did on the exam. Zach responded with the retort that "I don't compare myself to them." Zach set his own goals. He didn't compare himself to others.

I was reminded of the inaccuracies of other people's perceptions at one of Zach's soccer games. As I sat in the bleachers at the end of the fall season, the mother next to me was unable to contain her curiosity any longer. Apologizing for being so bold she asked, "Do you or your husband have some type of secret government clearance? Are you or David connected to the CIA or FBI, or some classified part of the government?" Was this soccer mom on drugs? How and why would this woman perceive that we had any high level security clearance? Responding to the look of disbelief and shock on my face, she explained, "Remember that flight from London? We were on it with you and your family two summers ago. Well, how did you get through customs ahead of everyone else?"

I remembered the flight and speeding through customs that day but had forgotten that we saw this woman's family among the hundreds of faces on that plane. I remembered the flight because it was an example of a time when I was sorry to be right. On this particular occasion I told the Prince, who was sitting next to Zach, that his son was about to hurl. Mothers have a unique ability to predict the future. Mothers immediately perceive that miserable look on a child's face just before he loses his cookies. The slight mouth drop and the green hue are unmistakable signs that the status quo is about to change. It wasn't the cookies he'd eaten that made him sick that day. It was the turbulence and the loss of air conditioning on the last part of the flight. The Prince was focused on the end of his movie, rather than the shade of green his son was turning. Alerting David to the upcoming disaster, the Prince responded by discounting my advice and suggested that Cinderella shouldn't worry so much. David told me to relax. He said Zach was "just fine." Just as Hans Gruber fell to his death at the end of David's movie, Zach vomited part of his in-flight breakfast of strawberry yogurt and cheese omelet. Nobody on the plane wondered what Zach had selected for his in-flight breakfast. Zach's shirt and jeans were like a 3-D menu. David was happy that he was able to see the climax of his movie, but felt Zach used very poor judgment in not relieving himself in the airsick bag that remained in the seat back pocket. I felt bad that I couldn't sit next to all three children on the flight. While it was painful to see my son feeling humiliated, I wondered if this would be one of those teachable moments for Prince Charming. Unfortunately the Prince thought that Cinderella was simply psychic, and he was not.

Most kids feel better after the plane lands and the source of the air-sickness has been eliminated. Whether because of residual omelet and yogurt in his stomach or simply the smell of his own gastric acid, it was clear to me that Zach still had more breakfast to lose. Making my way to the front of the line in customs, I quickly explained the situation to the customs agents. Fortunately, even though the customs agents were not psychic, they appreciated the potential gravity of the situation and rushed us through customs. When Zach made it to the restroom to relieve himself of the remaining portion of his in-flight breakfast, the Prince commented on how lucky we were. Cinderella muttered under her breath that we were lucky the customs agent, who hurried us through the line, was a woman.

The perceptions of the people on the flight that day were each quite different. David thought Zach was fine. I thought he was about to vomit. In spite of his appearance or the smell that was obvious to anyone within a 10 foot radius, this soccer mom totally missed the fact that Zach was covered in his partially digested breakfast. Instead, all she saw was the speed with which we passed through customs. Her perception of our relationship with customs agents was inaccurate. If she had paid closer attention, perhaps she would have realized that the only thing that should have been attributed to our family was a propensity for motion sickness, rather than some secret connection to customs agents. If the Prince had accurately perceived the insight of Cinderella into her children, David would have retrieved the air-sick bag himself before Zach was in need of it. Sometimes we don't realize that our perceptions are wrong until it's too late.

C. Hotels.com

Prince Charming and his partner Bob are both attorneys. They opted out of their careers as attorneys to start their own company, which became known as Hotels.com. Hotels.com was not always a household name. The predecessor company was a call-center business known as Hotel Reservations Network. David and Bob had been partners since the day we returned home from our honeymoon, 30 years ago. H.R.N. was their child. David and Bob were law school classmates at Cornell. Although they have been incredibly successful financially, the value of a dollar remains the same to them in spite of their success. Some people perceive that David is cheap. That perception is inaccurate. He's not cheap. He is careful with money. David would never shop for clothes at the mall if Sam's or Wal-Mart carried something comparable. David doesn't buy new cars, because they lose too much value when you drive them off the lot. Yet, he has happily paid thousands of dollars for the education for our kids and other relatives because education is invaluable.

David's perception of the value of a dollar has remained the same, regardless of how much money he has earned. Twenty years ago David would never order a soft drink at a restaurant, as they were over-priced. Soft drinks in restaurants are still over-priced, and David still won't order one…but he'll drink mine. A penny found on the ground is like treasure to David, so the security check point at the airport remains one of his favorite places. He still empties the refrigerator of left-overs for his lunch. David calculated that if he saved the money he might spend eating lunch away from the office, at retirement he'd have saved $750,000.

David helped Katie, our youngest daughter, raise money for the Salvation Army as part of her mitzvah project for her Bat Mitzvah. He helped Katie appreciate how hard it is to earn a dollar. We visited the Salvation Army and saw kids living with their moms, in a room smaller than a college dorm. They had a single twin bed, to be occupied by the mother and all of her children. Katie immediately realized the importance of being able to support herself. Until that visit to the Salvation Army, Katie had never thought that having a picture of herself was special. She perceived that everyone could afford a picture of themselves. That day at the Salvation Army gave her new perspective.

When Katie went to Peru on a mission trip, she captured images of poverty-stricken children on her expensive digital camera. The pictures reflected the tragedy of children living in poverty, and the hope of a brighter future. Her pictures accurately reflected her perception of the poverty in which the children lived. However the Peruvian children didn't think that they lived in poverty. From the children's perspective, everyone lived as they did. As they posed for pictures, they had no idea of the value of a digital camera. They had never seen one.

When Anna studied with a tutor for the ACT, the tutor felt sorry for her because she thought our family couldn't afford the tutoring. Anna's modest appearance was misleading. Maybe it was unusual for one of the tutor's 17 year-old students not to drive up in their own new car. We never received a bill from the tutor. Anna tried her best to correct the tutor's misperception that we couldn't afford the lessons. The more Anna insisted on paying her fee, the more the tutor resisted. The tutor's perception was wrong.

Ralph was an attorney at the firm where I started and ended my career as an attorney. Ralph was older, more distinguished, and a graduate of Harvard. He thought of himself as smarter, and more accomplished, than any young woman who graduated from O.U. Ralph used a computer when the rest of us were using Dictaphones. He paid full price for his perfectly fit suits from Saks Fifth Ave. I bought mine at Macy's, on sale. They were not tailored to my every curve but they fit well enough to convince a jury that I was a lawyer. Ralph's clients were involved in sophisticated business litigation. My clients were involved with alcoholic beverages while stopping a motor vehicle just beyond the crest of a hill to admire the scenery. Ralph had children and a wife he supported. Ralph was very proud to attend the Baptisms, First-Communions, and High School graduations of each of his children. He never painted his feet to make footprints with his kids. His hands never got dirty hunting fossils with his kids. Ralph was part of the elite. If he had given me any work, it would have been to carry his briefcase. In 12 years of practicing law at the same firm, in the same department, Ralph never asked for me to work on a case with him.

When I quit my job as a Senior Partner at the firm to be a stay-at-home mom, Ralph and some of the other senior partners viewed my departure as validation that women were not fit to do the job that a man could do. Ralph's perception was that I was more suited to changing diapers, cooking dinner for my husband, and dusting the furniture. Perhaps he thought that a Harvard graduate would always be smarter than an O.U. graduate, which prevented Ralph from ever wanting to work with me. Maybe it wasn't a male/female thing. Whatever the reason, Ralph's perception of me was that I was his inferior.

The day that I walked out of the law firm for the last time, Ralph had no idea how hard that day was for me. To him I looked as I had every other day of my twelve years at the firm. I was wearing my dark blue suit, freshly pressed, and conservative navy heels. The modest string of pearls around my neck almost matched the color of my silk blouse. My auburn hair had been pulled back in a bun, attempting to convey my professionalism as a dedicated senior trial partner. The tie around my neck had a fabric similar to his, but mine was tied in a bow. His hung flat against his chest. He had no idea that inside I was a mess!

Four years later, I was wearing jeans, tennis shoes, and an old comfortable sweat shirt as I sat on the floor of LaGuardia Airport. I rested my head on my carry-on bag. Flights were delayed due to weather. The airport was packed. The floor wouldn't have been my first choice of seats, but it was my only choice. I was tired. Fortunately I had changed out of my suit in the restroom, so it didn't matter if my jeans got a little dirty. Knowing that this would be a really arduous trip, I remembered to bring my pillow. The pillow cushioned my carry-on bag so that I was prepared to be comfortable for as long as it might take the weather to clear. Most people thought it looked strange, and a little foolish, for a grown woman to travel with her pillow. I thought that I was pretty smart because I was the only person who thought to bring a pillow.

As I looked up at the first-class passengers who were waiting to board the flight first, I thought I recognized the man in the gray pin-striped suit. The last time I'd seen him he had more pepper than salt in his hair. Now his hair was almost totally white. His gray suit was still stylish; without a wrinkle. His shoes were almost at eye-level so I could see my reflection in them. Ralph and his client were waiting in the First Class line to board. They'd be greeted by a flight attendant who would hang up their suit coats. She'd get them the beverage of their choice before takeoff. As soon as the wheels were up, the flight attendants would serve warm nuts to tide them over until their three course meal could be served. My seat was in coach. I didn't need any nuts, warm or cold. I had a granola bar and a half-full Diet Coke bottle in my backpack.

It would have been rude for me not to say hello to Ralph. Rising from my pillow, I approached my former partner. He had been looking in my direction but hadn't recognized me. I'd like to think the lack of recognition was because my hair was down instead of being tied up in a bun. I was wearing a sweatshirt without a bow tie, so nobody would expect Ralph to recognize me. The surprised look on Ralph's face when I said "hi" eliminated any doubt that he failed to recognize me. Being the proper gentleman that he was he introduced me to his client. Ralph forgot to mention in the introduction that I had previously been one of his partners. Being caught off guard, Ralph was unable to fathom why I was in New York, dressed as I was, without children in tow.

"So....why are you here?" he finally asked, more out of politeness than genuine curiosity. It was obvious that Ralph assumed I had come to New York for something as inconsequential as shopping or perhaps a women's conference on breast feeding. As matter-of-factly as I could, I mumbled "Oh, I came to be with my husband when he opened trading on NASDAQ today." Ralph's face turned as white as his hair. His incredulity was unmistakable. Admittedly, I was enjoying every moment that it took for Ralph to compose himself. "It wasn't one of those.....dot com companies, was it?" he stammered. Unable to disguise the smile on my face, I admitted that it was. "It was Hotels.com." I explained. His shock and disbelief were a reward I hadn't anticipated. Ralph's client began asking lots of questions about David and his business. Ralph stood in line, speechless, which is an unusual state of existence for any trial attorney. Ralph's client understood what it meant to be married to a man who was the CEO of Hotels.com. Ralph was unable to overcome his perception of me as that girl who was a trial attorney, but gave it all up to stay at home and change diapers. Ralph didn't understand why I gave up my career. He didn't understand why I wasn't dressed in a designer suit, riding with him in first class. Ralph's definition of success was different than mine. He didn't understand why I originally chose to wear jeans at home with my kids. He couldn't understand why I was still wearing jeans on the plane home. Why was I sitting in coach, when I could clearly afford a better seat?

I was not particularly impressed with Ralph when we both worked at the firm. He was still unimpressive as he stood in line with his mouth open. He had on a beautiful, expensive, gray suit. He carried a handsome leather brief case. He was riding in first class. Ralph failed to perceive my commitment to my husband and children when working at the law firm, and while sitting on the floor at LaGuardia airport. Ralph's perceptions of me were wrong when I was a partner, and when I was a stay-at-home mom. He didn't get it when I was dressed in my business suit and he still didn't get it when I was in my jeans and tennis shoes. Ralph considered appearances and little else in evaluating people. His perceptions were wrong then, and now.

D. Thrifty

Prince Charming doesn't pay full price for anything. David has always been frugal, and proud of it. Years ago, before he was a successful entrepreneur, we decided that we'd buy a ping pong table. Not wanting to spend the extra money for delivery, David came up with an ingenious way to transport the table home. Accompanied by his brother, David visited a new car lot that offered some beautiful new pick-up trucks. Thinking that they had a real buyer, the salesman at the dealership was glad to give the Prince the privilege of test driving one of their trucks. Part of the test drive for David, included evaluation of the width of the truck bed for the transportation of wide loads, such as ping pong tables. When David returned the truck to the dealership he explained that he would seriously consider that truck when he made his final decision about which new car or truck to buy. That was 25 years ago and, unfortunately for that dealership, David still hasn't bought a new car…or truck.

Even after the sale of his business, David is still frugal. Fourteen years after the sale of Hotels.com, we sat waiting for the commencement of Katie's college basketball game. David announced he was hungry. Realizing his aversion to spending money foolishly, I knew that David's idea of obtaining sustenance would be a visit to the grocery store several blocks away. He would opt not to visit that high-priced, fast food establishment around the corner that sold turkey sandwiches for $3.00. When he returned to the gym just before tip-off I was surprised that he had returned with a large bag of potato chips. The selection of potato chips was inconsistent with David's approach to food selection. Typically, he would opt for a healthier choice of shaved turkey or fresh fruit. After watching him eat the chips for about 5 minutes, I too was overcome with hunger. I deviated from my quest to also make healthy choices. Retrieving one chip, I placed the entire morsel into my mouth. In an instant I realized the horrible mistake I'd made. Because I was sitting among other parents, in a public place, I refrained from my initial impulse, to forcefully expel the chip. Only with the assistance of a full bottle of soda, was I able to swallow the Jalapeño potato chip. In twenty-eight years of marriage to Prince Charming I had never seen him consume one Jalapeno potato chip. Now he was eating an entire bag? As I tried to catch my breath, and prepared to ask him why he chose the Jalapeno flavor, I stopped. As I got a better glimpse of the bag of chips, the answer was self-evident. On the bottom of the bag of chips was a round orange sticker advertising that the chips were 20% off. Mystery solved.

One of the parents at the game inquired as to who my daughter was. When I told her the mother's eyes lit up. She inquired about my husband, and whether he was the one who previously owned Hotels.com. As I admitted that he was, I was tempted to tell her he was also the one who had just eaten an entire bag of Jalapeno chips, and was currently unable to speak. Instead I simply patted Prince Charming on the back and answered in the affirmative.

Wealth is a relative concept. It is the people who feel insecure who are the poorest, not the ones with the least money. The children in Peru, depicted in the images Katie brought home, didn't feel poor. The parents who live in a modest two bedroom, one bathroom, apartment that have a great marriage, and successful kids, enjoy wealth beyond their dreams. Others who live in mansions and enjoy financial wealth, may be dealing with personal disappointment and distress.

Sam Walton was the wealthiest person in the United States during the 80's.[265] The founder of Wal-Mart and Sam's Club, Sam Walton, was content to drive his old pick-up truck and wear clothes from Wal-Mart.[266] His friends in Kingfisher, Oklahoma, where he was born, were still his friends when he died. Most of the people in Kingfisher were Sooners of modest means, but they were friends with one of the wealthiest men in America.

Tulsa, my home town, is a big city compared to Kingfisher. Yet the people across Oklahoma are very similar. Sam Walton could have easily been mistaken for one of the guests at my Aunt Mary's annual 4th of July party. From the time I was three years old, we celebrated every 4th of July at my Aunt Mary's house by saying the Pledge of Allegiance around the flag pole. We wore patriotic t-shirts and sang God Bless America. We didn't watch someone else shoot fireworks. We shot out own firecrackers and bottle rockets, without regard to the risks to our own personal safety. Aunt Mary lived in rural Oklahoma so shooting fireworks was not only allowed, but expected. We ate fried chicken and barbeque. We pitched horse shoes and shot skeet. At least eighty people came to Aunt Mary's 4th of July party every year. Nobody cared what anyone did for a living or who had the most impressive portfolio. Nobody cared what brand of automobile, pick-up truck, or tractor transported the guests to the party. Sam Walton would have felt right at home. For all I know he could have been there.

Having come from humble beginnings, I learned to value character rather than possessions. The type of car somebody drives isn't nearly as important as whether they offered a friend a ride. The names dropped in conversation are not nearly as impressive as the names of the charities on their check ledger. The people who use balance sheets to choose their friends are not worth having as friends. When I left Law School I was so broke that I had to borrow money to pay my moving expenses, even though the firm would ultimately reimburse me. Yet I was rich! I was optimistic. I was filled with excitement about the possibilities ahead. I had an education so I was empowered to determine my own destiny.

David has been extremely successful financially but his greatest joy and success in life has been his family. His only regret is that we didn't have more children. His greatest hope is that his children will live near him when they are finished with college. At the time the kids were young, I felt they needed more time from a parent. David didn't understand. I explained to David that he would have to help me more with the kids or I would have to quit my job. He reluctantly concluded that I should quit rather than compromising his business. He never considered taking time off to take the children in for their annual check-ups with the pediatrician, to the dentist, to the orthodontist when braces were needed, or to the eye doctor when glasses were required. If one of the kids had to go to the emergency room, it was my job to take them. He would stop by after work.

Each of the kids had their tonsils removed. We told him about our day in surgery that night when he came home from work. The Prince never attended a school Valentine's Day party or the school Halloween parade. He made it to the events that were scheduled at night after work. Soccer games we always on the weekends so he could make those. When it was time to move to a new home, it was my job to facilitate the move. It was David's job to remember to come home to the new address.

Now that the kids are grown, David is running another big company. He appreciates just how valuable his time is with his kids. He's traveled across the country to cheer at almost all of Katie's college basketball games. The Prince has taken each of the kids on vacations, just the two of them. Initially he did it for their 12th birthdays. Now he travels with them every chance he gets. He's hiked the Appalachian Trail with Zach. He traveled to Brazil with Anna. Katie experienced the elephants of Africa, the art of Russia, and the Sophia in Istanbul with her father. Not a day passes that he doesn't communicate by phone with at least one child. David is wealthy because he has children who love him, and Cinderella still adores him. When the kids have to plan their father's funeral, they'll probably mention that he was a successful businessman. However most of the conversation at his funeral will be about what a great father he was and how he enriched their lives. They'll be able to afford a beautiful resting place for their father's body, with a glorious headstone. The headstone will probably read "successful business man." It will surely read "beloved father." David has had it all, but not at the same time.

David loves the time he can spend with our kids now, because I spent time with them as they were growing up. Kids can have problems in spite of the best of parenting. Kids can survive to be great people in spite of the worst of parents. However if we are to give every child the best chance for success and a happy life, parenting is critical. There is no substitute for devoting time and energy to our children. Whatever parents say to justify their absence, children perceive that the choices we make, and how we spend our time, are the best indicators of our priorities and values. Mom may have to work two jobs to put food on the table. Her son realizes that she would prefer to watch his soccer games than go to work. However, supporting the family is her priority. By going to work, mom demonstrates her commitment to her children. However if mom is an attorney, and chooses to work long hours at a higher paying job than a job that would provide less financial support and more time at home, the kids understand that as well. Children learn by our example. If we tell them family is important but we fail to make time for them, it isn't a mystery where our priorities are. If a parent is too busy to help with homework then that parent is probably also too busy to notice when his/her child makes a D on that homework assignment. When a parent tells a child to make A's in school but can't find the time to help edit a paper the message is clear…"do what I say, not what I do." Time is the most valuable asset we have. How we spend that asset speaks volumes about our priorities regardless of what we say about those priorities.

Raising the next generation is a critical job. It is critical for success of our families and society. Women make a variety of contributions to society, by holding public office, through philanthropy, and running businesses. We are teachers and professors, policewomen and soldiers, doctors and nurses. All are vital to our society. Women have won Nobel prizes and Pulitzer prizes. We play golf and clean houses. We are engineers and scientists; musicians and artists. We are entertainers and CEO's. But the importance of enriching the world through raising the next generation should never be trivialized. It is hard work. Stay-at-home moms and dads receive no financial compensation. We never receive promotions. If we are really successful our children become independent…and leave home. We are often disrespected. But we are wealthy beyond measure because our children become a reflection of the time, love, and devotion we have dedicated to them. We pass on character and values only by being with our children long enough to teach them by example. Wealth is something stay-at-home mothers and fathers possess, even though bankers sometimes underestimate our net worth.

Professional women often worry that if we opt to stay at home, we are setting a bad example for our children. Yet it seems the opposite is often true. The woman who devotes time to her career, instead of to her children, inspires resentment in her children. When children are resentful they don't want to be like their mother. Instead of inspiring children to become successful in their careers, some professional women inspire their children to reject careers totally. Worse yet, if we neglect our children they have a way of getting our attention through destructive behavior.

When a wife devotes twenty years to raising children, the children become a gift to her husband and to society. The true measure of 'WEALTH' isn't money or financial success, but the relationships we have with family and friends. Every mother is different. Some mothers achieve a balance between professional success and raising children. By doing so she may be able to provide the emotional support her children need as well as the financial support needed to provide for college, travel, and even help with beginning a career. Some women attain wealth through relationships with friends. Some women attain wealth by sacrificing income for more time with their children. The important thing is that every woman with kids has to assess whether their needs are being met, and set her priorities accordingly.

As a nurse providing care for patients facing life threatening injuries or illnesses, I had the opportunity to listen as people reflected on the high points, and the disappointments, of their lives. Not one patient, male or female, ever expressed regret that they had not worked harder or devoted more time to their job. Instead many expressed regret at their choices to spend less time with their children or the people who were important to them. Unfortunately those patients had lived their lives trying to impress others instead of identifying their personal goals and working to achieve them. They never realized their **happily ever after**.

E. The Stool Collector

Filling out forms is an unappreciated art form. Some unfortunate soul has to dedicate herself to creating forms, handing them out, collecting them, filing them, and eventually somebody has to throw them away. The one job that nobody is ever hired to do is read them or to use the information contained in the form in any meaningful way. We have each filled out paperwork to start a new school year, an application for a credit card, a college admission application, an IRS tax return, an application to a summer camp, or a health form at the doctor you have visited every year for the last twenty. We spend hours of precious time filling out forms that nobody will ever read. The real question is why? Nobody cares what you put on the form, but only that you filled it out. If you wrote in Sanskrit would anyone care, or even notice?

For many women, and especially stay-at-home moms, the most annoying part of the form is the line for occupation. If you are a medical doctor or attorney it may not register that there is anything annoying about this question. However if you are a stay-at-home mother, what is an appropriate answer? The possibilities are endless: acquisition coordinator, dispute resolution specialist, aspiring chef, frustrated nutrition planner, amateur photographer, zealous videographer, well-intentioned scrap-booker, medical specialist, neophyte repairwoman, child activity facilitator, homemaker, psychologist, tutor, first-aid specialist, insightful advisor, repairman coordinator, party planner, creative costume designer, discount home interior decorator, frustrated counselor, ingenious cake decorator, crazed driving instructor, expert college counselor, employment application specialist, hygienic consultant, ingenious diaper disposer, experienced seamstress, esteemed tooth fairy, Santa Claus, laundress, lifeguard, athletic coordinator, homework enforcer, facilitator, hair stylist, and transporter. I suspected that it didn't really matter how I filled in the space labeled "occupation." Does a proctologist perform a colonoscopy differently on a lawyer than on a stay-at-home mother? Does the child of an attorney get a better room assignment at camp that the child of a stay-at-home mother? Why does the credit card company care if your income is derived from mowing lawns or cleaning port-a-potties? There came a time in my life when I had an opportunity to put my theory to the test.

A trip to Jamaica caused the longest period of illness and distress that my girls have ever experienced. No trip to Jamaica is complete without a trip to Dunn's River Falls. The Falls are world famous for their beauty, energy, and slippery surfaces. Being the ever-vigilant mother that I am, it seemed too dangerous for a 5 year old and a 7 year old to attempt to climb the treacherous rocks that the adult tourists ascend every day. Even the adults hold hands and navigate the falls with caution. The girls would be happy playing in the water at the base of the falls. As a clever mother I knew that a broken bone in Jamaica would present a much greater risk than a similar injury treated in Dallas. For at least one hour I played with the girls in the pool of water at the base of the falls, gladly sacrificing the personal thrill of experiencing the treacherous falls with the other adults in our group. In the stillness of the water we eliminated any risk of injury from the slippery rocks and the rushing water. The girls were happy and left the pool of water with all bones in-tact. What a great mother I thought I was!

Unbeknownst to me that stagnant pool of green water was much more treacherous than the slippery rocks of the falls. Some unidentified bacteria or parasite was lurking in the stillness of that infested water. Both girls must have ingested it as they became violently ill a week after we returned to Dallas. Katie missed three weeks of school. Anna missed five. Katie had horrible diarrhea for 3 weeks. Anna had stomach spasms that would cause her to scream out in pain, night and day. After the doctors decided that they had been exposed to something in Jamaica, the goal of treatment was to identify the particular bacteria or parasite that was playing such havoc with their intestines. The only way to do that was through analysis of their feces. We're not talking about those little cards that the doctor gives you with instructions to wipe a smidgen of stool on the sample card. We are talking about vials of excrement. The stool collector must first gather the poop in a plastic potty hat. It's called a hat because the brim of the bowl fits nicely over the edge of the toilet. The tall part of the hat, when turned upside-down, serves as a receptacle for the bowel moment you are trying to analyze. Once the child has had the opportunity to use the potty hat, the stool collector simply scoops the poop into a glass vile. The expert stool collector knows how to collect the stool, and then clean out the "hat" in preparation for the next use without splashing any excrement onto the stool collector's clothing. Fortunately, the vile used to hold the feces is clear so you can visualize whether you have collected a sufficient quantity, or whether you must wait for the next defecation to gather the appropriate amount of excrement. The really amazingly gross thing is that until time to leave for the lab, the vials must be stored in the refrigerator, next to the cheese sticks, juice boxes, chocolate milk, and ketchup.

For three weeks, I retrieved stool samples from both girls on a daily basis. I stored them in the kitchen refrigerator. Several times each day I cleaned out the potty hat placed it in the toilet to collect the stool. Every day for over three weeks I transported the samples to the lab. I became quite adept at stool collecting! If there were a market for books on stool collecting techniques, I could have authored a best-seller. If there were a speaker's circuit for stool collectors, I would have been in great demand. Because there was no market for books or speeches on stool collecting, I was destined to remain an unappreciated, unknown, expert stool collector.

Once the doctors gave the girls the right medicine they returned to school, and recovered completely. Thank God stool collecting is a talent that I have never had to use again. However it's like riding a bike. No matter how long it's been, you never forget how to collect a proper stool sample. In recognition of my new-found expertise David had business cards made for me to ensure that anyone interested would know that I possessed invaluable, uncommon, and often under-appreciated, expertise. I was a talented nurse, and a good trial attorney…but I became a great Stool Collector.

For at least four years thereafter, every time I had to fill out a form and list my occupation, I wrote "stool collector." Nobody ever asked or even commented about my job or expertise. Suddenly it was clear that nobody really cared what I did for a living, or how good I was at it. What they cared about was whether I filled out the form.

F. My Perceptions

Perceptions are notoriously inaccurate. When I perceived that Mrs. Gibson previously had "normal" sexual relations with Mr. Gibson, I was wrong. When a fellow soccer mom perceived that I was embarrassed by Anna running past the out-of-bounds line on the soccer field, she was wrong. When another soccer mom perceived that I had some inside connection to customs agents, she was mistaken. However occasionally perceptions are accurate as the customs agents are trained to be particularly observant. They could tell right away that Zach's shirt and pants were missing part of his breakfast.

Ralph's perception of me was never accurate. He knew that I was a successful trial attorney but he thought there was something wrong with me if I was willing to give up what he had, to stay at home and bake cookies. Ralph's perception of me in the LaGuardia airport was equally inaccurate. I had gone to the NASDAQ opening to support my husband rather than because I wanted my picture to be featured in Times Square. I wore jeans and carried my pillow, attempting to sleep on the trip since I was traveling at times that I would normally spend sleeping. I traveled in the early morning hours and late at night to limit time away from my kids. I was much more interested in sleep, than impressing someone in the airport with a designer suit.

The type of car people drive is not always an indication of their wealth or success. The old pickup truck Sam Walton drove, was not intended to convey anything about his net worth, which was estimated to be around $65 billion dollars. It simply served its purpose. He had no need for a better or fancier truck. That old blue Cadillac I drove, before David sold his business, was the same car I drove after he sold the business. He owned the business before the sale. After the sale we simply had the cash value of the business. Theoretically, we had the same net worth both before and after the sale. David and I perceived that our net worth was the same. Other people perceived it to be much different after the sale became public knowledge.

David continued to be the CEO of Hotels.com for a period of five years after the sale. Hence he still went to the same building, doing the same job, before and after the sale. Yet people's perception of him changed. Before the sale they thought we had no money, so they perceived that my reason for driving an old Cadillac was to be frugal. After the sale they knew that we had money, so now they assumed that we would soon be buying a new car. Surely we would opt for a nicer car if we could afford it. Their perceptions were wrong, both before, and after the sale of the business. I drove that old blue Cadillac before the sale, because it was a good car. The sheer size would protect the kids in the event of an accident. After the sale, it was still a good deal. It would still protect the kids in the event of an accident.

Success for yourself is different than success for others. Be cautious in thinking that someone else needs to meet your perception of happiness. There is no *one size fits all.* You will never know all there is to know about someone who may appear to be incredibly successful in their professional or personal life. The managing partner of the most prestigious firm in town may be embezzling money from his clients. He may have a wife who is an alcoholic. He may have a child who is a drug addict. The person flying in coach, dressed in tennis shoes and jeans, may be the wealthiest person on the plane. The man who is so frugal that he'd rather test drive a truck, than pay somebody to deliver a ping pong table might be the wealthiest in the table tennis store. The one who consumed an entire bag of jalapeno chips in order to save 20 cents, might have the most money. Yet he might not be the wealthiest because of the numbers on his bank statement. The better test of wealth may be the number of phone calls received every month from his grown children, who call to tell him that they love him.

Every person and family needs a minimum amount of financial security. Food, shelter, education, and medical care are essential for every family. While any amount of money beyond the minimum is nice it does not necessarily enhance or promote happiness. Because you never really know the financial status of others, you can't keep score. Don't try. Wealth for the sake of wealth, will always be a disappointment. There will always be somebody who has more. Act like you have less, and enjoy the feeling of success.

What we do for a living is not who we are. Whether I list my occupation as an author, a nurse, a Business Law instructor, an attorney, a stay-at-home mom, a trumpet player, or a stool collector, I am the same person. I have even told people at cocktail parties when asked what I do, that I am a stool collector. The funny thing is that they usually don't ask another question. Perhaps either they don't really care what I do for a living, or they are too embarrassed to admit that they don't know what a stool collector is. Either way, it is important to evaluate people for who they are, rather than what they do. Once we accurately identify our goals, it is our responsibility to take action to ensure the desired outcome. Cinderella was lucky the Prince came along. However if the Prince had gotten lost along the way, Cinderella knew where the castle was. It was her responsibility to find the Prince. Snow White was a victim of the evil queen. However, she should have taken responsibility not to eat the fruit given to her by a stranger. Sleeping Beauty's mother should have taken responsibility to teach her daughter about the danger of spinning wheels. Ariel was victimized by the Sea Witch, Ursula, who forced her to give up her voice in exchange for legs. However, Ariel should have accepted responsibility by simply telling Eric that she loved him, rather than trading her voice for legs. Belle should have been responsible for keeping her promise to the Beast, returned to the castle as promised, and told him of her feelings. Strong, successful women accurately perceive their own strengths and weaknesses. Each of the Disney women knew what she wanted. Having identified their goal, each woman should have each taken responsibility to ensure that she achieved her happily ever after, rather than waiting for a prince to determine her future. Magical things happen in Disney movies, but most of us live in the real world. In the real world we have to be our own fairy god mothers.

"In the long run, we shape our lives,
And we shape ourselves.
The process never ends
Until we die.
And the choices we make
Are ultimately our own responsibility."

-Eleanor Roosevelt [267]

CHAPTER VII. RESPONSIBILITY

Women must recognize men for who and what they are. Some men are pigs, abusive and perverted. Others can be our best allies. It is essential to a woman's happiness, that she accurately identify the character of a man. He may be a fellow executive, boyfriend, partner, fiancée, or spouse. Because of the importance of his role, it is critical to determine what type of character he has. Once we identify the fundamental nature of a man, it is essential that we take responsibility for making decisions to maximize our happiness with that man. For example, if a male executive demonstrates his lack of respect for women, it is a woman's responsibility to refuse to tolerate his demeaning attitude. She may quit her job, ask for a transfer to another department, confront her boss, or even go back to school to prepare herself for another line of work. If a husband is unable or unwilling to participate in cleaning the house, it is the woman's responsibility to demand that he share in the domestic chores. To prevent resentment we must insist on equal participation of the man and woman, whether to each clean or each participate by paying our share of the cost of a housekeeper. If we simply do the house cleaning ourselves, we become resentful and bitter. If spending time with the children is a priority of ours, but not our spouse, then it is the woman's responsibility to spend the time she perceives the children need. How could we expect our Prince Charming to compromise his career if we are unwilling to do the same?

Having identified the personality of a man we must take responsibility to accommodate his goals, while working to achieve ours. Until we take responsibility for our futures it is unlikely that things will just magically happen or change. Cinderella said "it's possible for a plain yellow pumpkin to become a golden carriage…it's possible." The problem is that most of us don't have a fairy-god mother who can make our cares disappear with a wave of her magic wand. If we are to achieve happiness and success we must make it happen. We can be Cinderella by being our own fairy-godmother, the mechanic in the construction of our own vehicle that transports us toward professional success, or the architect of our own castle. Whichever path we choose we must take responsibility for our choices. Our future depends on it.

We now have the power to make choices that women didn't have 100 years ago. We no longer have to rely on a man to support us. If we encounter discrimination in the work place, we have options. We can leave and find a more supportive environment. We can rely on fellow women for advice and guidance. There are strong women in powerful places who serve as role models and resources.

Women are working to improve conditions in the workplace for other women. The problem is that we don't have the luxury of waiting for twenty years for the men making the advancement decisions to retire. By the time they realize that they should be promoting the best and the brightest, whether they are men or women, we may have missed a critical time to start a family. In twenty years an employer may be more supportive of a woman who needs to take time off for a child's doctor appointment. However if we wait for twenty years to take the child, it won't be the pediatrician the child will need. It will be a psychiatrist, because mom was never around to meet the needs of her child. We can't wait for twenty years to have a child and take maternity leave. In twenty years our eggs will be old and a child conceived later in life has a greater chance of having developmental issues. We probably won't be able to conceive a child in twenty years. If we are able to conceive, it may be with the help of hormone therapy. That could lead to multiple births which could make the pregnancy harder. Child care challenges might become insurmountable. If the child is born with disabilities, the challenges of balancing career and family increase exponentially.

People of all races and socio-economic groups treat women differently than men. It may be the Home Depot clerk that assumes you don't know what an Allen wrench is. It may be the car salesman who asks if you need to consult your husband before making a selection. Women face disparaging and thoughtless remarks every day. It is our responsibility to choose how best to respond. While a lawsuit might be successful, it might cause you to be shunned from future employment opportunities. It may be time consuming and expensive. Sarcasm can be an effective tool that can facilitate education of the person who has been disrespectful to you. It can also cause the simultaneous disembowelment of the person who has disrespected you. When you are getting that famously abrasive feeling, sarcasm may be the perfect solution. For example when the Home Depot Clerk asks if you have one of those "L shaped little screw thingies" at home, you can simply answer him by saying that "if the little screw thingies he's talking about fit wrench sizes .035 to 3/8 inches, or metric sizes from 0.7 mm up to 10.0 mm, you've already got one of those screw thingies." Tell him you don't want another one unless the directions indicate that a bigger one is better. The used car salesman might ask if you need to consult your husband before buying a car. As you exit the store you simply tell him, "No, I already asked my husband and he told me that he didn't care what type of car I bought, as long as the salesman wasn't an asshole." It's not a woman's fault if somebody disparages her simply because she is a woman. She is only responsible if she allows it to happen a second time.

We must take responsibility for making choices in our personal lives regarding every aspect of our lives. We must decide who to marry. It is our decision when and if to have children. It is our responsibility to make decisions in the work place that will facilitate success. If we are unhappy or dissatisfied, it is our responsibility to make a change. The solutions may be varied but we cannot afford to simply complain that we are being treated unfairly. We must be proactive in seeking solutions for ourselves. Whether it means taking a part time position, accepting the idea that a promotion will not happen, going to work at a competing firm, starting our own business, changing careers, quitting a job to be present for all of our children's performances and sporting events, we must take responsibility for our happiness. The unhappy women are those who refuse to accept responsibility for their own success. If we wait for someone else to rescue us it is likely that we will remain a victim of our circumstances. If a husband is physically abusive to his wife, the wife may not be responsible until the second time he hits her. If a boss passes over a female employee for promotion in favor of a less-competent male, the woman can only blame the boss the first time it happens.

Women can be assertive without being aggressive. We can be strategic without being manipulative. But above all, we must accept responsibility to demand a change once we become aware of an intolerable situation. There will always be a misogynistic doctor, a judge who is a dirty old man, or a husband who is happy to allow you to do it all. Women may not have the ability to prevent those circumstances from happening the first time, but we must ensure that there isn't a second time.

A. The Little Red Hen

Mom often read to me the story of the ***Little Red Hen***. Contrary to popular belief, the moral of the story was not that women who eat home-made bread will get plump like a chicken. The message of the story was that everyone who benefits should help. When my brothers heard the story they didn't think to themselves that they should do their part around the house. They simply concluded that the Little Red Hen was a selfish bitch not to share her bread with the other people in her family. They thought the old stingy fowl deserved to gain weight from eating the bread all by herself. It was their conclusion that the bitter old hen should be lonely and depressed as she sat at home alone, eating her disproportionate share of starch. There was no cock, or baby chicks, at her table to recognize her prowess in the kitchen. Her homemade bread might have been the best in the county, but no cock was around to marvel at her achievement.

The Little Red Hen's goal wasn't to have it all. She didn't want to plant the seed, cut the wheat, take it to the mill, and bake the bread all by herself. She wanted her companions to help. They knew if they refused to help, she'd do the work anyway. When the hen was so resentful that she refused to share her bread, she realized that she had done it all. The accomplished chicken had proved she had expertise in farming, milling, and baking. She excelled in both professional and domestic endeavors. As the Little Red Hen sat alone, in the darkness of her kitchen, eating her delicious bread all by herself, she wondered if a better course would have been to opt for happily ever after, rather than having it all at the same time.

The story of the Little Red Hen epitomizes the American woman. Too often we think we should do it all, regardless of the unwillingness of others to help. We undertake all domestic responsibilities, even though we are working as many hours outside the home as our husbands. If we buy the store-bought bread we feel guilty. If we demand help, we feel weak. If we fail to share the fruits of our labor, we feel guilty and selfish. We must learn to ask for help. If we don't get it, we should demand it. If assistance is still not forthcoming, it may be time to re-evaluate our goals. Perhaps the home-made bread is not as important as our relationship with the other animals. Maybe it is better to opt out of the bread making endeavor and opt instead for a relationship-promoting endeavor. If we allow others to take advantage of us we will end up doing all the work, feeling resentful, and angry with those who chose not to help. Either others have to help, or we can all manage with store-bought bread. Having home-made bread was the Little Red Hen's goal, not that of the other animals. We must take responsibility to demand help achieving a goal set by the couple or family, and stop making it so easy for others to take advantage of us. Otherwise, we might make the best bread ever, but we'll be eating it all alone.

B. Shock

I made it! It was the end of my senior year in college. No more setting the clock for 5:30 a.m. I was finished fretting about tests, patient care cards, and annoying labs. Never again would fellow students practice the art of giving an injection or starting an I.V. on me. The injections weren't so bad but I still have nightmares about that Naso-gastric tube being put through my nose and reaching its final resting place in my trachea, instead of the desired location in my stomach. "Whoops" was the word that I most feared hearing from a fellow student in lab. The wound dressing lab should have followed the I.V. lab, so that the wounds left by students attempting to start I.V.'s could have been treated.

Now it was time to test my leadership skills in the real world. I had mastered the skills necessary to fully assess a patient including a detailed analysis of the ramifications of rheumatoid arthritis on the sex life of an 87 year old woman. I had inserted a Foley catheter in an elderly patient, by holding his penis with my right hand, and inserting the Foley with my left, learning not to flinch as his face contorted and the rest of his body stiffened in pain. I had picked maggots out of a wound and suctioned thick green phlegm from a patient's tracheotomy. In the real world, nursing students experience the most grotesque of human experiences. Yet we did not experience leadership unless we concluded our educational experience by serving as the head nurse in a remote rural hospital. If we stayed in a metropolitan area we would be allowed to work as a staff nurse. However, the staff at the more modern hospitals in the larger cities had the good sense not to be led by a nursing student. However a nursing student about to graduate was more knowledgeable than the nurses in some remote hospitals. Being the high achiever that I was, I opted to go to a smaller, rural hospital for my leadership experience. In this small remote, general hospital, I was permitted to work as the head nurse on one of two floors in the hospital.

On the third day of my leadership experience, I reported to work as the head nurse on the second floor for the 3-11 shift. As usual, the head nurse from the 7-3 shift gave report. Her description of the events from her shift was unremarkable except for the patient in 243. The patient in 243 was a 28 year-old female who had undergone a hysterectomy earlier in the day. She returned to the floor around 11:30 but "wasn't doing very well." Why would a 28 year old woman need a hysterectomy? What did the nurse mean by the comment that the patient wasn't doing very well? Was there a real problem, or was the nurse giving report simply over-reacting to the patient's lack of friendliness?

The minute report was completed, I went directly to room 243. As I entered the room, the look of distress on the face of the patient's husband conveyed the sense of urgency that had been lacking in the head nurse's report. I was unable to ask the patient any questions since she was unconscious. Shock is a medical term that I had studied in books, describing patients who had recently sustained a serious injury causing the loss of a large quantity of blood. I had never seen a patient in shock. I had not expected to see one in a hospital unless in the

Emergency Room, or ICU. I wasn't in the E.R. or ICU, but this patient was unquestionably in shock. The blood soaked dressing on the patient's abdomen would have suggested to a five year old that this patient was bleeding internally. The patient's blood pressure was low and her pulse rate was fast; both classic signs of shock. I had read about cyanosis of the lips causing them to turn blue, but I never expected to see it in a patient of mine. My patient's lips looked as though she had painted them with blue lipstick.

Shocked by the lack of attention to this critical situation, I immediately summoned a fellow nurse. "Call the surgeon immediately" I instructed her. I was emphatic. The doctor had to come right away. I explained I would stay with the patient, thinking to myself that I didn't know how much longer the patient might live. Shock was my reaction when the nurse returned and advised me that the doctor was annoyed. He explained that the patient was merely slow to wake up following surgery. That moron said that I should let one of the regular nurses take over for me since they knew more about surgical patients than I did. Without hesitation I called my nursing instructor from the patient's bedside. I tried to convey the urgency of the situation without causing the husband to panic. Although my instructor suspected that I was over-reacting, she came to the room within two minutes. As the instructor entered the room the look of shock on her face told me I hadn't overreacted. The instructor had access to the Chief of Staff at the hospital. She called him immediately. I don't know what she said to the Chief of Staff, but the surgeon came to the floor within a few minutes.

I met the surgeon in the hall, not wanting to scare the husband. Due to the urgency of the situation, I began giving report to the surgeon as he approached. The surgeon appeared to be close to seventy, with leathery wrinkled skin, and a nose as red as Rudolph's. Even as he sped past me in the hall it was hard to miss the divots in his red nose, characteristic of an alcoholic.

"Get one of the regular nurses to take care of my patient" he blared at me. I could only see the back of his head as he passed me in the hall. He was unwilling to pause to speak to me. Determined to give him a full report, I followed him into the room. Before I could speak, and before even examining the patient, the surgeon began explaining to the husband that the nurses had failed to properly medicate his wife with pain meds following the surgery. He said she had thrashed around in bed and her stitches had come loose. According to the doctor, that was the reason for the patient's bleeding for which he'd have to take her back to surgery. Of course I knew that if pain medication had been given to a patient with a blood pressure as low as hers, it would likely have killed her. The blood on the dressing didn't appear to me to be the result of stitches coming loose, but maybe I just didn't have the experience to know. I had never closed a surgical wound, but I knew how to sew. It was obvious to me that the stitches were still tight. The blood was just oozing out between the stitches.

The patient was being taken back to surgery so I had done all I could to save her. When my shift was over at 11:00 that night, I stopped by ICU to find out if my patient would survive. The report of the second surgery wasn't on the chart yet so I spoke to the ICU nurses about what the surgeons had found when they returned to the operating room. One of the ICU nurses had overheard the two surgeons talking. She gave me a full report. The surgeons found that they had failed to tie off a blood vessel in the original surgery. The patient had so much internal bleeding that two units of blood had to be given. The surgeons also found that during the first surgery they had punctured the patient's bladder. To cover it up, they did an "exploratory" procedure on the bladder in the second surgery. The patient had survived, so I was thankful for that. Thankfully, the Chief of Staff, my nursing instructor, the nurses on the floor, and the nurses in the ICU knew that I had saved the patient's life. I took responsibility to demand immediate intervention. However, being right about this patient wouldn't prevent the same tragedy from happening the very next day…and the next.

The next day my curiosity got the better of me. Even though the patient was still in I.C.U., I wanted to read the surgery report. I couldn't believe my eyes. The operative report of the second surgery had no mention of the internal bleeding caused by the blood vessel that the doctors had failed to tie off. There was a description of an exploratory procedure on the bladder that failed to identify any problem. The surgeon lied. He recorded that the reason for the second surgery was loosening of the sutures from thrashing around in bed.

Turning to my nursing instructor, I sought an explanation. She had none. The final two weeks at this hospital were filled with nurses reporting outrageous things to me that this doctor had done. It seemed that this doctor regularly wrote orders for so much I.V. fluid, that the I.V. fluid alone would have caused heart failure. The nurses didn't want to incur the wrath of the doctor, so they simply charted that they had given the ordered amount of fluid when, in fact, they had given only half. But that was only the beginning of the nightmare. I learned that the doctor had already had his obstetric privileges taken away. How many babies he had killed before the physicians on staff were compelled to act? I learned that the last three surgeries he had performed with this same assistant surgeon had each returned to the operating room for a second operation to correct a problem caused by the first. After completing my leadership experience, my instructor informed me that the surgeon had previously suffered from a mental breakdown, requiring hospitalization. When I left the hospital at the end of my leadership experience, that doctor was still on staff.

Surely this was not typical of most doctors, hospitals, and nurses? Surely most doctors were more competent than this one? Surely in most hospitals, the Chief of Staff would take action to prevent such outrageous conduct of one of her doctors? Wouldn't most nurses speak out against such blatant incompetence? Was this about men feeling superior to women, rather than being concerned for a patient's life? Surely the fact that all the doctors in this hospital were men, and all the nurses were women, had nothing to do with the blatant malpractice that was being repeatedly inflicted upon patients in this hospital? Was it just coincidence that the patients whose lives were being threatened by this monster were all women and children?

It seemed that I should speak out against a system of medical care that would allow women's lives to be threatened. I wasn't even a graduate nurse, much less a licensed nurse. How could I take on three medical doctors, including the Chief of Staff at this small rural hospital? Why would anyone believe me, rather than a licensed nurse with many years of experience? I resigned myself to believe that this hospital, and this surgeon, must be an aberration. If I limited my employment to only those hospitals in metropolitan areas, surely this attitude would not be tolerated?

Unfortunately, I came to realize that my experience in this small rural hospital in 1979 wasn't so uncommon. While the standards of care in the '70's, in a larger city might have been better, the attitude of doctors who were almost always men, towards nurses, who were almost always women, was intolerable. Even though many nurses had four years of college and spent eight hours of the day with patients, many doctors treated nurses with a total lack of respect. It was unclear if this was the natural result of doctors filling a supervisory role as the boss of the nurse, or because doctors were men and nurses were women, or a combination. Whatever the explanation, it was unacceptable. While I preferred to be in a supervisory role, if I respected my superior, I was glad to follow orders. If I was treated with respect and as part of the team, I was more than willing to defer to a superior. However, the summer after graduation I learned a valuable lesson. My personality was not compatible with deference to a man if I perceived that a patient's life hung in the balance. I'd rather be wrong, and incur the wrath of the doctor, than to remain silent as a patient died. Being famously abrasive seemed necessary when a patient's life was at stake.

Patient care was rewarding for me. I loved learning about the science behind medical problems and the treatment of them. Working in I.C.U. offered the opportunity to treat the most challenging medical problems and to work with some of the most competent nurses and doctors. Because many of my patients were critically ill, when their conditions improved, the families and patients, were eternally grateful for both the compassion and the superior quality of care provided. The non-monetary rewards of being a nurse were immense. However, it became clear to me that continuing to put myself in a position to be treated with a total lack of respect, by any physician who might pass through the I.C.U., was intolerable. As I watched physicians insult and disparage more senior, accomplished nurses, I knew that I would not survive. I had to take responsibility for my future happiness. My options were either to go into administration or teaching. Both options would mean that I would have little or no involvement with patient care, which had been my original motivation for becoming a nurse. Before finding a solution to my dilemma, I was assigned to care for Joey.

Caring for Joey taught me several things about nursing. I learned that the real patient may be a family member. I also learned that no matter how deferential I might be, any physician could disrespect me at any time, without consequences. Joey's doctor was an expert in pediatric trauma. He was such an expert that if a child of mine had suffered a serious injury, I would have chosen this physician to care for my child.

Regardless of a physician's orders, I was responsible to ensure that every medicine I administered was the correct dose, of the correct medicine, administered in the correct way (i.e. I.V., injection, etc.), to the proper patient. It was no excuse that the doctor wrote an incorrect order for the wrong dosage or medicine. If I gave it, I was responsible. If the patient had a drug allergy, I was supposed to know it. Medicines given in I.C.U. were typically intravenous medicines which are potentially more effective and more dangerous because they become immediately present in the blood stream. It was critical that I know and understand all that I could about the medicines that I infused directly into a patient's blood stream.

When Joey's physician ordered four times the recommended dosage of an IV antibiotic for the treatment of his infected leg I was faced with a dilemma. Even though I assumed this was an appropriate attempt to save the child's leg, and even though I felt sure that the physician knew what he was doing, how could I know that the dosage written was appropriate without confirming it with the physician? If all the medical literature indicated this dosage could cause renal failure, how could I administer it without first confirming that the doctor understood the danger of this dosage for this patient?

Realizing that the doctor might think questioning his order was insulting, disrespectful, or threatening, I consciously planned the most deferential way to ask the question. "Doctor I know that I am inexperienced and new to this I.C.U., so could you help me understand what I should do when I'm sure that a physician's order is correct but the dosage is four times the recommended amount according to the literature?" Disgusted, offended, and outraged, the doctor began to shake. After he yelled at me loud enough to be heard by every patient in the unit, he concluded his tirade by advising me that if I didn't want to follow his orders I could get another nurse who would administer the medication without question. I thought this doctor was smart enough to appreciate the fact that I was paying attention. The fact that I was aware of the normal dosage would be an indication that I took my responsibilities seriously. Wouldn't he be glad to know that if he ever made a mistake, I'd have his back? Instead his attitude indicated that he preferred a nurse who would follow his orders, regardless of their appropriateness. As much as I loved nursing, I hated being so vulnerable. Some nurses had the ability to let this type of abuse roll off their backs. I didn't. That night I decided I would apply to Law School. I couldn't change the doctor. I did have the power to determine whether I would be subjected to this type of demeaning attitude again.

I had to take charge of my life. If I had remained in nursing, I would have been the person injured. It was clear that I would become consumed with resentment. I would have been right; but miserable. Even if I became a Nursing Administrator or Nursing Instructor, I would still be in a subservient role to every male doctor who chose to disrespect me. By going to Law School I transformed myself from a person whose importance was minimized by doctors, to a person whose advice they valued. Instead of viewing me as a thorn in their side, they viewed me as someone who could extract it. Instead of begging them to speak to me, doctors waited for me to return their calls. While the doctors were confident of the right approach when treating a patient, they felt vulnerable and victimized in court. Being their attorney transformed me from being an annoyance to doctors, to an essential advocate for them. Going to Law School was a way to take responsibility for improving my relationship with doctors. Instead of complaining that I was being mistreated, I gave them a reason to want to change. They changed, not because it was the right thing to do, but because they now viewed me as someone who was valuable to them. Instead of an annoyance, I became an essential part of their future. I like to think that my presence as a female attorney, who was respected by male physicians, helped change the perception of those same physicians about female nurses. When the jury came back with a verdict vindicating my client, the doctor immediately felt a sense of permanent indebtedness. Imagine the shock on the face of a male doctor when he realized that a female nurse just saved his reputation and insurance premiums.

By leaving I became a better nurse, a better advocate for patients. I became an example to male doctors of the importance of female nurses in their lives. I didn't abandon nurses. By going to law school I was able to significantly impact the role of nurses in patient care. I gained the respect of male doctors not by demanding it, but by earning it.

C. Summer Clerkship

Between my second and third year in law school I had the best job in the world. I was a summer law clerk at a large, well known firm in Dallas. Law firms hired summer law clerks hoping that upon graduation the best students would return to become associates at their firm. Once the associate was hired as a permanent associate, you were never entertained again by any member of the firm. As a summer clerk, 30 hours of work per week would be ordinary. After graduation, and passing the bar, a young associate had the privilege of working 70 hours each week. Although your salary as an associate was a little more than that of a Summer Clerk, the associate had to pay for rent, food, and entertainment. Those were all provided for the summer clerks by the law firms.

I learned much more that summer outside the work environment, than at my desk. Summer law clerks came to my firm from around the country. These rising stars were among some of the most distinguished law students in the country. The job of the attorneys was to entice the summer clerks to return to the firm as associates after graduation. The job of the law clerks was to be entertained. For lunch we were taken to the best clubs in Dallas, by some of the most senior partners in the firm. We were treated to the finest food, created by the finest chefs in Dallas. Little did we know that after accepting a position with the firm, we would not see those senior partners again until we were being considered for partner 7-8 years later, or until they needed a job done...yesterday.

All of the summer law clerks lived in the same apartment building, most of us next door to each other. We were close enough to each other to be able to hear one male clerk beat his wife around 7:00 p.m. every night. We were close enough to see a young male associate arrive at the apartment of a female clerk at 2:00 a.m., planning to spend the rest of the night in her bed. He had spent the previous two hours in bed with his paralegal, but the paralegal must not have wanted to see her boss in the morning. When a female clerk's boyfriend arrived to visit and stay in her apartment, he got the couch. The bed was already occupied by the senior associate, to whom the female summer clerk reported during the work day. Thus, the mere fact that I was dating David, another clerk, was of little consequence.

Although I thought that I would find a home in the litigation section of a good firm, the summer was a perfect time to try different types of law. Litigation was the only area of law I experienced during the first half of my summer, at my first firm. While I enjoyed the attorneys at the first firm, the smaller firm had smaller companies for clients. These smaller companies tended to be less accepting of a female attorney taking responsibility.

During the second half of the summer, I was not allowed to work in the litigation department of the second firm. Instead, I was assigned to a corporate-banking area. There were only two female clerks assigned to litigation. One resembled a prostitute. She was the one who greeted her advising attorney at

2:00 a.m., after he slept with his paralegal. As far as I knew that law clerk was evaluated for her performance in bed rather than in the court room. She must have performed well because the firm made her an offer of permanent employment. The other woman who clerked in the litigation section was not rewarded for her performance by the male trial attorneys. Her hair was long, scraggly, and brown. Pam's hair was red, hot, and stylishly cut. The other clerk was overweight and homely. Pam was thin, provocative, and alluring. The homely woman received an offer from the firm, but was not invited to be a trial attorney. Obviously the homely, overweight female clerk was smart enough to meet the firm's requirements, but not sexy enough to meet the requirements of the litigators, who were all men.

I received an offer to work in the litigation section, even though I hadn't clerked in that department. Whew! What a relief to know that I was attractive enough to merit a job offer. However, I feared that one day I wouldn't be sufficiently attractive to satisfy the men's strict standards, so I looked for other opportunities. Instead of trying to change the culture of the partners in the litigation section, I took responsibility to find a firm that was already more accommodating to women. Instead of accepting a job at the first firm, where I would have had more difficulty convincing their clients to trust me, I took responsibility to find a better fit. I found that firm by talking to other female clerks to determine what experiences and impressions they had at other firms. While I could have worked at both firms with whom I clerked, I knew that the road ahead would be treacherous. I took responsibility to find the firm that would treat me with respect the day I walked in the door.

D. Dirty Old Men

Until I began the practice of law the only "first-hand" experience I'd had with dirty old men was my encounter with Mr. Williams. As an attorney, I quickly learned that dirty old men were not limited to the one-legged kind that might be found in hospitals. They also included the kind with two legs, who wore black robes and harassed young women as they came into the courtroom. Judge Dee Brown Walker was a dirty old man. Everyone knew it. Nobody seemed to care. Because he was the Judge, whatever he did or said was the law in his courtroom. He didn't have to abide by the rules of court, or follow case law that other judges felt compelled to enforce. Judge Walker knew that most clients would not spend the money to appeal any decision he made, so he was free to remain unfamiliar, and unconcerned, with the law. Judge Walker was an elderly, short, overweight, white-haired moron. The lines on his face punctuated the same reddish hue that I had seen on the face of a doctor I once encountered during my leadership experience in nursing school. Because Judge Walker was biased, he never felt compelled to explain the logic of his decisions. There was none. He ruled for those he favored, instead of those favored by the law. Judge Walker favored me, but it was a blessing and a curse. It was a blessing because he would always rule for my clients. It was a curse because every time I entered his court room I was sure to be harassed. When I entered his court room, he stopped whatever he was doing to kiss me on the cheek. The other attorneys in the courtroom just watched in amazement. He called me every week at the office and asked for, among other things, some "tender loving nursing care." I could always plan on humiliation and harassment from Judge Walker.

As people at my firm learned about my challenges with Judge Walker, they made a point of sharing with me their experiences with him. For example, another litigation associate, one year my senior, told a story about a case that went to trial in Judge Walker's court. The key witness was on the stand testifying. In the middle of her testimony, Judge Walker stopped her and inquired about whether she had undergone a hysterectomy. The case had nothing to do with medical procedures or hysterectomies. As it turned out the witness had undergone a hysterectomy sometime in the distant past. Judge Walker immediately disqualified her from testifying. His only explanation was that if a woman had a hysterectomy, she became incompetent to testify.

Taking responsibility for the situation in which I found myself was not easy. It would be easy to simply blame the judge, play the innocent victim, and file suit. Of course I was the innocent victim and the judge was wrong. While I would surely be victorious in a discrimination suit against Dee Brown Walker, if I filed such a suit I would be banished from every major firm in Dallas. While all the lawyers in Dallas knew that Judge Walker was a dirty old man, it was equally well known that any woman who would file a suit against a judge was the very worst kind of feminist.

I had to find another solution. What I needed was something more subtle, but equally effective. It was a man who solved the problem. His solution was a permanent one. Jesse was ahead of me by one year in Law School at the University of Oklahoma. Upon graduation he and his wife, another law student, moved to Dallas. Each worked for different firms as litigators. I was at a cocktail party when I learned that Jesse lived directly across the street from Judge Walker. With that connection in mind, I mentioned my experience and frustration with Judge Walker to Jesse.

Roughly one year later I ran into Jesse while sharing lunch with a friend. Jesse greeted me and then began to laugh in his boisterous baritone voice. All the customers in the restaurant were anxious to hear the joke. I became anxious to hear the joke too. When Jesse calmed himself enough to speak, he asked if Judge Walker had bothered me lately. Realizing that it had been several months since Judge Walker had called I became quite anxious to discover what Jesse knew about this unexpected lack of attention from Judge Walker. Recognizing Judge Walker for the man he was, Jesse knew that appealing to the honorable side of Judge Walker would be unsuccessful. Judge Walker didn't have an honorable side to his decrepit, geriatric body. He had no fear of a lawsuit. He was buddies with all the other judges. However, fear of great bodily injury was something even Judge Walker would like to avoid. If you want to bring an end to sexism, you can spend years in court, or you can use the man's sexist attitudes against him. Instead of appealing to the offender's sense of morality, which was nonexistent, it was much more effective to identify that which Judge Walker feared most. Jesse understood this concept without being told.

One day when Jesse was out in his front yard, he observed his neighbor, Judge Walker, doing yard work. Jesse stopped by for a neighborly chat with the Judge. During the encounter Jesse brought up my name, suggesting that the Judge and I were good friends. It was just after Judge Walker's acknowledgement of our friendship that Jesse warned Judge Walker that his personal safety might be in jeopardy. Judge Walker was shocked to learn that I was engaged to one of the Dallas Cowboy Football players. Of course the football player was about 6'8," and strong as an ox. Jesse laughed as he imagined what the football player would do to any man who might be foolish enough to even consider pursuing me. Fearing for his life, or at least fearing for that portion of his anatomy that defined him as male, Judge Walker never called or kissed me in court again. This is the definition of poetic justice. A man convinced another man to stop harassing a woman, because another man might physically assault him for his sexist behavior.

Sometimes, men can be our best allies, if we identify those who have our best interests at heart. I knew Jesse was one of those people. He was always respectful. By his choice of wives, I knew that he respected professional women. Jesse was keenly aware of the struggle of women trying to be accepted in the court room by other attorneys and judges. In the case of Judge Walker, taking responsibility for changing an unbearable situation required patience and insight.

Filing a suit against a judge would have been devastating to my career, to my future employment, and to any future dealings with other judges. While judges today are surely more careful about the appearance of impropriety, women continue to be faced with difficult situations. Now the judges are even more subtle about any improper relationship they might have with a woman. Women have to take responsibility to be more subtle about the way we deal with an untenable situation.

E. Prince Charming

Zach was just about to turn one-year old. I had survived colic, ear infections, teething, sleepless nights, and catching up at work after maternity leave. I only worried about once a week that I was leaving my first born with a potential child molester. I had convinced the older trial partners, and my clients, that I could be a mom and an effective trial attorney. Prince Charming still loved me, even though he now had to share me with another young man. Christmas of 1989 was the third time I had taken Zach on the 45 minute flight to Tulsa. By that flight, I knew how to help Zach clear his ears and relieve the pressure babies experience on flights. As soon as the plane left the tarmac, I gave him a bottle to help him clear his ears. This limited his screaming to only the first five minutes of the flight. My sense of self-confidence was at an all-time high. I was living proof that women could have it all. I was confident of my ability as a trial attorney, a wife, and a mother. As I arrived in Tulsa for the holidays, I was overjoyed to have a week at home where I could enjoy my son, while having the assistance of grandma. For one week I wouldn't have to stay up till 2:00 am, working because I wanted to spend the time from 5:00 to 10:00 p.m. with Zach. To say that I was elated to be on holiday was no exaggeration.

That sense of elation lasted about 26 hours. My royal brother-in-law had agreed to feed the royal dogs while we were gone for the week. The day after we arrived in Tulsa the phone rang. Instead of enjoying a restful week of vacation, my entire world turned upside down as I hung up the phone. The pipes in the attic of our house had frozen, broken, thawed, and flooded the attic. When the attic could no longer hold the water, the vaulted 20 foot ceiling over the main part of the house gave way. The entire downstairs of the house looked like a hurricane had hit from within. When you know a hurricane is coming, you take precautions. We didn't know a hurricane was about to hit, so we had taken no precautions. Standing water ruins hardwood floors, furniture, sheetrock, carpet, and even marble floors. As soon as we heard about the disaster, David and I flew back to Dallas to survey the damage. The house was worse than we could have imagined. The Prince volunteered to stay overnight to meet with the insurance inspectors the next day. I returned to Tulsa to be with Zach. The Prince spent that night lying on our wet mattress, with the royal German shepherd at his side. The castle and its contents had been destroyed. Cinderella's fairy god-mother was nowhere to be found.

The same week that the castle was destroyed, another type of disaster ravaged the kingdom. A constable visited Prince Charming and served him with papers notifying him that his company was being sued. The constable had a little bit of difficulty finding the Prince since the castle was under water. No forwarding address had yet been sent to the post office. Somehow the constable located us at the condo where we lived for three months, while the workmen repaired the devastation from the hurricane.

Now *having it all* included rebuilding the castle, fighting with the insurance company of the castle, dealing with the contractor hired to repair the castle, and working with the restoration company hired to restore or replace all the furnishings in the castle, including the thrones and the royal window coverings. Even Cinderella's fairy godmother was frustrated trying to wave her wand fast enough to rebuild the castle, hold the insurance company accountable, direct the building contractor in the reconstruction of the castle, manage a full trial docket, spend quality time with a one-year-old child, locate and move to alternate living quarters while construction was underway at the castle, cook meals, complete house-hold chores around the temporary residence, and supervise the Prince's lawsuit. Every evening Cinderella fixed dinner, bathed and played with the royal baby until his bed-time at 10:00 p.m., and then cleaned up the kitchen. The Prince would be waiting patiently for Cinderella's help with his lawsuit papers, even if that meant waiting until 11:00 o'clock. The lawsuit papers were often soiled from food and beverage consumed during the football game while the Prince waited for Cinderella to review them. About 2:00 a.m. every morning, Cinderella was overcome with exhaustion. She knew that if she missed her precious 4 hours of beauty sleep, she might lose her regal appearance. Would the Prince still love Cinderella if she helped him with his legal problems but prematurely aged due to lack of sleep? As Cinderella crawled into bed she was careful not to disturb the Prince's slumber. He was really tired. His performance at work the next day might be adversely affected if he didn't get a good night's sleep.

By the time Cinderella and the Prince moved back into the recently renovated castle, it was unclear if the Prince and Cinderella would be sharing the same royal living quarters, or if they would occupy separate bedrooms in the new castle. Cinderella had proved that she could have it all, but the price she paid for having it all was too expensive. Cinderella was resentful of the Prince that he had watched as Cinderella abused her fairy-god-mother without offering to call upon his fairy-god-father for help. The Prince was clueless! He thought Cinderella was distraught that her glass slippers had been lost in the flood. If he had looked he'd have seen the glass slippers were still on Cinderella's feet but her feet were wrinkled from the water sloshing around inside the slippers. He didn't realize that the songs of his nightingale had been replaced with the screeching of an owl, searching for a place to sleep. Would the Prince be happy sleeping with the royal German shepherd on a permanent basis? Didn't the Prince realize that the fairy god-mother was never around when the dishes needed to be washed? How could he watch television every night, as his bride was desperately trying to have it all?

Cinderella was drowning in resentment. If she were to be rescued, it would have to come from a woman throwing Cinderella a life ring. Cinderella knew she needed to be rescued. She knew that it would be a woman who would understand and relate to the resentment she was feeling. Cinderella didn't want a Prince to wake her from her sleep with a kiss. She just wanted to sleep. Cinderella wanted the Prince to show his appreciation for all she did for him.

Just once the Prince could do the dishes. Just once a week the Prince could have given the royal baby his bath. Just one day a week the Prince could have dealt with the builder so Cinderella could catch up at work. Cinderella didn't want to fight the waves all alone. She wanted the Prince to battle the surf with her, or at least carry the surf board for her.

Finding a female therapist was easy. Any female therapist would do. What woman wouldn't agree with Cinderella that the Prince was worthless, insensitive, and uncaring? Surely any female therapist would advise Cinderella that she deserved to be treated better by her Prince. Surely it was the Prince's responsibility to realize that Cinderella couldn't navigate the waves without his help. Cinderella needed only the confirmation of one other woman to tell her that it was only fair that she should turn the Prince back into the frog that he was before she met him.

Cinderella only visited the therapist twice. To her utter dismay, the therapist advised Cinderella that the fairy-god-mother was a figment of her imagination. Instead of being critical of the Prince, the therapist suggested that Cinderella was responsible for telling the Prince what was wrong. Imagine the shock and disbelief Cinderella experienced upon being told that her Prince couldn't be expected to intuitively know that Cinderella's feet had grown too large for her slippers, or that her feet were tired and wrinkled from dealing with the hurricane. Instead of blaming the Prince for being so clueless, the therapist told Cinderella that she was to blame for treating the Prince like a Prince. How could the Prince know that Cinderella was dying if she was still breathing and if she had it all? The Prince would have gladly turned off the television, if he had known he needed to attend Cinderella's funeral, or visit her at the institution where she was confined.

The Prince thought Cinderella was happy because she had it all. The Prince's needs were simple. He just wanted to watch the game. He didn't want to have a career, deal with repair and renovation of the castle, cook dinner, and give the royal baby a bubble bath. He wanted to go to work, eat dinner, and watch the game in peace. Was that asking too much? As far as he knew Cinderella was happy to have a career, be a mother, be married to a Prince, select all new furnishings for the castle, and dance in her beautiful glass slippers. The Prince let Cinderella choose whatever type of furniture she wanted. It didn't matter to the Prince if the color of the royal drapes was White Linen, or Alabaster. Cinderella got to choose whatever she wanted to make for dinner. It was her choice what type of bubble bath to use while bathing the royal baby. The Prince was happy to eat any time Cinderella had his dinner ready. He never complained that Cinderella hadn't done the dishes until after the baby had been put to bed. The Prince was always polite and thanked Cinderella for dinner, even if he didn't really like the food. If Cinderella didn't have time to look over the Prince's lawsuit papers until midnight, the Prince never complained that he couldn't get Cinderella's input until the next morning.

Fortunately for Cinderella, she got the help she needed. Fortunately for the Prince, Cinderella's therapist refused to bash the Prince. Instead she insisted that Cinderella take responsibility for her happiness. Cinderella had to tell the Prince that she didn't like wearing the glass slippers anymore. Cinderella learned that having it all didn't mean doing it all by herself, at the same time. It was Cinderella's responsibility to tell the Prince that she had an incurable case of a deadly disease called *having it all*. Cinderella was willing to trade part of all for survival. Because the Prince was one of the most important parts of having it all, Cinderella wasn't willing to give him up, even though something had to give. Instead, Cinderella shared her frustration with the Prince. Together they found the glass slippers and placed them back in Cinderella's closet. She no longer wore them every day, but they were the perfect shoes to wear on nights out with the Prince.

Cinderella realized that men and women are engineered differently, and not just anatomically. Women perceive the world differently than men. When Cinderella's grandchild is born, Cinderella won't tell her about the events following her father's first birthday. That story might be too frightening. A better illustration of the differences between men and women might be the story of the day Cinderella was sitting in the den, six months pregnant with her third child. Zach and Anna were playing in the den. The Prince was watching a football game. Cinderella was eating an apple, by cutting it in pieces with a really sharp knife. When the knife slipped and cut a piece of Cinderella's hand, instead of the apple, the sight of the bloody gash in her hand was overwhelming. Cinderella fainted. Because Cinderella was already sitting in a chair she didn't fall or injure herself. Rather, Cinderella simply slumped backwards in the chair as if asleep. Cinderella awoke from fainting as a result of Anna, the two-year-old princess, screaming in an utter panic. Even in the haze of trying to awaken from her state of unconsciousness Cinderella immediately knew that something was terribly wrong with Anna. The volume and pitch of Anna's screams made it clear that Anna was the victim of some horrible tragedy. How badly was Anna injured? Had Anna broken a bone, suffered a concussion, or was she bleeding profusely? Cinderella fought to awaken herself as fast as possible to come to the rescue of her little princess. As she awoke, Cinderella realized it wasn't Anna's blood that was causing Anna's screams of terror. It was the blood of Anna's mother that scared Anna. At two years old Anna was perceptive enough to appreciate that something was terribly wrong with Cinderella. Anna knew that her mother didn't normally sit slumped over in a chair, mouth open, and blood dripping from her hand.

Wrapping a napkin around the wound in her hand, Cinderella grabbed Anna, comforting her. Cinderella reassured Anna, explaining that everything was alright. As Anna's sobs subsided, Cinderella surveyed the other members of the family to ensure they were not unduly worried about her bloody hand or Anna's screams of panic. Whew! The Prince was still watching the game. Whether he was worried that it was Third Down, or just laughing at the last Budweiser commercial, he hadn't noticed the blood on Cinderella's hand, Anna's screams, or his pregnant, unconscious, wife. Zach was playing pretend with his sword. Perhaps he thought Anna's screams were the damsel in distress that he was about to save with his shiny sword. In Zach's world of imaginary play the blood he saw was probably perceived to be a mortal wound he had inflicted on his adversary. David and Zach perceived that everything was as it should be.

My two year old daughter was more perceptive than my 36 year old husband, or my five year old son. Recognizing that the Prince and his son didn't always perceive the condition of women around them, I learned to take responsibility for telling them! I also took responsibility not to ever again cut an apple with such a sharp knife. I taught Anna, when she was older, that she should remove any distractions from men before telling them something important. I learned that if I needed to get Zach or David's attention turning off the television was essential. If I had something really important to tell Zach, I would gently place my hand on his face and turn it towards my face. This way I could see his eyes and he could watch my mouth as I conveyed my message.

F. Taking Responsibility

Women take responsibility for performance at work and chores at home. Too often at work, and at home, we fail to tell our male counterparts what seems obvious to us. When a man surprises us by treating us disrespectfully, the most urgent concern may not be to educate him about the importance of respecting women, at that moment. He might be distracted. It is a lesson he needs to learn, but sometimes it is better taught by the right man, under conditions where the transgressor is most likely to pay attention. Men can be our best allies if we let them. We must be perceptive about circumstances at home and at work, and position ourselves in a way to minimize any hardships we could otherwise avoid. Too often women make the mistake of failing to say what we think should be obvious to a man. It is our responsibility to speak up. If the result is still unacceptable then it may be time to make another choice. It is also our responsibility to be strategic about how and when to speak up. As Snow White was walking through the forest with the Huntsman, who was charged with killing her, that probably wasn't the best time to mention to him that he had abandoned his wife and children to do the queen's bidding. When the Prince had just killed the dragon with his magic sword and then used it to cut down the thorny branches that engulfed the castle, Sleeping Beauty should just be grateful. Sleeping Beauty would be making a terrible mistake to awaken and begin telling the Prince the many reasons that she wouldn't tolerate weapons around the house.

Women must be pragmatic in dealing with unfair and discriminatory situations. Fighting the system takes time. If a boss tells you that your daughter's first grade play isn't as important as an upcoming trial, he may be wrong but you don't have the luxury of proving him wrong. When the judge postpones the trial you can tell your boss that he was wrong, but the first grade play is already over. You will never be able to adequately explain to your first grader why mommy had to miss her play?

You may have to remain employed for 8 years and work long hours to prove that you earned the partnership position that you were denied. Better to ask yourself at the beginning if you really want to be a partner at a firm that discriminates against women. The best revenge for discrimination is not a lawsuit, or complaining to management. Instead why not go to a different firm that is a direct competitor and show your old firm what they missed by not treating you right? Why not entice clients to come to your new firm because half of the executives at the client's office are women? Why complain to a male adversary that he is disrespecting you? Nothing will teach him better about the power of a woman, than getting beaten by a woman in trial. Don't wait to speak up until you are so tired that you commit malpractice and get fired. Take a part time position, do a good job, and when you are ready to return to full time, you will have demonstrated what great work you do.

When hiring young men and women coming out of school you'll be able to attract the best and the brightest because they are smart enough to realize that they don't want to be associated with a firm that disrespects women. Family is important to men and women, but they have to have enough time to have a family to appreciate its importance. Today young men and women, married to other professionals, seek employment in an environment where their time with their family is respected and protected. Women are no longer the only ones who want to have it all.

By refusing to accept being treated as a subordinate, or inferior to a man, at home and at work, women are not "feminine-nazis," ball-busters, or bra-burners. We are just responsible. We can make the choice to change our circumstances, even if our husband is a Prince. The secret is to take responsibility to make the hard choices.

"I fought all my life for women to have the
right to make their own
choices, in their personal
and professional lives.
I made mine."

-Hillary Clinton [268]

CHAPTER VIII: CHOICES

A. Children

For centuries a woman's worth was determined by the number of children she successfully birthed. A woman with a lot of children was proof to the world that she was attractive enough to have a husband who wanted to have sex with her. The more children a woman had, the stronger the woman appeared to be. Children proved that their mother was strong enough to survive child-birth... repeatedly. The children's presence established that she was resourceful enough to keep her children alive. Women today have the ability to find validation through careers and professional success, so having children is no longer a necessary part of a woman's resume. With the advent of contraception, having children has become a choice rather than an eventuality.

There are many reasons not to have children. Pregnancy should be the first clue. Our bodies are stretched and distorted, often permanently. Our glass slippers have to be replaced with longer, wider, rubber soled shoes. Belly buttons change shape and become the most prominent part of our anatomy. The anatomical area reserved for the most private of bodily functions becomes the focus of video cameras, and the subject of dinner conversations. Does it seem odd to you that everyone in your office knows the degree of dilatation of your cervix? When you wake up one morning and think that a jeep left tire marks across your abdomen, you'll be relieved to know they are only stretch marks. Even the boss has them.

One of the forms of torture used in prison camps is sleep deprivation. That same form of torture is associated with both pregnancy and post-partum depression. No longer do we fantasize about sleeping through the night. Instead our objective becomes protecting the carpet between the bed and the toilet. The pressure of 9 lbs. of baby, and 8 lbs. of amniotic fluid on your bladder can produce an annoying trickle that can ruin your carpet. That insight becomes invaluable even after the baby is born, when coughing or laughter may result in a spontaneous burst. They tell you to buy diapers for the baby after delivery. However, nobody tells you to buy Pose pads to absorb those unfortunate and often unpredictable bladder bursts.

Once the baby arrives, your life is forever changed. Sleep deprivation intensifies. A new baby typically results in 400-750 hours less sleep for parents during the first year.[269] We forgo the pain meds prescribed for that tender episiotomy and/or delicate dry and cracking nipples that predictably result from breast-feeding. We are fearful that the medicine might be transmitted in breast milk to the baby. Our definition of a successful day is reduced to the successful completion of personal hygiene. The focus of conversation becomes the amount, coloration, and consistency of the baby's bowel movements. Never before could we imagine talking to a casual acquaintance about the degree of bleeding caused by breast feeding or the toughness of our nipples. Before your baby was born you're only concern about a long day in Court was that you might be so tired that Luther Vandross would put you to sleep, instead of putting you in the mood. After the birth of a baby a 12-hour day in Court means you must worry about whether the nanny can stay late, whether the baby will be asleep when you get home, and the potential for spontaneous appearance of spots on your silk blouse due to engorgement, because you weren't able to pump since lunch.

Until the baby arrived you probably didn't realize that stool softeners are available in a variety of colors. Until the birth of a baby, you probably thought that a woman with an electronic device sucking milk from her breasts would have been the subject of a documentary about self-mutilation. It would not be a part of the ordinary routine of a professional woman every morning before leaving for work. At your baby shower nobody gives you cute little bags to tie around the baby's neck to catch the projectile vomit, or stain remover to eliminate that hard-to-erase spot left on your favorite blouse from the iodine the nurse put on the baby's cord. Even the book **What to Expect when You are Expecting** doesn't adequately prepare you for the day the baby's diarrhea erupts from the top of the diaper, runs up the baby's back, through the baby's new outfit, and across the front of your white linen suit. Pregnancy, birth, and child care are messy.

For women who love to be mothers, no other experience can rival giving birth to a precious new life. There is nothing more rewarding or fulfilling than seeing a smile on your child's face.[mm] No salary or title could replace your child's hug good night. That picture he drew in first grade is more beautiful and more valuable than any piece of art in the most expensive of galleries. As you watch your child grow, the portraits around the house grow in number too. With each passing year we remember how much we loved our child when they drew that picture. Then they draw a better picture the next year. As we watch the child grow up in pictures we realize that our love grew proportionally. Just when you think you couldn't love a child any more, you do. Just when you think they couldn't get any cuter, they do. Just when you think nobody is as important in life as your child, you have another.

Fortunately, most women, even professional women, find that having a child is intoxicating. Even after 9 months of pregnancy and 24 hours of hard labor, the sound of your child taking its first breath, and crying its first sob, is a moment that cannot be duplicated in the realm of human experience. It's as if nothing else in life matters except your child. In an instant, priorities in life change. Relationships change. What was a sensation in your abdomen is now a human being stretching its arms. What was fluid passing in and out of the baby's lungs in-utero is now the sound of your child taking her first breaths. What was silence is now a voice that fills the emptiness. What was a couple, is now a family.

[mm] https://www.youtube.com/watch?v=F1m6g124YOM

What was a wife, is now a mother. Life is important because it belongs to your child. Your future is no longer defined by the years of your life, but those of your child.

People in your life change in an instant. Your mother becomes a grandmother; your siblings become aunts and uncles; your husband becomes a father. Just when you thought you had become skilled at your job, it changes. Mothers hold a unique position in society and in the life of their children. Mothers are the epitome of all that is good in the world. Most mothers think that their baby is adorable, even if everyone else thinks the child resembles an alien. Most mothers think their child can do no wrong, even when others perceive that their toddler is actually the child of Satan. The expression "only a mother could love" describes that person who is most disliked and lacking in any redeeming qualities.

Men don't have the same challenges. While I'm sure it has happened, I've never seen a new dad, sitting on a plane, trying to calm a screaming infant, while reading a story to his two-year old. If you ventured into a Men's restroom at the shopping mall they probably don't have a Koala Bear Care fold out table between the urinals for those pesky diaper changes. What father have you known who had to go home during the fourth quarter of the Super Bowl because he promised the sitter he'd be home by 9:45? There is probably a company that makes a masculine looking diaper bag, but the only person who'd buy one is a woman buying it for her husband. Have you ever attended a baby shower at the office for a father-to-be? Somebody has surely had one but I've never been invited to one. There is a reason that all the baby photos in the album are pictures of dad and the baby. It is because the mother was the photographer. You will never see a picture of mom and the baby in the album that would be embarrassing to mom. She is the one who took the pictures, printed the pictures, purchased the photo album, selected the pictures to feature in the album, put the photos in, labeled them, and put the album in a place it could be found years later when a 4th grade teacher asks for a baby photo.

Women create things. We knit, sew, and crochet. We bake, roast, fry, and sauté. We paint rooms and hang wallpaper. We scrapbook and decoupage. We make team t-shirts and decorate team photos. We make Christmas gifts for teachers. We make latkes at school during Hannukah, and pack snacks for campouts. We make locker decorations and design costumes for the school play. But our most important creation is the child we raise. That child becomes our masterpiece. We may only be capable of creating one, or a few, masterpieces during our lives. They take work, time, and energy. We may not fully appreciate the importance of this work of art at first, but by the time it is near completion we realize that it was the most important creation of our lives. Women may never be satisfied with their creation. We may spend a lifetime fine-tuning the portrait. Yet its beauty is apparent from the moment it takes its first breath. Sometimes a casual observer might miss the importance of your work. However, you didn't create this masterpiece for a casual observer. As with many artists, you may not be fully appreciated during your lifetime. As your children become contributors to society, the world will better realize the beauty of your work.

Unlike artists who may be capable of creating masterpieces throughout their lives, mothers have a finite time during which they can create their masterpieces. Women are limited to about 16 years during which we are able to spend a significant amount of time perfecting our masterpiece. Once that time has passed, it is never an option again. That time is unique. It can't be delayed or postponed. Once a baby is born the clock is running. A parent has a finite period of 16-20 years with that child. After that time, the child is an adult. There is only one first birthday. The child only takes its first step once. The first day of school only happens one day each year. There will only be one first soccer goal. Each child only loses their first tooth one time. The opportunity to be supportive when the child becomes the victim of hateful remarks by a bully at school may happen more than once. However, being there for the first time may minimize the effects of the second time. Teaching coping mechanisms when a child suffers anguish when the love of her life asks someone else to the dance, puts the child in the best position to handle the next rejection. Helping a child learn to be humble and gracious after scoring the winning goal enhances the possibility that she will score another winning goal, as a result of an assist from her teammate. But you have to be there to see the goal to have the opportunity to teach the child about humility. Unfortunately, many significant moments in the lives of our children can't be delayed until it is convenient for mom to be around. If financial support from mom is necessary, mom will miss these moments, but the mother and child each understand and appreciate the reason mom wasn't there. If however, mom chooses to work instead of making herself available to attend the child's games, concerts, or plays, both mom and the child will likely remember that mom wasn't there at a critical time.

B. Control

Strategic, successful women have a lot in common. We may excel in a variety of professions and have a multitude of domestic talents, but we have certain characteristics in common. We are organized. We multitask. We like to be in control. We protect, defend, and enrich the lives of our family members. Once we make the decision to expand the family unit, by adding a child or children, the need for organization, multitasking, and being in control, becomes even more important. Each child we bring into the world represents another member of our family who must be protected, defended, and whose life we feel compelled to enrich.

To the surprise of many newly pregnant women, it is challenging to stay in control. It's hard to feel powerful while hugging a toilet at home, in the grocery store, or at work. If nausea and vomiting are daily experiences during the first three months of pregnancy the only control we may exercise is choosing the grocery store with the cleanest restrooms. We may feel powerful by choosing the conference room nearest to the ladies' room. By being close, when we have to run to the rest room to get sick, we won't have to tell the client of the pregnancy. The only organization for which we can take credit, might be the packing of an air-sickness bag in our brief case, and keeping a clean change of clothes at the office. Pregnant professional women may fool themselves by bringing a laptop with them to the hospital when they are admitted for preterm labor so they could be at that all-important conference call while having contractions monitored. The painful reality is that if the labor becomes too difficult, the only contribution you will make during the conference call is to leave it. You could anticipate difficulty focusing on the client's needs, when the doctor is expertly placing your feet in stirrups and assessing your degree of dilatation. That gushing sound when the doctor breaks your water can be distracting to you, and annoying to your clients.

Pregnancy is boot camp for motherhood. No amount of planning or organization can prepare a mother for that call from the preschool teacher advising that her child has just fallen from the jungle gym and had to be taken to the hospital with unidentified injuries. Any woman who thinks she is in control has never taken her baby on a flight when the baby couldn't clear its ears, taken a 2 year old to the doctor for her immunization shots, taken a three year old to Chuckie Cheese and told her it's time to leave, taken a four year old on a hike only to find that the child had diarrhea, or tried to convince a five year old that aliens weren't going to take over the earth today.

A professional woman who hasn't had children might think that multi-tasking means cleaning her desk while talking on the phone. Professional women who have children would consider multi-tasking to be driving on a class field trip while utilizing GPS for directions to an unknown location, talking on the speaker phone with your secretary about how to deal with an unhappy client, while trying to take control of the 6 five-year-olds who are having a sword fight with your 12 year old daughter's art project, when a beep tells you that there is a call waiting, while eating your granola bar for lunch, as the car's engine light comes on.

Professional women without children might take pride in their organizational skills when they remember to put their yoga mat in the car so they don't have to stop home after work on their way to workout. A professional woman with children takes pride in her organizational skills as she reminds her daughter on Monday that there are homemade cookies in the freezer for her snack day at soccer practice on Wednesday, when mom will be out of town. That soccer mom is particularly pleased that she remembered not to put nuts in the chocolate chip cookies because #22 is allergic to nuts. It was also nice that the nanny speaks English so she would be able to call the coach and parents, to remind them that the practice will be on a different field this week. That mother had to be really organized to buy the new shin guards at the same store where she was buying the birthday gift her son would be taking to Jimmy's birthday party. The problem is that the shin guards were the wrong color so mom had to exchange them on her way to pick up dinner that Sunday night because the athletic store would be closed after her daughter's choir performance later that night.

A professional woman without children may ascend the corporate ladder faster than the one with children. She is better able to focus all of her time, attention, and energy on her profession. It's a choice and she deserves the promotion for making the commitment that she has. The professional woman with children has made a different choice. Her climb up the corporate ladder will inevitably be slower and the ladder may be shorter. She may never climb as high as the woman without kids. She may prefer to ascend to the top of a Jungle Gym instead of the ladder, moving laterally at times, to reach the top. However the same is true of men. If a man prioritizes his family over his profession, he too may find that his ladder isn't as tall as the man who has been divorced twice and was never home long enough to do his part to create a child. The reality is that regardless of whether a professional is a man or woman, we must all be adults and make adult choices. We must make our choices based on our individual definitions of success. When we reach our final destination, even if it's not as high, we'll enjoy the view because we have someone who will share our joy in reaching the level we did. Some people are satisfied to enjoy the view from the top, all by themselves, because that pinnacle is often so narrow that there is only room for one to stand. That decision is personal to each professional. Neither decision is good or bad. Each decision will be right if it's made considering each professional's goals.

C. Comfort with Chaos

If we are to have hope of a successful career, a fulfilling marriage, and happy children, we must learn to be comfortable with chaos. Because some level of uncertainty is inherent in any profession, flexibility is an important attribute of any successful executive. Because children, by their nature, are spontaneous and unpredictable, flexibility is an important trait for mom. If Kendra invites Katie to stay the night after she has spent the afternoon at soccer practice, Katie's teeth won't fall out if she doesn't brush till the next day. Sleeping for one night in her soccer jersey won't cause Katie to spend the rest of her life in dirty clothes. If Katie throws up during the night at Kendra's house, mom needs to bring Katie home. It may be 3:00 a.m., and you may have a 7:00 a.m. meeting, but you have to answer the call. If Kendra's mom tells you, as you are picking up Katie at 3:00 a.m., that Kendra has lice, you may have to re-schedule the 7:00 a.m. meeting.

The sign over my computer reads: "When the shit hits the fan it won't be evenly distributed." Some days you step in it, and some days you don't. Little Miss Muffet didn't have her breakfast interrupted every day by a spider. However, the reality is that spiders do make a pest of themselves occasionally. When they do, you have to respond or suffer the consequences. Because you can't predict which day you will need to run away, you have to be flexible enough to run away at any time. Organizing chaos for Miss Muffet didn't mean controlling which day the spider would come along. Instead Muffet wore her tennis shoes to work every day, so that when she was caught unexpectedly by the venomous assailant, she was prepared. Even though Jill knew that Jack was clumsy, she still couldn't predict when Jack would need a doctor who specialized in concussions. Yet Jill could organize herself so that the day that Jack fell down and suffered a blow to his head, she would have the emergency room number programmed into her cell phone, which she always kept in her pocket.

Parents must learn to be comfortable with chaos. Spending a day with a school nurse would be great training experience for any adult considering the possibility of having children. It was the school nurse that got a mother out of a business meeting to explain that Danny had dropped a 20 lb. rock on Steven's foot. Danny felt really bad about missing the ants with the rock, and hitting Steven's foot instead. Normally the nurse would have waited to tell the mother about the incident involving her son until after the business meeting was over, but the blood was still oozing out of Steven's shoe. The kids at carpool might have been scared. When a child is injured or ill we are forced to redefine success, adapt to our circumstances, become comfortable with other people's perception of our limitations, make hard choices, and take responsibility to realistically deal with our limitations. Nothing puts things in perspective faster than a sick or injured child.

D. The Choice to Make Choices

Albert Einstein said:

> "The definition of insanity is doing the same thing over, and over again, and expecting a different result."[270]

Women make choices every day. Should I wear the black or the blue suit? Even though Zach doesn't have fever is he well enough to go to school? Should I take Katie to have her arm x-rayed after she fell rollerblading? What will the kids eat for dinner without too much complaining? Should I fire my secretary for continually being late? Does Rick deserve a promotion? What should I get Prince Charming for his birthday? What should Anna be for Halloween? Should I have a doctor look at that hard place in my breast? How do I tell my mother she shouldn't be driving? Should I buy the Whirlpool dishwasher and save the money now or get the KitchenAid that costs more money but might last longer? Is that movie really appropriate for my kids? If I let Katie go to the concert will she be safe? Should I buy condoms for Zach before he leaves for college? Should I tell the girls about tampons or do they already know about them? Am I paying the yard guy too much? How do I know the nanny is not ignoring my baby?

While it may be unfair, it seems that most of the choices men have to make are at work. At home, the choices men have to make seem fairly insignificant. Men do have to decide if, and who, they should marry. After making the decision to marry, it seems that women make most choices. If I ask David which color of paint he prefers for our bedroom, he shrugs his shoulders. Obviously he makes hundreds of decisions in business every day. However it seems that the choices in his personal life fall into one of three categories: (1) What sporting event he will watch on T.V.? (2) What form of exercise he will do today? and (3) Which things does he need me to take care of in our personal life today? David and I worked out a system 30 years ago that has withstood the test of time. He makes all the big decisions. I make all the small ones. Fortunately, we haven't had any big decisions yet. Luckily for me, I seem to be very comfortable making choices. It has been said by some that I am often wrong, but never in doubt. Of course I'm sure that I'm right. The reason I might be described as never in doubt is not because I'm always sure that every choice will be a good one. What I'm sure about is that if there is a problem, the right choice is always to try to fix the problem. I might make the wrong choice, but the choice to try to fix a problem is always the right one. There may be a better way to fix the problem than the first one. A new option might need to follow my initial attempt to solve the problem. The only wrong choice is to make no choice at all. Failure to try ensures that nothing will change.

The biggest mistake women make is failing to make choices. Fear of failure can be debilitating. The woman who is the unhappiest is not the woman who made a bad choice, but the woman who failed to make any choice at all. The concept of a choice implies that we have control. We must recognize that which we have no control over and move on. Having high cholesterol is not a choice. Taking appropriate medication and refusing to eat chicken-fried steak, covered in gravy, are choices. Having M.S. is not a choice. Exercising regularly to stay as strong as possible is a choice.

The choices we make may be affected by circumstances that are beyond our control. We don't have unlimited choices. We don't make the choice to have breast cancer. The choice we make is how we deal with it. When I realized my leg was broken my only choice was what to do to maximize my chance of recovering as quickly as possible. When a young girl named Rion Paige learned that she had arthrogryposis multiplex congenital, a condition that caused blindness in one eye, and disfiguring contractures of her hands, she didn't become depressed and feel sorry for herself. Instead she took responsibility to develop her amazing voice. She became a musical sensation. Audiences hearing her incredible voice were mesmerized, not only by her beautiful voice, but by her positive attitude and bubbly personality.[271] While Rion's arthrogryposis plagues her with devastating disabilities, it was probably that condition that helped her get noticed. Her mother was there to share that special moment when Rion performed on the X Factor.[nn] If her mother had been at work that day, it wouldn't have been the same for Rion, or her mother. Rion made the choice to maximize her strengths. She found her **happily ever after,** in spite of her limitations.

The first goal for every woman should be to maximize her choices. The best way to do that is to get an education. We may later choose to pursue a different line of work, or career, but having an education gives us options. With education comes financial independence which also improves the number of options available. Working to get an education is choosing to be respected, knowledgeable, and independent. Women have already figured this out. In 1994, 63% of female high school graduates attended college. Only 61% of men went on to college. Over the next eight years the percentage of women in college increased to 71%. During that eight year period the percentage of men in college remained the same (61%).[272] Having higher education increases our awareness of the choices before us, and helps us make better decisions at every stage of our lives.

Being the best you can be at whatever you do, gives you more choices. If you place yourself in a position to be the best in your field, suddenly potential employers become accommodating. An employer who identifies you as special, or particularly well qualified, is much more likely to make the accommodations you require to balance your job and personal life. Being the best at something opens many doors. Everyone wants the best. If you are simply a marginal or

---

[nn] https://www.youtube.com/watch?v=11oMu365xYU

below average attorney, no firm wants to hire you, especially if you are pregnant. However, if you have distinguished yourself as one of the best in your chosen field of law, you will have many opportunities, pregnant or not. The law firm you are currently employed with is much more likely to accommodate your maternity leave request if you are invaluable to them. If you are a below average associate and you request a year off to have a child, they'll probably give you much more than a year to stay at home with your child.

I always assumed that I'd go to college and study to be a nurse. However, before even finishing my B.S. degree I knew that I would likely be unhappy. Having an advanced degree would expand my choices exponentially! I might have found a job in nursing that would make me happy, but it seemed that my chances for happiness were greater if I obtained a Law Degree. All the nursing students and teachers seemed to feel that my decision to go to Law School was a rejection of them instead of a personal decision for me. I knew that if I didn't like practicing law that I could make a different choice. Becoming a lawyer opened doors and created possibilities that I could never have imagined. Even though I have not practiced law for 20 years, I still earn respect because I'm an attorney. I still understand legal concepts. My ability to support myself and my children has not changed. It is because I have the ability to support myself and my children that I am independent, even though I now rely on financial support from my husband. Education gave me that choice. My kids only remember me as a stay at home mom. Yet they know that I was a Senior Partner at a well-respected firm. My choice to stay at home to raise the next generation of Litmans means even more because they know what I gave up for them. Because I earned the respect of my husband, before opting out of my career, he knows that my decision to become a stay-at-home mother was not motivated by a sense of dependence. It was a sense of devotion to our family that precipitated the change.

When I began writing my blog, I immediately earned respect when readers learned that I was an attorney. When asking to be considered as a speaker at women's conferences, I was taken much more seriously because I was an attorney who became a stay-at-home mother.

After 4 years of college, 3 years of law school, and 12 years of legal practice, I had achieved all I could have hoped for when I began my career. I loved the thrill of courtroom drama. I enjoyed success persuading juries. The only case I lost was the first one. Even the best attorney has a hard time convincing a jury that it's reasonable to drink beer and watch prostitutes, while driving a car. I found that being a woman was an advantage in the court room. Juries are more likely to believe a woman than a man.[273] Women are more honest than men.[274]

I was often invited to give lectures at Continuing Legal Education conferences. It was rewarding to find that even if men in the audience thought they knew more than me, by the end of the presentation they had pages of notes to make sure they remembered all the things I taught them. The longer I practiced, the more independent I became. As a young associate, I was dependent on various senior attorneys to give me work. By the time I was a Senior Partner, I had enough clients of my own that I kept myself and several other attorneys busy. After 12 years in practice, it was particularly rewarding that I had earned the respect of the other lawyers with whom I worked, who were primarily men.

I made the choice to reduce my hours at work after Zach was born, but I failed. Instead, the only thing I reduced was my income. After Anna was born I tried to rely more on the Prince to help with the kids. Inevitably the Prince always seemed to be busy when I needed help. Thus the older the kids got, the less sleep I got. Everyone thought I was the perfect example of a woman who had it all. The reality was that, had I continued on that path, I would have lost it all. More clients than ever were paying for my services, while more children than ever were in need of my services. As much as the Prince enjoyed watching our net worth grow, our marriage was failing. Even though friends loved my sense of humor, they missed hearing me laugh.

Listen to your heart. The only wrong choice is not to make any choice. Once we recognize that we are not happy or fulfilled doing that which we are currently doing, we must adapt and change. Whatever we choose, and however long it may take to change, the important thing is that we are trying to identify and react to a problem or dissatisfaction. It is all too easy to blame someone else for a problem, especially a spouse. If we accept total responsibility for the household chores, planning meals, shopping for groceries, cooking, cleaning, child care, paying the bills and doing the laundry, what husband wouldn't be thrilled? Who wouldn't love to take the afternoon off to watch the game? Why would any husband, or partner, do the dishes if somebody else would do them, without even being asked?

Eighteen years after giving up my job, I have one child in college and two that have graduated. Each child, now an adult, will be a positive addition to the next generation. Each child is smart, motivated, and has the character of a person that knows they are truly loved. I'm still married to my first husband, Prince Charming. My background as a nurse, a lawyer, and a mother are all helpful in writing my blog. Laughter is part of every day, and even more so when the kids are home. The children each have a sense of humor. That sense of humor makes the time that we share even more special.

People still ask me if it was hard to give up my career. They just don't get it. I never gave it up. I still benefit from my education and career every day. I have just moved on. I have made the choices that were necessary to adapt to the circumstances of my life. I will always be a trumpet player, a mother, a nurse, and an attorney. I'm no longer playing Boogie Woogie Bugle Boy, breast feeding, starting I.V.s, or trying cases. However the experiences of each aspect of my life have become a part of the person that I am today. The satisfaction and confidence I gained from each phase of my life is invaluable in all that I have done since. We are the sum of our experiences. At every step we have the opportunity to grow and expand ourselves. As a trumpet player I didn't only learn to play the trumpet. I gained an appreciation for the difficulty of executing a precision performance as part of a marching band or drum and bugle corp. If anything, my respect for musicians who devote their lives to music is greater, not less. As a nurse I didn't only learn about the side effects of medicines. I also learned about life and death. As an attorney I learned not only about the law, but about the value of hard work and persistence. As a mother I learned not only how to predict when a child is about to vomit. I learned about the critical importance of instilling character and values into the next generation. As an author, all my life lessons are part of what I write. Thirty years ago I didn't plan to be an author. It was just the best choice given my circumstances.

I'm not done. I am still learning valuable lessons of life. I still have many stops along the way. If I live to be 80 years old, I still have 23 years to go. In my first 25 years of life I was a student, a nurse aide; I worked in a bank; I sold insurance; I was a Registered Nurse working in the I.C.U. and Burn Units; I was a Business Law instructor at O.U.; a law student; and an attorney at a major firm in Dallas.

During the second 25 years I became a Senior Partner at Thompson & Knight, a mother of three, a stay-at-home mom, the President of the Pre-school Parents Association, the designer and creator of spook houses, play centers, Halloween costumes, birthday cakes, green smoking witches brew, and bulletin boards at school with three-dimensional decorations. Some kids remember me best for Dinosaur Day complete with erupting volcanoes, dinosaur bone excavations, and custom decorated bags for each child. Some teachers remember the teacher appreciation lunches I organized with freshly made omelets and buttermilk waffles that were served hot off the griddle. Some parents remember the decorations that filled the school cafeteria for Grandparents Day, and the props and scenery that I made for the 4th grade play. I was the ultimate soccer mom, organizing sports teams for all three kids, including basketball, volleyball, softball, and soccer. I ordered uniforms and reserved practice fields. I decorated frames for team photos and hosted end-of-the-season parties. Even though the players are grown, they are still special. Their parents are among my closest friends.

The third 25 years is still a work in progress. Women volunteer more than men.[275] Perhaps I'll do more volunteer work during the third 25 years. The amazing thing about the third wave of feminism is that I can do, or be, whatever I want. The fact that I was a stay-at-home-mother may mean that some doors have closed. Inherent in the notion of a choice is the implicit understanding that something will be forfeited. However when one door closes, others open. When Katie comes home for Spring Break with her basketball teammates from college, I'll use my skills at making buttermilk waffles once again. If one of the girls gets hurt during the week, I'll rely on my nursing skills. If one of the girls is hurt in an automobile accident, I'll help her obtain the settlement she deserves from the insurance company. I gave up my career as a nurse and an attorney, but I didn't forget how to administer first aid. I'll never stop being an advocate. If we go to the symphony, I might comment on the exceptional trumpet player. If we go to the Opera I'll introduce the girls to my friend. She's the second chair violinist who needed an assist the day her daughter broke her collar bone during a basketball game that I attended, but she could not.

Because I am no longer tied to a professional career, and not motivated by the need to make money, I am free to spend the next chapter of my life making a difference in the world. By enriching the lives of my children, I hope that I have already made a valuable contribution to improvement of the human condition. For the next 25 years I hope to make a different kind of contribution to improvement of life in America. Now I am prepared to reach a broader audience because my children are grown, independent, and contributing to society. Instead of devoting myself to success in trial to help a single client, I am able to devote time to women's issues, hoping to impact the lives of many women. My audience is broader than the 12 people on the jury. Now I realize that my departure from the practice of law was a springboard into my next career as a champion of women's rights.

*"If you could choose one characteristic
that would get you through life,
choose a sense of humor."*

-Jennifer Jones [276]

CHAPTER IX. LAUGHTER

Rosy is my companion in torture. Some people love exercise. People report the rush of adrenalin and the release of endorphins when they exercise. For eight years I have worked-out with Rosy twice each week. The only rush I feel is the eruption of pain coursing through the affected portion of my body. The only release I feel is the sensation I experience when exiting the weight room. I hate exercise. What I love is the time I share with Rosy. Because she is one of my very best friends, Rosy was able to motivate me to exercise when nothing else worked. Rosy and I share laughter, tears, and pain. The work-out is a gift we give to ourselves; to our bodies and our spirits. While keeping our bodies as physically strong as our ages might allow, the work-outs keep our spirits youthful and robust. We share the mundane parts of our lives.

The very best part of our exercise regimen is always the exercise of those under-used muscles in the face. The masseter muscle is all too often neglected in an ordinary work out. Many people totally neglect the masseter muscle, except for chewing. It is one of the strongest muscles in the body. Undoubtedly, it is critical to survival. Of course it is required for chewing. However, it is equally essential in its role allowing people to laugh. It connects the jaw to the cheek bone. It is usually associated with mastication, more commonly known as chewing. However equally essential to sustaining life is its function as one of the muscles involved in smiling and in laughing. It is the only muscle I actually enjoy exercising. Every woman must take responsibility to ensure that her masseter muscle stays in tip-top shape. It seems no amount of exercise is ever enough for the masseter. When all muscle groups have lost tone due to age or illness, it is the masseter that can rejuvenate every part of the body. Laughter provides momentary relief from pain. It transforms an intolerable experience into a simple annoyance.

Laughing with a friend can make the good times better and the bad times bearable. Mourners at a funeral are grateful for a funny anecdote about the deceased. When consumed with anger because your teenager just totaled the car, it's nice to laugh. That insurance company that overcharged you for adding your son as a driver, will now have to buy you a new car. Laughter makes life richer. It enhances our relationships, and allows us to survive stressful or embarrassing situations. Laughter puts things in perspective. If we can laugh at the toothless repairman, we can assuage our anger. If we can laugh at the product that had a life-time guarantee, but died after one week, we are better able to deal with our grief. If we approach all aspects of life, searching for humor, we can achieve great things. All of my favorite anecdotes end with a good laugh.

A. Condoms

Some parents always look like they just came from a Brooks Brothers' photo shoot. These parents are spared the humiliation of having flatulence. They never burp. Their nose doesn't produce boogers. They never appear in public with their zipper unzipped. Toilet paper doesn't stick to their shoes. Umbrellas are always located in their cars when rain unexpectedly falls from the sky. Colon polyps don't run in their families, so there is no need for a colonoscopy. Their mouths don't make saliva, so they never drool while reading a book, and they don't have anything to choke on when they aren't eating food. The crotch of their pants is reinforced so they never get holes in embarrassing places. Instinctively their children know they should never stare at a special needs child. No explanation is necessary for their children to understand the difference between a short person and a dwarf. Their child has never greeted a fellow shopper by saying "hi fat lady!" Some parents are perfect.

Unfortunately, I'm not one of these parents. Years ago, I had to learn not to worry about impressing other people. Because I'm not a person to be worried about perceptions, jeans and tennis shoes are much more practical than linen suits, leather high heels, and designer jewelry. As I drove down Midway on my way home from carpool one morning, I realized that I was approaching Wal-Mart. I knew my jeans and sweat shirt would be inconsequential to the other Wal-Mart shoppers. Being the organized, practical, mother that I am, I learned a long time ago that if there is something I need at Wal-Mart, the time to go is right after morning drop-off of the kids at school. Nobody shops at Wal-Mart at 7:45 a.m. so you can accomplish any task in half the time, if you go first thing in the morning. The problem with shopping immediately after dropping the kids off at school is that my shopping attire looks identical to my sleeping attire, with the addition of pants. I may not have had the benefit of a hot shower before being welcomed by the Wal-Mart greeter. Cosmetics are often unfamiliar early morning companions. The image of me strolling the aisles of Wal-Mart at 7:45 a.m. is not a pretty one.

One morning, after drop off at school, I remembered that I had promised to help a teacher at school. Most teachers are special people, but this one is a gem. She became my friend, and a role model for Katie. Lisa is always perfect when you ask how she is. She lives her life as if nothing can get her down. Her sense of humor helps her continue to be perfect. Every year Lisa makes a trip, on her teacher's salary, to help kids she has adopted at an orphanage in the Dominican Republic. The orphanage gets little or no assistance from anyone other than Lisa. On the trip, she takes needed items for the orphans that may be donated by anyone who knows Lisa is going and wants to help. One year I simply told Lisa to let me know what was on her list to take that she didn't have donated by someone else. I would complete the shopping list. When she was about ready to leave she reported that there were only two items left that she hadn't received. Lisa needed 12 back packs, and as many condoms as I was able to donate.

Condoms for an orphanage? What kind of perverted orphanage was this? Orphans in the United States didn't need condoms, so why would anyone, except a child molester, need condoms in an orphanage in the Dominican Republic? As it turns out the condoms were not for the orphans, but for the parents of the orphans, to help prevent the creation of more little orphans.

Evidently the kids at the orphanage did have parents. The parents simply didn't have enough money to care for the children. Thus the kids went to the orphanage during the day for food, school, and recreation. They went home to their indigent parents at night. The parents of the orphans did not have access to any type of birth control so they continued to make more orphans. Not only did they have a complete absence of financial resources, but they also had no access to any store to provide essential pharmaceuticals. They knew how to use condoms…they just didn't know where and how to find them when the need arose. It was a vicious cycle. The fewer condoms they had, the more back packs they needed.

Wal-Mart was the one-stop shopping experience that would satisfy all my charitable needs. An experienced shopper could locate both back packs and condoms at this single location. Because it was 7:45 a.m., I knew that I could retrieve the back packs and condoms in a matter of minutes. Upon entering the store I quickly identified the need for a shopping cart. The Wal-Mart greeter, covered in lapel pins, was happy to retrieve a cart for my shopping convenience. Being the efficient shopper that I am, I immediately deduced that I should select the condoms first, being the smaller of the items on my shopping list. While I had not previously purchased condoms at Wal-Mart, my shrewd powers of observation led me to the pharmacy. Making a bee-line for the pharmaceutical section of the store, I immediately identified the aisles dedicated to condoms, diaphragm jellies, and spermicidal creams. I was, after all, the mother of three children so there would be no embarrassment associated with the selection of items from this area of the store. Because I was unfamiliar with the vast variety and selection of condoms, I found myself in a bit of a conundrum. Being unfamiliar with genitalia of men living in the Dominican Republic, I was unable to identify the size and brand that would best suit their needs. Should I choose the ones designed from a woman's perspective since a woman was buying them? Would men in the Dominican Republic prefer the "thinner, stronger, and silky soft" condoms which were guaranteed for a "sensuous natural experience," or would they prefer the ribbed variety? Then there were flavored condoms. They had Strawberry, Vanilla, Grape and Mint, but not banana. When I think of the Dominican Republic, I think of bananas. I don't know if the Dominican Republic women like bananas or if they are tired of the flavor. I do know the Dominican Republic has beaches so maybe they would prefer the seashell-like curves of the Inspiral condoms. To make matters even more confusing, I saw that they had red, white, and blue tri-colored condoms. Perhaps I should remind the users of the country that provided their condoms? In the end I purchased the largest boxes that had the best prices, regardless of size, color, shape, or flavor.

The best value were the mega-man condoms in the value pack. I selected all the mega-man boxes the store had to offer which comprised a total of 656 condoms. I was feeling pretty generous as I imagined the excitement of the parents as they opened their surprise gifts from America.

Six hundred fifty-six condoms is a lot of condoms. The boxes pretty much covered the entire bottom of my Wal-Mart shopping cart. For a brief moment I panicked. I was mortified as I contemplated the expression of shock and disbelief of the checker as she scanned the life-time supply of condoms. The checker might wonder whether I was just being a responsible manager of a house of prostitution, or whether I thought a water balloon fight utilizing condoms would be more fun than the traditional latex variety of water balloons. There were enough boxes of condoms to fill the entire conveyer belt, and then some. Should I stack them several boxes high or would they be less embarrassing if placed side to side, spanning at least five feet of the conveyer? Oh wait,…not to worry…Wal-Mart has self-checkout lanes! Whew! Realizing that I had solved a potentially embarrassing check out experience, it then occurred to me that I would have to show my receipt as I exited the store. I could only imagine what my receipt might look like. A receipt for all these condoms would be two feet long. How could I keep a straight face as I exited the store if I had to show a recordation of my purchase of so many condoms? Not to worry. That lady by the exit recognizes me and will see me checking out so she'll just wave me by. I pride myself on knowing that I am a strong, resourceful woman.

Smiling to myself and imagining all the funny remarks I could make about needing 656 condoms, I traveled to the end of the aisle dedicated to sexual health. Planning to re-direct my path toward the back-pack aisle, I turned the corner. Immediately I was overcome with a torrential flood of emotions. I wanted to laugh and to cry; to scream and to hide; to forget and record this moment for all time. This was a moment great comedians live for. There at the corner of the aisle was the mother of a child in Katie's class, having just finished a Brooks Brothers photo shoot. She was looking perfectly coifed in her linen suit and silk blouse. Her makeup was perfect. Not a hair on her head was out of place. There I was in my jeans, tennis shoes, stained sweatshirt, no makeup, disheveled hair, and pushing a shopping cart with nothing but 656 mega-man condoms. Thank God I hadn't gotten the banana flavor!

Quickly identifying my options, I realized that my choices were simple. I could greet this June Cleaver look-alike as if there was nothing unusual about shopping for hundreds of mega-man condoms at 7:45 in the morning after my brief stop in the carpool lane…or I could ask if she were wondering why I had 656 mega-man condoms in my basket on this fine spring morning. I chose the former. I greeted this perfectly dressed mother with a friendly "hey, funny to run into you this morning" and chose not to mention anything about the contents of my shopping cart. Surely this mother had the good taste not to mention anything about my apparent obsession with mega-man condoms. As I proceeded towards the back pack aisle, it was a challenge to wipe that funny grin off my face. Any other shopper who happened to pass me on the way to the backpacks would simply assume that my giggling was either the result of some mental disorder, or simply the elation inspired by my anticipation of the rest of my day…or week…or month…or year.

I survived this prophylactic predicament because I knew that very soon it would have great value for its therapeutic effects on my masseter muscles.
Remembering this shopping extravaganza would brighten even the worst of days in the years ahead.

B. The Masculine Mystique

More than 90% of Americans will marry during their lifetime. In the 70's and 80's the divorce rate was reported to be 50%.[277] However, now the divorce rate is actually dropping. Seventy percent of marriages that began in the 1990's reached their 15th anniversary, up from 65% in the 70's and 80's. The increase in marital success has been attributed to shared incomes and the increase in sharing of domestic responsibilities between the husband and wife. As the median age for marriage has increased, so has the success of marriages. In the 1950's the median age for marriage was 23 for men, and 20 for women. By 2004 the median age was 27 for men, and 26 for women.[278] I was 26 when I married the Prince. He was 27. Thus from the perspective of age, we were average. However because we married in the 80's we had not evolved to share domestic chores. Our biggest fights during the first years of marriage related to domestic chores. The solution was not for the Prince to do more around the house. We hired a housekeeper. We were each glad to share the financial burden of a housekeeper. Yet that wasn't the end of marital conflicts. Both the Prince and Cinderella felt they should each be in charge of all things that related to their personal lives.

Ninety-two percent of women who are married, have husbands who demand to be in control. Recognizing the need for men to maintain the appearance of control is a life-changing event for a woman and her marriage.[279] When a woman recognizes that it is the *appearance* of control that is important to men, women can take control of things that are important to them if they are strategic. As long as the man feels in control, any decision is less threatening. In my Big Fat Greek Wedding, Tula's parents epitomize the traditional roles of men and women in a relationship. Tula's mother teaches her daughter that even though the man may be the head of the house, the woman is the neck. She can turn his head any way she wants.[oo]

While some might suggest that this is a form of manipulation, I prefer to describe it as strategic planning. Timing, atmosphere, and negotiation are all familiar considerations for men in positions of authority, who are involved in sophisticated business negotiations. Men aren't perceived as sophisticated manipulators. Rather, they are viewed as shrewd negotiators. Wives need to refine those skills too. We must choose our battles. We must choose when to fight them. We must be strategic in the negotiation process.

When a man and woman are in the car, who drives? In couples who have stayed married more than 5 years it is almost always the man. The car was the source of many arguments for the first years of my marriage. I drove myself everywhere from the time I was 16. For ten years before marriage, I had my own car. I found my way even before anyone became dependent upon GPS. I drove to

---

[oo] https://www.youtube.com/watch?v=8fJoPI-xytM

depositions and Court Houses in distant locations. My husband drove to his office and back home every day. I never caused a wreck, and never got a ticket. Prince Charming caused a wreck and had two speeding tickets. After children, I drove carpool, being responsible for the lives of several children. I put twice as many miles on my car as the Prince did his. However, the day that I stopped being logical about who was the better driver, and realized that the issue of who should drive was an emotional one, I was able to rationalize allowing my husband to drive.

That experience is typical of most men in heterosexual relationships in Dallas, Texas. In a random survey of men and women in Dallas, in cars at hotels, churches, and schools, 98% of cars occupied by men and women, were driven by men. A national survey in 2010 determined that men are at least four times more likely to drive when women are in the car. Even in households that identify themselves as feminist, the man still does most of the driving when both partners are in the car. Predictably, when car companies advertise, it's almost always the man who is driving.[280] Some have explained the phenomena as a control issue. "Letting women take control is considered emasculating in our culture. Even pro-feminist men are not immune."[281]

The same dynamic can be seen with remote controls. What family doesn't have the dad in control of the remotes?[282] Several television studies have found that men, and young men in particular, covet remote controls. Control of the car is similar to control of the remote. Men like to feel as if they are in control.[283] They maintain control by driving and holding the remote.

From the moment my older brother tried to dominate and control the television, when I was 11 years old, I resented any man trying to exert control over me. However because the men in my life are physically stronger than me, it is important for me to recognize their need to perceive that they are in control. Being strategic about how and when to let them win is critical to my ultimate happiness. I never gloat when I get what I want. Instead I compromise on the big issues, like who drives my car or who holds the remote. On the small issues like which house to buy, which car to buy, or where to go on vacation, I make those tiny decisions. The Prince and I can laugh about the difference in our roles now. Previously we didn't laugh about it, as we never talked about it.

Having a sense of humor about all the big decisions that our husbands will make is essential. Men are fundamentally different from women. How many times have you heard a man suggested that you should watch him?

- Hold my beer and watch this…[pp] (The really amazing thing is how often the man filming is simultaneously laughing.)

[pp] https://www.youtube.com/watch?v=1Ybqsis4A64

- Watch me go fast.[qq]

- Watch how oblivious I can be?[rr]

- Watch, I know what you need![ss]

- Watch me do what you can do, only better.[tt]

- Watch me try to determine what you want?[uu]

- Watch me kiss her?[vv]

- Watch what I will eat![ww]

- Watch me blow-up shit.[xx]

- Watch me go to work.[yy]

- Watch how fast I can run![zz]

In my home, Price Charming doesn't own the power drill, I do. If he did, he couldn't find it. This is not a character defect. It is simply a characteristic that I need to embrace and celebrate. People aren't born handy. Home repair is not something that people are genetically engineered to do. Y chromosomes aren't necessarily linked to skills of auto repair, home repair, and technical savvy. There is nothing instinctive about putting together a tricycle or repairing the back door that you slammed so hard the door knob fell out. The mistake many make is assuming that home-repair is a masculine characteristic. Prince Charming has many attributes, but he has never received a Father's Day gift from Home Depot. David is not a do-it-yourself kind-of-a-guy. One of David's goals in life has been to make enough money to be able to hire a handy man to do all the things around the house that are handy. As my M.S. has progressed, the number of things around the house that I am unable to do has increased. For example, climbing a ladder to change a light bulb is incompatible with Multiple

---

[qq] https://www.youtube.com/watch?v=riBA-FsJJmY
[rr] https://www.youtube.com/watch?v=TIy3GqS-cd8
[ss] https://www.youtube.com/watch?v=-4EDhdAHrOg
[tt] https://www.youtube.com/watch?v=-YFRUSTiFUs
[uu] https://www.youtube.com/watch?v=WsJSRP7cZVo
[vv] https://www.youtube.com/watch?v=iGoC8FTLKSI
[ww] https://www.youtube.com/watch?v=QuB3kr3ckYE
[xx] https://www.youtube.com/watch?v=_hdl86mhxMo
[yy] https://www.youtube.com/watch?v=eVXKKaWJTls
[zz] https://www.youtube.com/watch?v=fE9_MtJ-1aY

Sclerosis. However Prince Charming doesn't have an excuse. He is just incompatible with ladders, for any reason. Prince Charming would rather help someone else take pride in their ability to accomplish something handy and limit the unemployment rate in America.

During pregnancy, women learn about limitations. When pregnant with my third child I had already learned that there were just some things that I could not accomplish. By my eighth month of pregnancy, I was as big as most women when they are at full term. I'd like to blame it on my unusually large babies, but even a 10 pound baby couldn't account for the massive girth of my abdomen. At least part of the expanse of my stomach was related to the milk shakes I craved. I was unable to limit my encounters with ice cream, but I did have enough sense to avoid encounters with ladders.

One Saturday when I was about 8 ½ months pregnant with our third child, Prince Charming was feeling especially motivated to handle some of the home maintenance that I had been unable to accomplish since my fifth month of pregnancy. Maybe the Prince was afflicted with that nesting thing. In one day he changed the air filters on the air conditioner, and put new light bulbs in the ceiling fixture in the nursery. Having successfully completed these tasks he became inspired to change the light bulbs in the den ceiling which was 20 ft. high. Because of the height of the ceiling, the only way to reach those light bulbs was to go into the attic and change them from above. With a spring in his step, the Prince bounded up the stairs to the attic. He would show me that he was equally capable of home repair. He may have even thought that he was actually superior to me in the speed with which he could complete any given task. While David was in the attic, Zach and Anna were mesmerized by a Barney the Dinosaur video. I took advantage of this rare moment of peace, to lie down to rest my aching back. Almost two minutes had passed before I heard what sounded like a bomb going off in my house. Zach was yelling. Anna was crying. The Prince was moaning. As fast as I could elevate myself from the bed, I waddled into the den to assess the source of the explosion and evaluate the extent of the injuries to my children. As I entered the den I was immediately relieved to see that neither child had a bone out of place or blood oozing from a recent wound. However, to my dismay, the legs of the Prince that are typically appended to his torso, appeared to be appended to the ceiling. The slight wiggling motion of his feet and lower extremities told me that the appendages hanging through the 20 ft. ceiling remained connected to my Prince Charming. The fact that his legs were moving indicated that he had not lost consciousness.

Zach stopped yelling. Anna was no longer crying. The Prince was still moaning. A shower of small white flakes of sheetrock continued to float through the air. Fearful that David was about to fall from the 20 foot ceiling, I mimicked Zach's yells and called to Prince Charming to ensure he was alright. As I learned that a 2x4 had broken his fall, I felt a sense of relief that it was only the Prince's pride and groin that were injured. My laughter, after determining he was alright, calmed Zach and Anna.

The hole in the ceiling had not yet been repaired when the air conditioner went out. Being 8 ½ months pregnant, repair of the air conditioner was a true emergency. I had a repairman out within 4 hours of my discovery of the tragic failure of the air-conditioner. Fortunately for me it only took the repairman a few moments to identify the problem and make the necessary modifications to the air-conditioner. When he asked me if somebody had recently changed the air filter, I didn't understand what he thought was so funny. When he emerged from the electrical closet with a cone-shaped air filter, I got the joke. The Prince failed to follow the royal directions. He put that tricky air filter in upside-down. The problem with air filters is that they are rather persnickety about being positioned in the unit in their proper orientation. The air conditioner shut itself off after being unable to suck any more royal air through what became a cone shaped filter, lodged deep inside the air conditioner. Evidently, even a Prince can't reverse the flow of air through an air filter. That evening I took the opportunity to enlighten the Prince about the critical importance of the arrow symbols for streets, microwave popcorn, and air-conditioners. The Prince explained to me about the critical need to keep Americans employed.

Workmen were repairing the sheetrock in the ceiling when the breaker flipped off. The scent of something burning was unmistakable. Unsure of the source of the problem, I called an electrician. Looking at the fuse box, the electrician was able to tell that something was wrong in the nursery. Although I thought that the smoke smell had been coming from the nursery, I couldn't see any sign of smoke or fire in the nursery. Why would the nursery have an electrical problem? The baby hadn't even been born yet. Nobody was using that room. It wasn't until the electrician removed the glass fixture in the ceiling that I realized the source of that burning smell. The sheetrock around the light bulbs was charred black. The electrician was standing on the ladder, inspecting the damage, when he began to laugh. He asked me if anyone had recently changed the light bulbs. I admitted that my Prince Charming had recently ascended the royal ladder to help me. The electrician suggested that next time the Prince should use three Royal 40 watt bulbs, instead of three 200 watt bulbs. I told the electrician that I would make sure that going forward, I wouldn't get pregnant so that the Prince wouldn't have to change any more light bulbs. That evening I explained to the Prince, very tactfully, that more is not always better. To illustrate my point, I gave the Prince very tangible examples of situations where more isn't necessarily better… wine, medicine, and wives. I'm not sure he understood the reference to the wine and medicine, but the image of a multitude of wives, laughing at his home repair skills, convinced him that more isn't always better. I could laugh because no harm had come to the house. The Prince laughed because he wouldn't have to change light bulbs ever again.

C. Favorite Quotes

Sometimes other people inspire us to laugh and help us keep our perspective in life. Mom used to make a cake when she was having a particularly bad day, but cakes are full of calories. After I eat a piece of cake, I feel worse about myself. If I find something to laugh about it puts everything in perspective. A multitude of sources of humor are easily available. I find that refrigerator magnets and signs around my desk remind me of some of my favorite reasons to laugh. Here are some of my favorites:

"Why do people say grow some balls? Balls are weak and sensitive? If you really wanna get tough, grow a vagina. Those things take a pounding." Betty White

"Women who seek to be equal with men lack ambition."
Timothy Leary

"I'd much rather be a woman than a man. Women can cry, they can wear cute clothes, and they are the first to be rescued off of sinking ships." Gilda Radner

"Here's all you have to know about men and women: women are crazy, men are stupid. And the main reason women are crazy is that men are stupid." George Carlin

"If women ran the world we wouldn't have wars, just intense negotiations every 28 days."[aaa] Robin Williams

"The problem is, God gave man a brain and a penis and only enough blood to run one at a time." Robin Williams

"I'm sorry, if you were right, I'd agree with you." Robin Williams

"God made Adam first because he didn't want any advice from Eve about how to make Adam."

"I am the boss in this house, my wife told me so."

"If I agreed with you, we'd both be wrong."

"Behind every great man is a woman rolling her eyes."

"Someday, when you have your own kids, you will understand why Mommy drinks."

[aaa] https://www.youtube.com/watch?v=MAp8j4c2LGs

"Women are not moody! We simply have days when we are less inclined to put up with your shit."

"I am fluent in three languages…English, Sarcasm, and Profanity."

"Oh, interesting. Let me just write that on my list of things I don't give a shit about."

"When a woman says 'what?' it's not because she didn't hear you. She's giving you a chance to change what you said."

The other day someone told me that I could make ice cubes with leftover wine. I was confused. What is leftover wine?

"Men think women dream of finding the perfect man. What every woman really dreams of is eating anything she wants without getting fat."

"The speed in which a woman says 'nothing' when asked 'what's wrong,' is inversely proportional to the severity of the shit-storm that's coming."

"A husband is someone who, after taking the trash out, gives the impression that he just cleaned the whole house."

"When a man gives his opinion, he's a man. When a woman gives her opinion, she's a bitch."   Bette Davis

"No woman gets an orgasm from shining the kitchen floor."
     Betty Friedan

"I hate housework. You make the beds, you wash the dishes, and six months later you have to start all over again." Joan Rivers

"I hate women because they always know where things are."
     James Thurber

"I have an idea that the phrase weaker sex was coined by some woman to disarm some man she was preparing to overwhelm."   Ogden Nash

"I prefer the word homemaker, because housewife always implies that there may be a wife someplace else."
     Bella Abzug

"I would rather trust a woman's instinct than a man's reason."
Stanley Baldwin

"Is the reason we have so few female politicians, because that it would take too long to put make up on their two faces?"

"Men are from mars, women are from "Do I look fat in these?""

"Sometime I feel conflicted. Breast augmentation- or secretly perform an ice pick lobotomy to try and save the world from more idiocy."

"I meant to behave, but there were so many other options."

"Everything happens for a reason…but sometimes the reason is that you're stupid and make bad choices."

"People always ask me, 'Were you funny as a child?' 'Hell no' I respond, 'I was an accountant.'"   Ellen Degeneres

"My grandmother started walking five miles a day when she was sixty. She's ninety-seven now, and we don't know where the hell she is."   Ellen Degeneres

"I'm pretty sure if I smacked the stupid out of you, there'd be nothing left."

"I don't have a bucket list, but my fucket list is a mile long."

"Don't think of yourself as an ugly person. Think of yourself as a beautiful monkey."

"I'm not arguing. I'm simply explaining why I'm right."

"I got expelled from school on pajama day. It wasn't my fault. I sleep naked."

"Oh, you have a cold! How rude of me. I just laid an egg, and now my body is violently ripping down the walls of my uterus. But can I get you a tissue?"

"I don't want to brag or make anybody jealous, but I can still fit into the earrings I wore in high school."

"If it walks out of the refrigerator, Let It Go!"

"Some call it bitching. I call it motivational speaking."

"I wasn't yelling. I was just being emphatic."
Malia Litman

"You could file a complaint, but my supervisor doesn't care either."

"I just found out I'm awesome. You might want to get yourself tested."

"The first 50 years of marriage are always the hardest."

"Dear Lord, Please put your arm around my shoulders and your hand over my mouth."

"Anyone who says they don't need a girlfriend, just hasn't found a good one yet."

"I always wanted to be somebody, but I realize I should have been more specific."   Lily Tomlin

"If you haven't got anything nice to say about anybody, come sit next to me."   Alice Longworth

"God created man…then he had a better idea."

"We will be friends until we are old and senile…then we'll be new friends."

"Sometimes a gal has to pull herself up by the Fallopian tubes and just soldier on!"

"Some people say that behind every successful man is a woman, but nobody seems to realize that women choose only successful men."

"Whatever you choose, however many roads you travel, I hope that you choose not to be a lady. I hope you will find some way to break the rules and make a little trouble out there. And I also hope that you will choose to make some of that trouble on behalf of women."   Nora Ephron

Jesus was a woman. If you're looking for proof, just remember:

"Jesus fed a crowd at a moment's notice,
when therewas virtually no food.
Jesus kept trying to get a message across to a bunch of men,
who just didn't get it.
Even when Jesus was dead,
She still had to get up becauseThere was still work to do."

"Three Wise Women would have...
Asked directions,
Arrived on time,
Helped deliver the baby,
Cleaned the stable,
Made a casserole,
Brought practical gifts, and
There would be peace on earth."

D. Sharing Laughter

Laughter is infectious and contagious. Laughter has been shown to strengthen the immune system, boost energy, diminish pain, and protect from the damaging effects of stress. It's hard to stay mad, stressed, or depressed if you are laughing. It is no wonder that over 9 million people have watched babies laugh. The reason for the laughter of each infant was insignificant. It was the laughter itself that made us smile.[284] The contagious nature of laughter is best illustrated in the video clips of twins,[bbb] triplets, and quadruplets laughing.[ccc, ddd]

Scientists have shown that laughter:[285]

1. relaxes the whole body

2. boosts the immune system

3. triggers the release of endorphins

4. protects the heart

5. eliminates distressing emotions

6. assists in relaxation

7. changes perspective

Laughter is especially important to share with the entire family. A couple or family that can laugh together, usually stays together. Dinner together may be the best time to share the funny moments of the day.[286] Whether at work or home, laughter is an invaluable tool to bring people closer. It is also essential to any woman trying to balance the conflicting demands of professional and personal life. If we can find something to laugh about, we can tolerate most stress in life. It doesn't matter why we laugh, but only that we do laugh.[eee]

[bbb] https://www.youtube.com/watch?v=L49VXZwfup8
[ccc] https://www.youtube.com/watch?v=WxUulGkLu4I
[ddd] https://www.youtube.com/watch?v=zZH0sNsaAz4
[eee] https://www.youtube.com/watch?v=Z4Y4keqTV6w

"A woman has to
live her life,
or live to repent
not having lived it."

—D.H. Lawrence, Lady Chatterley's Lover [287]

CHAPTER X. AMAZING WOMEN

Incredible women have made their presence known throughout history.[288] Long before anyone had heard of the feminist movement or women's liberation, women courageously fought to make the world a better place. Everyone knows the stories of Queen Esther, Joan of Arc, and Queen Elizabeth I, Harriet Tubman, and Sacajawea. Zach wrote a paper in Middle School about Marie Curie. In third grade, Anna learned about Eleanor Roosevelt, and her famous advice: "No one can make you feel inferior without your consent."[289] Katie was always interested in famous female athletes.[290] I love to learn about women who were amazing mothers.[291] The Prince always talks about Golda Mier. Whether mothers, athletes, political leaders, scientists, performers, executives, clergy, or soldiers, women have distinguished themselves throughout history, and across the globe.[fff]

When we talk about feminism, the discussion in America often relates to female executives. In May of 2013, Caroline Howard of Forbes Magazine published her list of the 100 most powerful women.[292] The list gives a true representation of how far women have come in our evolution. Her list is certainly not exhaustive, but it is representative of the amazing accomplishments of women around the world. Eleven women on the list were the President or leader of their country. Four managed charitable foundations. Twelve filled a major role in their governments. Six were celebrities or in the entertainment industry. One was the First Lady. Another woman was also a First Lady, and might be the First Female President of the United States. There was a research scientist and the President of Harvard University. Some were Editors of national newspapers, magazines, and anchors on national news shows. Forty nine were Executives of some of the largest and most successful companies in America. None had ever worn the crown of Miss America. None have ever worn glass slippers. Some were single. Some were divorced. Some were married with no children. Some were married with children. All faced the daily challenge of defining success and adapting to new circumstances in their lives. None were perceived as powerful because of the success achieved in their home life, but surely some of them valued that above their professional success. Some measured success by their professional accomplishments alone. All mastered the second wave of feminism to have achieved their powerful positions. Many are still working on mastering the third wave. Amazing women are all around. Even if women don't know other famous women personally, we can learn from their examples.

[fff] https://www.youtube.com/watch?v=lANb0BAYupE

A. Sandra Day O'Connor

Justice O'Connor is my hero! July 6, 1981 was the day Sandra Day O'Connor received a call from President Reagan asking her to be the first woman appointed to the United States Supreme Court. I was 23 years old, and was a summer law clerk. It was only 11 days later that the Prince would arrive at the firm where we met. Justice O'Connor was identified as one of the most powerful women in the world.

Justice O'Connor graduated from Stanford in 1950 with a B.A. in economics. She attended Law School at Stanford. After graduating at the top of her law school class, and working as an editor of the Stanford Law Review, the only legal position offered to her after graduation was as a legal secretary. She married in 1952, five years before I was born. Justice O'Connor and her husband, John, had three children. She was not appointed to the Supreme Court until she was in her early 50's.

I graduated at the top of my Law School Class in 1982 and served on the Law Review too. However, jobs for women in law were significantly better in 1982 than thirty years before. Dallas Texas in 1982 was not a hot bed of liberal thinking or a haven for liberated women. Nevertheless, women were getting jobs as lawyers. Although I was often confused for a secretary, I cashed a pay check every month that was the same as that of the male associates. Prince Charming also brought home a check identical to mine.

Justice O'Connor will be remembered as the first female member of the United States Supreme Court. She will also be remembered for the role model she is for all women, in her professional and personal life. She is my hero not simply because she was the first woman on the Supreme Court. She is my hero because she was one of the most outstanding Justices on the Court, irrespective of gender. As a judge of integrity, she set the standard for honesty and fairness. She was one of the true intellectuals on the Court. The fact that she was the first woman made her an invaluable asset for women struggling for acceptance and equal treatment in the courtroom. Although a liberated woman, Justice O'Connor was never perceived as a radical feminist. She was happily married and the mother of three children. She has been a stay at home mother, a Trial Judge, an Arizona Court of Appeals Justice, and a member of the U.S. Supreme Court. This amazing role model reached the pinnacle of success for an attorney. Yet she was able to raise three boys and remain a devoted wife. When her husband was very sick with Alzheimer's, Justice O'Connor retired in 2005 after 24 years of service on the Court. She knew that there was no other person on the planet who could take her place as the wife of her ailing husband.

When Justice O'Connor's husband died, she adapted to her new circumstances. Justice O'Connor returned to the 2nd Circuit Court of Appeals where she works as a visiting Justice. She has also dedicated herself in her retirement years to various causes including serving as the Chancellor of William and Mary

College, serving as a member of the Iraq Study Group, and teaching a two week course at the Univ. of Arizona College of Law called "The Supreme Court." In February 2009, O'Connor launched a website which is now known as iCivics.org. She is responsible for creating interactive civics lessons for students and teachers.

She currently serves on the Board of Trustees of the National Constitution Center in Philadelphia, which is a museum dedicated to the U.S. Constitution. The resume of Justice O'Connor could fill an entire book. What would probably not make it on her resume would be Master Surfer. As a Master Surfer she has devoted herself to her country, to her family, and to becoming a role model for modern American women. She has successfully mastered the art of surfing the last two waves of feminism.

O'Connor was born in 1930, just ten years after women won the right to vote. Throughout her early years women faced constant challenges as a way of life. While Sandra Day O'Connor faced blatant discrimination she navigated the tumultuous waters to put herself in a position to be considered to serve as the first woman on the United States Supreme Court. By 1982 when she was appointed to the U.S. Supreme Court, she had proved herself worthy without alienating the men who had the power to promote her to a position on the highest Court in the land. She never filed a suit for discrimination. She balanced the professional and personal parts of her life for over half a decade. Having mastered the second wave of feminism, Justice O'Connor spent the next 24 years affirming the importance of a woman's voice on the Court. She ruled with fairness, and a firm hand. She earned the respect of men and women, conservatives and liberals. Justice O'Connor was appointed by President Ronald Reagan, who was generally recognized as a champion of the Republican Party. She received the Presidential Medal of Honor from President Barack Obama, a Democrat. President Obama is one of the most liberal Presidents of the last century. Yet both men honored Justice O'Connor.

Women of the 21st century don't want to be perceived as radical feminists. Women simply expect to be treated fairly, by their boss, and by their Prince Charming. The desire to have it all is the realization that women are smart enough to compete with men in the work-place, but compassionate enough to be willing to compromise their careers if necessary. Without announcing her mastery of the third wave of feminism, Sandra Day O'Connor retired from her position on the highest Court in the land to be with her ailing husband. Having been elevated to the pinnacle of success as a judge, she proved herself a compassionate and devoted wife. When she was appointed to the Court, her husband compromised his career for the sake of hers. He recognized that this appointment represented an historical opportunity for his wife, and for women across the country. When John became ill and was in need of his wife's unique love and devotion, Justice O'Connor compromised her career for her husband. She knew that nurses could be hired to care for her husband's physical needs, but nobody could provide for his emotional needs as she could. Without asking for the approval or blessing of anyone, Justice O'Connor had the courage to do what she determined to be right for her family.

Sandra Day O'Connor has mastered the third wave of feminism. She has shown by her example that women can achieve greatness professionally, and be willing to compromise professional success for the sake of family. No one will ever question Justice O'Connor's competency as a member of the U.S. Supreme Court. Upon her retirement from the Court, she has become a role model for all professional women struggling to master the third wave. She has not told others how to live their lives. However, she has demonstrated, by example, how to make choices that best satisfy individual goals. By considering her unique circumstances, she has taught women everywhere that we must rely on our own judgment when dealing with the circumstances of our lives. She has also shown by her example that we can fill different roles at different times in our lives. Each can be gratifying and each can be critical for the success of ourselves and our family. She had the courage in her professional life, and in her personal life, to re-define success at each stage of her life. Sandra Day O'Connor has charted the course. We must follow her lead. When she left the Supreme Court, she didn't quit being Justice O'Connor. She didn't quit being the first woman to serve on the Court. She didn't give it all up. She simply adapted. We respect her more now than ever for having the courage to leave the Court when she did.

B. Barbara Walters

I made it to my seat. Most people attending the Yale graduation for the class of 2012 were proud of their young graduate. They hadn't even thought about the accomplishment of walking the few blocks necessary to get into the courtyard for the commencement speech. As I pulled my walker up to the end of the white plastic chairs, I sat down relieved to find a resting place. As I glanced down the row, my mother was beaming, wishing that my father could have seen his grandson graduating from Yale. The girls were looking around. They were not nearly as impressed as their parents at the magnitude of the accomplishment for Zach, and for his parents. My son was graduating from one of the most prestigious colleges in the country. He had earned a spot at another prestigious college to pursue a PhD in Chemistry. When I graduated with a B.S. Degree in Nursing, from the University of Oklahoma, I was proud. However, I wasn't nearly as proud that day as I was this day watching my son graduate. Watching my son, who had overcome so much, graduate from Yale, in such a challenging major, with such good grades, was a fantasy. Even Cinderella wouldn't have thought of asking her fairy-god-mother for this reward.

Barbara Walters was the Commencement speaker that day. Until she began speaking, I had not expected to feel that the speech was being given for my benefit. I assumed her presentation would be directed at the graduates. Any importance placed on her words of wisdom by the parents would be secondary. As I sat waiting for the ceremony to begin, I realized in that moment of solitude, that the commencement ceremony was a celebration for me, as much as my son. His accomplishment was graduating. Mine was the validation that I had made the right decision to devote myself to raising the next generation. Zach had put in the laborious work of overcoming dyslexia and achieved a goal that most young men, who had no disability, could have never hoped to realize. For me I was celebrating not only my success in walking to the ceremony, but I was also celebrating a decision made 17 years before when Zach was only five years old. There were times when I wondered if I would one day regret leaving my career to be a stay-at-home mom. Would I one day wake up and realize that raising children was not as fulfilling as I had hoped? Would I feel that my child's success was enough satisfaction to justify limiting the personal satisfaction of being a successful trial attorney? Was I unfairly taking credit for my son's accomplishment? I knew it was Zach's day, and Zach's accomplishments. However, I was willing to be the one making the assist. Zach scored the winning goal, but he knew who passed him the ball to him.

Katie asked what I was smiling about. I shrugged my shoulders, hoping that one day she would understand. I couldn't tell her about the thrill of surfing the third wave of feminism and reaching the shore. One day I hope she will understand the importance of mastering the third wave. She is pursuing professional success in college, so she's still working on mastery of the second wave. It will likely be several years before she has to master the third wave. When it hits, she'll have so many more tools than I did to find success and happiness. Because she's a great athlete, she'll probably glide to shore the first time she attempts to master the third wave. I'll stand by, just in case she gets hit with an unanticipated wave.

As Barbara Walters began to speak, I felt she was celebrating with me. Her speech was a tribute to her accumulated wisdom while mastering all three waves of feminism. As an 82 year old female icon, Barbara Walters stood before the Yale graduates of 2012, sharing her insights for the men and women graduating.[ggg] She tied her advice to wisdom she acquired from famous people she had known or interviewed over the past 50 years.

Barbara's paternal grandmother, Lily, explained to her 7 children that she was still a virgin. When the kids tried to correct their mother, she acknowledged that while she had to have sex to get pregnant, she never participated. Barbara explained that it was important to participate in all that we undertake to do. Even though Barbara was somewhat intimidated to give the speech that day, she accepted the challenge. According to Barbara the students graduating were smarter, better educated, and younger, than she. However she was determined to participate. I think her message was to Lean In, to whatever you choose to do. Whether a stay-at-home-mom, or the President of the United States, people should always try their hardest to do the best job they can. As Lord Chesterfield said: "If it's worth doing, it's worth doing well."

Professor Joseph Campbell was one of Barbara's college professors. He taught his students *to follow your bliss*. Barbara explained to her audience that they might not yet know what their bliss is. However the advice of Professor Campbell was to search for your bliss. When you find it, don't be afraid to follow it. It was clear that Barbara's message was to search for happiness. If we find our bliss we will live happily ever after.

Ms. Walters identified Hillary Clinton as one of "the most admired women in the world." Barbara prefaced her question to Hillary by saying that "life is about choices." What is the biggest choice you made? Hillary answered,

> "Staying married to Bill." Hillary explained that "…everyone has a choice every single day about how to live your life, and many people looking at my life would say how tough. I look at it differently. I look at the lessons I've learned and the opportunities I've had."[293]

Barbara then asked Hillary what was the most important lesson she had learned. Hillary responded:

[ggg] https://www.youtube.com/watch?v=7lIYZ2XqLX4

228

"Life is a gift, and we learn as we go. Love, and hope, and faith, are truly the most important gifts that we can have, and that we can give to one another. When something difficult happens you have to decide what's important to you and decide what your priorities are. You have to listen hard to your own heart. There are always going to be people who have different ideas about decisions and choices that you should make, but ultimately we are born alone, and we die alone, and the life we make, the journey we take, is up to us."[294]

The Dalai Lama of Tibet was the next person Ms. Walters mentioned. Unlike most people Barbara interviewed, the Dalai Lama explained that the purpose of life is to be happy. We achieve happiness through compassion and warm-heartedness.

Barbara shared her personal story, explaining that she really didn't have much family. Her friends filled that role. Barbara cautioned the graduates to appreciate that the friends made during their college years might be the best part of college. Treasure them. Treat them with compassion and warm-heartedness. Realize their importance in your life.

Barbara specifically mentioned Kathryn Hepburn in the context that some men and women might expect to have it all. Barbara reminisced about her conversations with Kathryn Hepburn. Ms. Hepburn died at age 96, content with her life, even though she never had children, and was only married for a few short years. Kathryn Hepburn was very definite about things. She saw things in black and white. Ms. Hepburn explained that she lived as a man. She didn't think you could successfully combine marriage, children, and a career. She said that she had done what I damn well please. Because she made enough money to support herself and wasn't afraid of being alone, Ms. Hepburn was happy with her life. Ms. Hepburn mastered the first wave of feminism as a teenager when women won the right to vote. Ms. Hepburn mastered the second wave in 1928 when she began her acting career. Her mastery of the third wave was clear by her acknowledgement that she was happy with her life, even though she never had children and was only married a few years. In her mind, she had it all because she found a way to live happily ever after.

Margaret Thatcher was born in 1925 and is best known for her service as the Prime Minister of the United Kingdom from 1979 to 1990. Ms. Thatcher's advice related to failure. Ms. Thatcher experienced being removed from office by her own party. Barbara Walters told the story of her own experience with failure and explained that most people can't go through life without some form of failure. She cautioned against the tendency to sink into despair or to blame someone else. Ms. Thatcher and Ms. Walters used their own disappointments as an opportunity to re-invent themselves. Each found new purpose and meaning.

Christopher Reeve was the last interview Ms. Walters mentioned. Mr. Reeve was an athlete and best known for his role as Superman. Superman was the epitome of a handsome, virile, well built, young man. He was in the prime of his life when he suffered a broken neck as a result of a fall from a horse. He was left permanently paralyzed. Barbara Walters explained that the lesson taught by Superman was that life sometimes brings enormous challenges; that you can and will bear them. Mr. Reeve's wife gave him the choice of ending his suffering by pulling the plug. As he was contemplating his decision, a famous doctor came in the room. The doctor introduced himself as a proctologist and ordered Mr. Reeve to turn over. The doctor was Robin Williams.

Mr. Williams made Mr. Reeve laugh. It was his ability to laugh that gave him the strength to push through the pain. He let his mind and spirit take over. He had a reason to live.

The insight of Ms. Walters in that graduation was perhaps the most helpful and inspiring advice I've been given. Most of the Yale graduates have probably forgotten her advice. I won't forget.

C. Anne Marie Slaughter

Anne Marie Slaughter is a professor of politics and international affairs at Princeton. She is the mother of two teenage boys. From 2009 to 2011 she served as the Director of Policy and Planning at the State Department. Most people recognize her as a result of an article she published in the Atlantic magazine in July of 2012 entitled *Why Women Still Can't Have It All*.[295] The turning point for Ms. Slaughter in her quest to have it all, was a glamorous reception she attended with the President and the First Lady. The reception was a prestigious affair with foreign dignitaries, and various other important people in attendance. The guests sipped champagne and nibbled on fancy hors d'oeuvres. Instead of enjoying the spectacularly impressive list of people attending, and the exquisite food and beverages, Ms. Slaughter was thinking about her teenage sons at home. They needed her. She needed to be with them. They were in need of their mother's guidance through their difficult teenage years. She realized that she not only needed to be home with them, but she wanted to be with them. Even though she was unable to identify any role models for guidance, she made an incredibly difficult decision. She quit her job in D.C. and went home. She described her decision to spend time with her children as deeply satisfying. Ms. Slaughter identified the irreplaceable simple pleasures of baseball games, piano recitals, waffle breakfasts, family trips, and goofy rituals. She concluded her article with the observation that her boys were doing much better. The boys benefitted from having their mother home.

Reading this article, I agreed and related to the observations made by Ms. Slaughter, from the struggle to be the best she could be professionally, to her overriding desire to be at home with her sons. Within four days one million viewers had read Ms. Slaughter's article. The article was insightful, relevant to women around the country, and well written. The only problem with the article is that Ms. Slaughter's conclusion was wrong. Ms. Slaughter did have it all. She identified that which was most important to her and she did the necessary to achieve it. She did what she wanted to do. It was deeply satisfying to her. Her time in the State Department makes her lectures at Princeton, teaching about policy and international affairs, much more impressive. Her background gives her credibility that could never be achieved had she not previously served in the capacity she did. By quitting her job in the State Department she didn't lose that experience. She was just moving on. She prioritized things in her life that made her happiest and found a way to achieve a balance. By moving home, she was able to teach at Princeton, while simultaneously being with her husband and sons. For the first time since she began working at the State Department, she found balance in her life. What is having it all, if not to do that which makes you happiest? In a few years her teenage sons will be grown and gone. She will then be in a position to reassess what would make her happy. Maybe she will return to the State Department? Maybe she will decide that she doesn't want to live apart from her husband? Maybe one of her sons will play a sport in college and she might desire to be able to travel to see his games? Whatever the answer, only Ms. Slaughter will know what is right for her. Now that she has learned to define success for herself, and found her happily ever after, Ms. Slaughter will adapt to her new circumstances and find the right solution for her. Ms. Slaughter has mastered the third wave of feminism.

D. Sheryl Sandberg

In 2013, Sheryl Sandberg published *Lean In*. The book has been described as a "manifesto for getting women into leadership and helping them balance work with the rest of their lives." Fourteen Thousand *Lean In* Circles around the world have evolved as a result of sales of over 1.6 million copies.[296] Ms. Sandberg's book has been touted as a very positive influence in helping women address the challenges women face both at home and at work. However *Lean In* is not intended to be a guide for finding balance. It is a guide to achieving further success in the work place. The goal of Ms. Sandberg is to help women achieve greater professional success.

Ms. Sandberg is one of the richest women in the world. She is one of a handful that has achieved incredible wealth from her own professional success, instead of that of her father or husband. Certainly there has been criticism of Sandberg's advice regarding getting ahead in the work-place.[297] However, it's hard to argue with the notion that women often "leave before they leave."[298] Sandberg suggested that in planning for a family, women often take a lesser role in their professional lives, thinking that one day they will need flexibility during their child-bearing years. Unfortunately, the book focuses only on achieving professional success. Ms. Sandberg has been incredibly successful in her professional life. Her net worth of over One Billion Dollars, is proof of her dominance as a professional. Yet, the only reason the book has been described as providing insight into balancing professional and personal life, is that Ms. Sandberg was married, and has two children. The text of the book illustrates Ms. Sandberg's frustration and difficulty in managing the conflicting demands of professional and home life. No one could criticize Ms. Sandberg's decision to pursue professional success. Who could walk away from one billion dollars? However, *Lean In* illustrates the extreme challenges faced by professional women who are extremely successful at work, which makes the challenges of balancing children and work even harder. Sandberg, the COO of Facebook, admits that it has been very difficult for her to balance two children and professional success. For example she writes:

1. By age 25 Sandberg had been married and divorced. Ten years later at age 35, she was the COO of Facebook, remarried, and had just given birth to her first child.$_{p18}$

2. Ms. Sandberg's first child was born in 2004, when she was 35 years old.$_{p3}$ Until the birth, she'd been working a minimum of 12 hours every day from 7:00 am to 7:00 pm.$_{p126}$ When her son was born Sandberg wanted to take the 3 month maternity leave that Google offered, but she worried that if she did, her job wouldn't be there when she returned.$_{p126}$ Sandberg reported returning e-mails from her hospital bed the day after her son was born.$_{p127}$ That "maternity leave was a pretty unhappy time."$_{p127}$ Sandberg acknowledges that she "let herself down." When she returned from

her non-leave maternity-leave, Sandberg reported crying as she left her baby at home to return to work.$_{p127}$ Her husband was the "primary caregiver" for their newborn.$_{p105}$ It was her husband that taught her how to change the baby's diapers when the baby was 8 days old!$_{p105}$

3. After kids, Ms. Sandberg tried to solve the problem of finding a balance, by sleeping less.$_{p132}$ She admits that "If I could go back and change one thing about how I lived in those early years I would force myself to get more sleep."$_{p132}$ Unfortunately Ms. Sandberg doesn't offer any ideas about how she would find the time to get more sleep.

4. "…no matter what any of us has---how grateful we are for what we have ---no one has it all."$_{p119}$

5. "There are many powerful reasons to exit the workforce. Being a stay-at-home parent is a wonderful and often necessary choice for many people. Not every parent needs, wants, or should be expected to work outside the home….No one should pass judgment on these highly personal decisions. I fully support any man or woman who dedicates his or her life to raising the next generation. It is important and demanding and joyful work. What I am arguing is that the time to scale back is when a break is needed- or when a child arrives –not before, and certainly not years in advance."$_{p95}$

6. Sheryl Sandberg had her second child when she was 37 years old.$_{p97}$ She agrees that it is not always time to lean in.$_{p97}$

7. "Choosing to leave a child in someone else's care and return to work is a difficult decision. Any parent who has done this, myself included, knows how heart wrenching it can be. Only a compelling, challenging, and rewarding job will begin to make that choice a fair contest. And even after a choice is made, parents have every right to reassess along the way."$_{p103}$

8. Ms. Sandberg admits that she is "not completely comfortable" with her choice to go back to work.$_{p137}$

9. It was the nanny, not mom, for whom Sandberg's son cried.$_{p137}$

10. In spite of a net worth of over one billion dollars, and incredible success as a professional woman, Ms. Sandberg still counts the hours away from her children and feels sad when she misses dinner or a night with them.$_{p137}$

11. Stay at home mothers can still make the COO of Facebook feel guilty and intimidate her. There are moments when Ms. Sandberg

feels like they are judging her.$_{p167}$ Sandberg recognizes that it is the stay-at-home mothers that constitute a large amount of the talent that sustains our schools, nonprofits, and our communities.$_{p167}$

12. Ms. Sandberg admits that her marriage isn't perfect and is a "work in progress" with "bumps along the way."$_{p111}$

The clear message is that Ms. Sandberg chose a dangerous path. By waiting to have her first child until 35 years old, she was three times more likely than a 30 year old mother to have a child with a chromosomal defect.[299] At age 37, when she had her second child, she was four times as likely. By allowing her husband to be the primary care giver to her baby, she would have likely lost custody of her baby if her husband had sought a divorce. If she made more money than her husband, she would predictably have to pay him alimony if he had sought a divorce. Certainly the choices made by Ms. Sandberg have resulted in incredible wealth and happiness. Few men or women would opt to stay at home to raise their children, instead of pursuing a profession that would result in a net worth of one billion dollars. For another woman in similar circumstances, who made the same choices, the result could have been dramatically different.

Why didn't Ms. Sandberg choose to stay at home with her baby as I did? Why was it so hard for me to opt out of my career? If Sheryl Sandberg describes child care as joyful work, why wouldn't she choose to stay at home to enjoy the work of child-rearing?$_{pg95}$ Of course the financial reward for Ms. Sandberg makes her choice seem to be inevitable. However remember that when Sandberg made the choice to work after having children, she had not yet made her billion dollars. Remember that every time Ms. Sandberg appears to give a speech about women's issues, her book, or the great balancing act, she is taking time away from her children. Her children are still young enough to live at home. Perhaps the audience that is most in need of her input and advice are the two children at home. In 10 years, when the kids are gone, there will be plenty of time for speeches to large auditoriums full of people.

E. Advice from Accomplished Women

Sometimes, hearing the advice of other women gives us comfort that one solution doesn't fit all. However, hearing different approaches may give us insight into solutions that we may have not considered.

a. Angela Ahrendts was the CEO Burberry. She has recently taken a job with Apple as the Senior Vice President in charge of retail and online stores. She is Apple's only female executive. Ms. Ahrendts has three teenage children, and describes her jobs as a wife, a mother, and chief executive. She gets up at 4:35 a.m. She regularly declines sought-after invitations, such as the Oscars, because her family is more important. She tries to limit herself to one night out a week. Even if traveling, she always tries to be home by Friday night. She says:

> "Balance is really important to me. You can't do it all, not all at one time. It is my job to set an example. We have a lot of working women here (at Burberry) and I always tell them they are mothers first. Those children are their legacy and they have partners and that's a big obligation." "I don't want to be a great chief executive without being a great mum and a great wife."[300]

b. Susan Bates is Medical Doctor but a stay-at-home mother to five children.[301]

c. Ursula Burns is an African American woman and the only Black woman to serve as the CEO of a Fortune 500 company. Ms. Burns was raised by a single mother and has a daughter and step-son. The head of Xerox Corporation said:

> "As long as I've been alive discussing this, and even before, this concept of having it all — that's not the point…" " Pick the places where you want to be great, focus your energies there, and then go do it." "You're not going to be great at everything, and then relax."[302]

d. Nora Ephron was a journalist, essayist, playwright, screenwriter, novelist, producer, director, blogger, and the mother of two boys. Ms. Ephron was married three times. Nora said:

> "Maybe young women don't wonder whether they can have it all any longer, but in case any of you are wondering, of course you can have it all. What are you going to do? Everything, is my guess. It will be a little messy, but embrace the mess. It will be complicated, but rejoice in the complications. It will not be anything like what you think it will be like, but surprises are good for you. And don't be frightened: You can

always change your mind. I know: I've had four careers and three husbands."[303]

e. Bethenny Frankel is a television personality, talk show host, author, and entrepreneur. She has been married and divorced twice and has one child. She said:

"No matter where you are right now, no matter how far along you are on your own path, don't wait to 'have it all' to celebrate. You're never going to figure it all out. Make being happy your business, all along the way. Life can't be one long, tough haul, with a little party at the end. What good is that? Life should be punctuated with celebrations and you have to build them into your time because being happy isn't easy."[304]

f. Melinda Gates attended Ursuline Academy which is located less than one mile from my house. Ms. Gates graduated from Duke with a B.S. degree in Computer Science. She earned a MBA in 1987. She met Bill while working at Microsoft and they married in 1994. Melinda left her job shortly thereafter to begin having a family. She and Bill have three children born in 1996, 1999, and 2002. Ms. Gates is a trustee of the Bill & Melinda Gates Foundation which is the largest private foundation in the world. The endowment was reported to be $42.3 Billion Dollars. Ms. Gates said:

"Progress for girls and women means progress for all."[305]

"I care much more about saving the lives of mothers and babies than I do about a fancy museum somewhere."[306]

"I think it's very important that we instill in our kids that it has nothing to do with their name or their situation that they're growing up in; it has to do with who they are as an individual."[307]

g. Ilene Gordon is the Chairman, President, and CEO of Ingredion, a company that exceeded sales of $6 billion dollars in 2012. Ms. Gordon is one of only 21 women to run a Fortune 500 company. She said:

"In my mind, there was never a choice of career vs. family. I was going to do both. I had my kids in my young 20's. My husband was very busy traveling as a consultant, so we hired a lot of good help. I'm a big believer in delegation and being organized. Every Sunday night was family night. We'd have dinner and lay out a plan for the week and month. Sometimes my daughter would say: I have a big paper due, and I'd like your input. I would copy the chapter she was working on, take it with me, and call her from the road so we could talk about it. Once, I gave her a spelling test from the back of a taxi. It was a lot of energy and you have to be willing to do it, but I never thought for a moment it wasn't possible. You have to have a plan. We had a backup nanny, and a backup to the backup. My attitude was: We'll figure it out."[308]

h. Kristen Houghton is a lifestyle journalist and author of *AND THEN I'LL BE HAPPY!* Ms. Houghton writes:

> "During the last 40 years or so, we women have been told that we can have it all. We can always look great, run errands with ease, balance family and work seamlessly, throw fantastic parties, have decorator homes and never miss a beat in being fashionable and in the know. But while you and I may admire the women we see in the media or read about who seem to be able to do it all, we also have a certain dislike for them and have thought, I can't do it all. Is there something wrong with me?
>
> Actually there's nothing wrong with imperfect you. What you don't know is that the perfect woman runs her perfect life at great expense. The expense isn't monetary, but if you try to do the same, it will become a personal cost to you in terms of stress. You will pay with both your physical and emotional health, and the cost gets higher as the years go on."[309]

i. Christine Lagarde is a French lawyer, twice divorced, and mother of two sons. She is the first women to serve as the Managing Director of the International Monetary fund. Ms. Lagarde said:

> "I think you cannot have it all at the same time. I think you can in a way have it all as long as you can afford to be patient. But you cannot have it all at the same time. You must accept there will be failures."[310]

j. The Levo League is a career cockpit for the first phase of a woman's professional journey. The Levo League's website features this quote:

> "…you decide what you want to do, who you want to be, and how you're going to get there. Success means something different to each of us."[311] Caroline & Amanda

k. Marissa Mayer is 40 years old and is the President and CEO of Yahoo. In 2014 Ms. Mayer ranked 6th on Fortune's 40 under 40 list[312] and 18th on the most-powerful business women in the world.[313] Her primary residence is the Penthouse at the Four Seasons Hotel in San Francisco.[314]

Ms. Mayer has one child. She announced she was 6 months pregnant in July of 2012, a few hours after Yahoo announced she had accepted their offer to hire her.[315] Ms. Mayer worked while she was away from the office after giving birth. She returned to work just two weeks after the birth of her first child. Nine months after she returned to work Ms. Mayer changed the policy at Yahoo regarding leave after the birth of a child. Under the new policy fathers get 8 weeks of paid leave after the birth of a child, and mothers get 16 weeks.[316]

Ms. Mayer explains that:

> "You can be good at technology and like fashion and art. You can be good at technology and be a jock. You can be good at technology and be a mom. You can do it your way, on your terms."[317]

l.   Indra Nooyi is the President and CEO of PepsiCo.[318]

Fortune ranked her the #1 most powerful woman in business in 2009[319] and in 2010.[320]

She was born in 1955 and has two grown daughters. She said:

> "At the end of the day, don't forget that you're a person, don't forget you're a mother, don't forget you're a wife, don't forget you're a daughter."[321]

In another interview, Ms.Nooyi explained that "having it all" is just an illusion that comes with painful sacrifices and tradeoffs. She advised that:

> "You have to cope...because you die with guilt. You just die with guilt."

She realizes that her daughters may not feel she's been the strongest of mothers, but "the person who hurts the most through this whole thing is your spouse. There's no question about it."[322]

m.   Michelle Obama, the First Lady, and mother of two said:

> "I think that in order to be successful, women have to figure out what they're passionate about first. No matter what you aspire to, you've got to love what you do in order to be successful at it. I also encourage young women to set high goals for themselves and be confident in their ability to achieve them."

"The truth is, women can do anything they want. There is absolutely no limit on what we can achieve, and I hope that every young woman approaches life that way. We can become even more successful if we support each other, empower each other, and mentor the next generation so they can stand on our shoulders."[323]

n. Norah O'Donnell is a print and television journalist. She currently serves as the co-anchor of CBS This Morning, a position she has held since July 2012. She is married to her first husband and has three children. Norah said:

"No, I don't care for (the phrase "work-life balance") I think it sets up these scales of justice where for me they're the same---work and life---and that they're supposed to be equal. I spend more time at work during the week than I am at home. I spend time with my children during the night, but they're also at school during the day—I mean, they have lives too.

My biggest thing is that the guilt has to end -- this guilt that men never suffer about work and home has got to end. When I've done interviews, and then I ask other women about work-life balance, they're like, how can you ask that, you hate that phrase, so I find myself in a contradiction. But I think women are mostly fascinated with how other women do it, because it is really hard, and it's not a one-size-fits-all about how we do it."[324]

o. Oprah is a media mogul, talk show host, actress, producer, and philanthropist. She has never married. Her only child died shortly after birth, when Oprah was only 14 years old. Oprah said: [325]

"You can have it all. Just not at once."

"If I had kids, my kids would hate me."

"They would have ended up on the equivalent of the Oprah show talking about me; because something [in my life] would have had to suffer and it would've probably been them."

p. Gwyneth Paltrow is an actress, singer, author, and comedian. She has two children. Ms Paltrow said:

"You can't have it all. I don't care what it looks like.... I look for an interesting supporting part about once a year. That's the most I can manage. Some women can do it and that's fantastic, but I can't."[326]

q. Sarah Jessica Parker is an actress, model, singer and producer. She is married and has three children. The Sex and the City star said:

> "The question is not only how you do it, but why? If you don't have to juggle career, children, and husband for financial reasons, why choose to? The beauty of the times we live in is that we do have choices. For me, it has been hard to say no. I wanted a family and I was a career person. I tried to marry those two things; sometimes it's successful and sometimes it's not."[327]

r. Christine Quinn is a politician and the first woman to serve as the Speaker of the New York City Council. She now serves as the special adviser to Governor Cuomo. Ms. Quinn is openly gay. She has never been married, and doesn't have children. She explained:

> "I think having it all is a phrase I don't particularly like. You need to have what you want. All seems to me to be an imposed list, an imposed definition by society of what 'all' is supposed to be. As women, we should be able to decide what we want, how we want it, and (how we) get there. That means it won't be perfect, there will be mistakes, but that's fine, that's human. All should be a determination of what we want, not what somebody else or society says."[328]

s. Sheryl Sandberg is the COO of Facebook. She has been married twice and has two children. She said:

> "Having it all is the worst. No matter how much we all have and how grateful we are for what we have, no one has it all, because we all make tradeoffs every single day, every single minute."[329]

> "If I had to embrace a definition of success, it would be that success is making the best choices we can...and accepting them.... The secret is there is no secret –just doing the best you can with what you've got."[330]

t. Lauren Sandler is a journalist and author. She is an only child, and has only one child. She has written the book *One and Only*. Ms. Sandler explains:

> "Even so, women who choose not to become mothers are finding new paths of acceptance. As their ranks rise — and as the community of adults without kids diversifies in terms of race, education levels and political affiliations — so do positive attitudes about being able to lead a fulfilling, childless life. Along the way, these women are inventing a new female

archetype, one for whom having it all doesn't mean having a baby."[331]

u.   Anne Marie Slaughter is a professor at Princeton. She and her first husband have two sons. She said:

> "You can't start off with work-life balance and be successful. Period. If you're not willing to acknowledge that, then there are certain lines of work that you shouldn't go in. I think maybe people haven't quite accepted that reality. They just haven't accepted it. They're just kind of stumbling into it and then they realize it, discover it.[332]

v.   Deborah Spar, is the seventh president of Barnard College and the author of several books. She is also married and the mother of three. She said:

> "It wasn't supposed to be this hard. Like many women, I grew up believing we were equal to men, that we could have sex whenever we wanted, children whenever we chose, and work wherever we desired. For years, as a professor at Harvard Business School, I was the only woman in a room of alpha men, and still I always felt equal. And I was. Then five years ago I was offered the chance to become president of Barnard College. There was barely a man in sight, and the change gave me a front-row view of what women are thinking and feeling now. We have opportunities today—to choose our educations, careers, spouses—that would've stunned our grandmothers. But now we're dazed and confused by all the choices. Feminism was meant to remove a fixed set of expectations; instead, we now interpret it as a route to personal perfection. Because we can do anything, we feel as if we have to do everything."[333]

w.   Gloria Steinem was born in 1934, the same year as my mother. Ms. Steinem is a feminist, journalist, and a social and political activist. She became nationally recognized as a leader of the women's liberation movement in the late 1960s and 1970s. She didn't marry until she was 66 years old. Her husband died three years later, so she has been single the vast majority of her life. Ms. Steinem never had a child of her own. The leader of the feminist movement said:

> "It's impossible for women to have it all, if they have to do it all. It is ridiculous! We tried to kill [that saying] off for years. It blames the person instead of the structure."[334]

x.   Meryl Streep is an actress who has appeared in theater, movies, and television. She is widely regarded as one of the most talented actresses of all time. Meryl Streep, at 62 years old, is still at the top of her game. She has been married 33 years to Don Gummer, a sculptor. They have four children. However even with four children, Ms. Streep indicated she needed another outlet when asked if she could be happy being a full time mother.[335]

When she thinks about the future, she hopes for grandchildren.[336] Her secret to a long lasting marriage is goodwill, a willingness to bend, and to shut up now and then. She said, "There's no road map on how to raise a family: it's always an enormous negotiation. But I have a holistic need to work and to have huge ties of love in my life. I can't imagine eschewing one for the other."[337]

When speaking about her husband, a sculptor, Ms. Streep explained: [338]

> "My husband understands the compulsion to create things. With somebody who had a regular job, I think it might have been harder to translate those creative impulses and the need to satisfy them ... I think you have to have somebody as a partner who shares what you value in life."

> "I'm not sure we think about it as compromising as much as it is trying to keep a certain balance in the relationship. We're lucky to have found each other, and we both recognize that. Our marriage and our four children and their future well-being inform all the decisions we make. Of course, we're fortunate that our lives are flexible enough to accommodate everybody's changing needs."

She is also credited with saying:[339]

> "Motherhood has a very humanizing effect. Everything gets reduced to essentials."

> "My family really does come first. It always did and always will."

> "I have a very busy life, and not many people who have a career and four kids go out a lot to the movies."

> "I have four to five months, tops, per year to give to my acting work."

y. Kerri Walsh-Jennings is an Olympic athlete who won gold medals in beach volleyball in 2004, 2008 and 2012. She is married, and the mother of three children. After winning gold in 2012, she disclosed that she was 5 weeks pregnant during the competition. Jennings said:

"Having it all means something different to every single person in the world. For me, having it all means having my family, having a great career, and having my faith, and those are my priorities in life, and I feel like if I'm paying attention to each one of those categories, then I feel like I have it all."[340]

"For what it's worth:
it's never too late,
...to be whoever you want to be."

- Eric Roth[341]

CHAPTER XI. SOLUTIONS

A. The "Assist"

Michael Jordon is regarded as the greatest NBA player of all time.[342] Among the statistics that justify that distinction, Michael Jordon made a total of 5,633 assists, for an average of 5.3 per game.[343]

The mere fact that the NBA records assists is a testament to its importance.[hhh] Team sports require the players to work together to be successful. The whole is truly greater than the sum of its parts.

Title IX is a part of the Education Amendment of the 1972 Equal Opportunity Education Act. Title IX provides:

> *"No person in the United States shall, on the basis of sex, be excluded from participation in, be denied the benefits of, or be subjected to discrimination under any education program or activity receiving federal financial assistance."* [344]

In 1971, the year before Title IX became the law, there were 310,000 girls and women in America playing high school and college sports.[345] I was never an athlete. I was already in high school before the passage of Title IX. By that time I was playing the trumpet in the marching band. Sports had never been an option. After the enactment of Title IX, women began to compete in team sports like never before. Today there are more than 3,000,000 women playing high school and college sports.[346] That represents ten times the number of women as in 1971. My daughter Katie is a college athlete, and has been on sports teams since before kindergarten.

One of the advantages Katie has as a result of her years of playing sports is the understanding and appreciation for the assist. When Katie scored a goal on the soccer field it was often preceded by a pass from a teammate. When one of her teammates spiked the volleyball to score a point, it was the result of an artfully placed set by Katie. In the high school championship basketball game, Katie scored the final winning basket. However she was only able to score the winning basket because her teammate, Hannah, saw that Katie was open and made the critical assist. Everyone in the stands understood the importance and contribution of both Katie and Hannah. Girls today have the advantage of playing team sports that women born in the 50's didn't. Perhaps, that is why professional women over 40 years of age are hesitant to accept help, or acknowledge the importance of the assist that we provide every day, to each other, to co-workers, and to our families.

[hhh] https://www.youtube.com/watch?v=xQwTJsY50l4

When we compromise our professional goals for the sake of our children, we put ourselves in a better position to assist them in pursuing their dreams. By making ourselves more available we are more likely to be there to assist. By giving up my job, I was available to pick up Zach the day that he had a crisis at school. I was available to arrange violin lessons for Anna. When she determined that she didn't want to become a concert violinist, I was there to help in the transition. When Katie's team needed a new soccer coach, I found one. When David's business was sued, I was able to provide support by providing an independent evaluation of the legal issues they'd be facing in Court. When he was in need of an attorney to represent him in the sale of his business, I provided an invaluable service by doing the interviewing and screening of potential transaction attorneys. Literally hundreds of things happen every year in the life of an average family that require an assist from someone. A child or spouse could survive without help, but getting an assist from mom enhances the experience for everyone, and increases the potential for success. The amazing thing is that all too often mothers and wives, fail to take credit for the assist. We may brag about the success of our child, but we don't brag about our involvement helping them reach their goals.

Working moms need help too. As a stay-at-home mom I have provided an assist to many professional mothers. When someone got caught running late, I was glad to pick up her kids. I was the one who thought to get the coach a gift to be given at the end-of-the-season party. Shelbie could only accompany Katie to gymnastics after kindergarten, if I provided transportation. Shelbie's mom had an important job. When Anna was old enough to attend a summer camp in Austin, Texas, Anna and her roommates had to get to Austin on a work day. The mother of her roommates had an important job. Since I wasn't working, I was glad to assist in driving all the girls to Austin. It was only a three hour drive each way, so I still had time to make dinner after I got home. I was glad to drive the girls, but wouldn't have wanted to ask for any help. I should be able to do the driving myself?!

In the past women have been hesitant to take credit for the success of a mother they helped, or their husband and children. Today it is important that everyone appreciate the value of having the help of a stay-at-home adult. The spouse, the children, and other parents all benefit. If we are a team member, and we provide an assist to anyone in the family, we should be proud of our contribution. As long as Prince Charming acknowledges my contribution, it is not necessary that the world know what I did, or how much I contributed. What matters is that my team won. When we define success for ourselves, if we are on a team with a spouse or children, then it is essential that we define success as success for the team. When the team reaches a goal it is important for us and the family to acknowledge the contribution of mom to the team's success. Just as an illness of one member of the family can be devastating to the entire family, the success of one can be gratifying for all.

The mothers of school-age children who have careers may have time to bring food for the teacher appreciation lunch. They don't have time to organize the volunteers, set up the lunch, and clean up after the teachers feel appreciated. Professional mothers may feel a sense of accomplishment when they locate the perfect costume at the costume shop for their child who is the star of the school play. Just finding that single costume was a huge accomplishment. However they couldn't possibly help with the design or construction of the ship known as the "Citizen-ship" that would be guided by their child in the school play. That professional woman needed help from a stay-at-home mother who had time, and was willing to design, construct, and set up the ship for the play. When the mothers are seated next to each other, watching the play, it is imperative that they each appreciate the contribution of the other. Their children both benefitted from the experience. Both mothers provided an assist. The professional woman provides a role model of a professional woman to all the young girls in the play, demonstrating that she can have a career, locate a costume for her child, and attend the play. The stay-at-home mother provides a different kind of role model, but one that is equally important. Without her help the students would be citizens, in great costumes, but without a ship to transport them on their journey.[iii]

When the teachers convene after the play for their teacher-appreciation-lunch, they will need utensils to eat their pasta. If the stay-at-home mother didn't step forward to organize the luncheon, the teachers might have to go without lunch. There might be food to eat, but nothing to transfer the food from the serving bowl to the mouths of the hungry teachers. Both the mother who brought the pasta and the mother who organized the utensils contributed. Both helped achieve success for all the children, parents, and teachers. Without the contribution of mothers who are willing to accept the job that results in no financial remuneration, and will never result in a promotion, the ship would never set sail. The teachers might not ever feel appreciated. Everyone would pay the price.

We think we should be able to do it all. If we have to ask for help, we perceive that we aren't doing our job.[347] The reality is that we all need help from our husband, our spouse, a friend, a relative, or a fellow employee. By accepting their assistance, we increase the likelihood of success for ourselves, for our families, and for the next generation. Women who accept help, allow others to participate and share in that woman's success. Women who provide the assist should feel gratified that their invaluable contribution made all the difference.

Perhaps because women born in the 50's didn't play team sports as we grew up, the recognition and appreciation of an assist is something we never learned. Watching our children play sports, we have the opportunity to learn from their example. Just as they participate as a member of a team, and achieve success as

---

[iii] http://youtu.be/pfnz3ZopHDI

a member of that team, we can do the same. We are part of the family team. We may have initially hoped that our child would be the star of the team. Over time we modified our hopes and goals to want success for the entire team. We taught our children to think about doing that which is in the best interest of the team, rather than for the individual. We should take our own advice and allow ourselves to celebrate the success of those we assist.

B. Strategic Planning

Woody Allen said:

> **"If you want to make God laugh, tell him about your plans."**[348]

The very notion of planning implies control of our destiny. Girls learn at an early age that there are just some things we can't control. Certainly as a child, I was not consulted about how many obnoxious brothers I would have, which days the popsicle-man would drive down our street, or which nights I would have to eat all the tongue on my plate. I learned to manipulate what I could control. I learned to dominate my brothers who were stronger than me, with wit instead of brawn. I learned to keep money in a hiding place for that magical moment when I heard the popsicle-man broadcasting his presence on a steaming hot summer day. I learned that I could control my gag reflex while eating tongue if I covered the taste-buds of that loathsome bovine organ with as much Heinz ketchup as possible. I learned that Del Monte ketchup was way too runny to mask the nasty taste of tongue, although it was better than nothing. I wanted to take piano lessons but I could not find a way for my family to afford a piano. In fourth grade mom said I had to play an instrument in the band. I had no desire to add to the rigors of homework, washing dishes, and taking a bath every day. For me to be required to play an instrument in the band seemed like child abuse. I planned to play for only one school year. The instrument I chose was what I perceived to be the easiest to play. It was the one with only three buttons to push.

Things don't always turn out the way we plan. Because I played the trumpet, I had a lot more boy-friends than the flute or clarinet players. While making plans to quit playing a musical instrument, I surprised myself and learned to love music. When trumpet lessons came to an end, I began making plans to replace my old brass, dent-ridden trumpet, with a state-of-the art sewing machine. I didn't give up my trumpet playing to be a seamstress. It was simply time to move on. The value of the trumpet was minimal compared to the articles of clothing and costumes I could make with the sewing machine.

Strategic Planning for every woman should begin with a plan to seek higher education. It is undisputed that higher education is directly correlated to higher income.[349] Betty Friedan explained in the Feminine Mystique that "...education, and only education, has saved, and can continue to save, American women from the greater dangers of the feminine mystique."[350] When it was time to make decisions about college, my choices were to seek admission to the University of Oklahoma, Oklahoma State University, or Tulsa University. We couldn't afford out-of-state tuition. My idea of strategic planning was not whether to apply to an Ivy League school, but to determine how best to use my limited budget for application fees to state schools. When deciding to go to law school, my planning didn't include taking a course to improve my LSAT score, since that would have cost money. My dilemma was to identify the hospital where I would work if I didn't clear the waiting list to gain admission to O.U. Law School.

To maximize the potential for success and to minimize the potential for losing it all, women must be strategic in planning for the future. No longer should we assume that every woman should have a career, children, or husband. No longer should we ask little girls "What do you want to be when you grow up?" We are assuming they will be only one thing. It should never be assumed that women can only do, or be, one thing. What do you want to be presumes that the only thing important is what career the woman wants to pursue. A woman might be one thing in her professional life, or many different things at different times. In her personal life a woman might be a baby, a little girl, a big girl, a niece, a daughter, a granddaughter, a sister, a wife, a mother, a grandmother, and a widow. In a career, a woman could be an attorney for 50 years, or she could be a nurse, an attorney, an author, a blogger, and a political activist. The secret is to be strategic in planning, and to adapt to changes that may occur while we are making other plans.

Sheryl Sandberg recommends leaning in to your career and cautions not to leave before you leave.[351] While that may be good advice, it doesn't go far enough. The term *Lean In* is great advice for a profession, but it doesn't take into account the multiple challenges of balancing personal and professional life. Perhaps better advice would be to *Lean In the Right Direction, at the Right Time*. The problem is knowing which way to lean, at which time. Even Sandberg explains that she was married and divorced by age 25.[352] Then there was the time that she had the option to take a new job, but she was planning on a second child so she passed on the new job opportunity.[353] In real life a medical doctor who specializes in Obstetrics might be required to be on call every other day for 24 hours. That woman is predictably going to have trouble finding a babysitter to care for her infant, in the middle of the night, when she has to run to the hospital to care for a patient in labor. Instead, if the woman chose to be a medical doctor but in a different specialty, like dermatology, she would likely be able to limit the frequency of the instances when she might unexpectedly need a baby-sitter. However if she loved obstetrics, and would only consider that type of specialty, then she might seek a group practice that would limit her on call time to once a month. Either way, she could *Lean In the Right Direction* and put herself in the best position to spend time with her child or children.

We also make choices about personal success. If we marry, presumably we want to stay married. If we have children, presumably we want to spend time with them. Strategically, there are some choices that we make professionally, that make our lives easier or harder domestically. The choice of a specialty would have to be made by a medical student, in or upon finishing medical school. Even if that choice occurs before marriage, it is realistic to consider life styles when making such choices. Consequently, women must be mindful of the possibility of a family even before actually having children or a husband. We may need to *Lean In* to the right career, and to the strategic career path, that would allow the most flexibility when, and if a husband or family becomes an issue. Being the best at whatever you do professionally gives women the best chance of finding flexibility if a husband or children do become a consideration. *Leaning in* is always a good idea, but giving yourself choices and options is wise. By pursuing higher education and professional excellence before beginning a family, women give themselves the greatest number of options in the event they decide to have children.

The greatest challenge in strategic planning comes with the birth of a child. It is virtually impossible to predict how a new mother will react to the presence of a baby. Even a new mother herself may have a totally unexpected reaction to becoming a mother. Some women are unwilling to leave the baby with a sitter. Others can't wait to get back to work. For some taking a maternity leave may convince them that staying home with an infant is torture. For others, the importance of staying at home with their child is a necessity. Being strategic in the decision to have a child, or more children, may simply mean that women recognize that they can't predict how they will feel after the birth of any particular child.

Being strategic is also essential in deciding when and how many children a woman might choose to have. Unfortunately, planning when to have children, and how many, may be more complicated and more problematic than you think. The longer a woman waits to conceive, the more likely she will have problems getting pregnant. The women who are older mothers are more likely to have difficult pregnancies, multiple births, and/or children with problems at birth such as Down's syndrome.[354]

A woman's rate of ovulation undergoes a dramatic decline after age 35. She will have a precipitous decline in fertility after age 38.[355] A woman's most fertile years are ages 20-24.[356] I was 24 when I graduated law school. The Prince and I weren't even engaged at age 24. If I had chosen to get pregnant when I was 24, I had a 20% chance every month of getting pregnant. The risk of a miscarriage for a 24 year old woman is only 10%. The risk for a 24 year old women of having chromosomal abnormalities is only 1 in 526 pregnancies.[357]

As the chance for professional success improves over time, the chance for an easy pregnancy declines. The rate of C-sections is almost twice as high among women 30-34 as compared to women in their 20's. The rate of miscarriage for pregnant women between the ages of 30-34 increases to 11.7%. The risk for the same group of a chromosomal abnormality increases to 1 in 385. Additional risks to the mother over 35 include a higher chance of miscarriage (18%), and the rate of stillbirths is twice as high as compared to younger women. For women 40-44 who become pregnant the reality is that almost half of all pregnancies result in a miscarriage. One in 66 babies born to mothers 40 years old and older will have a chromosomal abnormality.[358] However if a woman determines to have a child, even if it is healthy and normal, that mother knows that life will never be the same.

Today 40% of babies are born to women over 30, and 14% are born to women over 35. The pregnancy rate for women 40-44 has increased steadily since 1991. While the possibility of health issues is greater for a child born to a woman over 40, some advantages have been documented. The children of mothers over 40 years-old, tend to have higher IQs, better vocabulary, and the kids are less accident prone.[359]

A critical consideration is often overlooked by women who plan to get pregnant later in life. If we wait till age 40 to have children, and our children wait that long, we may never experience the thrill of being a grandmother. When we are 35 years old, being a grandmother may not be a significant consideration. When we are in our late 60's, and contemplating retirement, the desire for grandchildren may be of greatest priority.

There is inevitable conflict in planning for the best time to get pregnant and the optimal moment to take time out of a career. The more experience and seniority that a professional woman has, the greater the likelihood she will have of flexibility if she decides to get pregnant. However, the more experience and seniority she has, the greater the likelihood that she will have problems getting pregnant.

Success or promotions at work may not coincide with the best time physiologically to become pregnant. There is unfortunately no way to provide general advice that works for everyone. The secret is to be willing to make changes if you are not happy. There will be time later in life to pursue professional achievement long after your child-bearing years have passed. It is important to remember that your time with your children is necessarily limited. Time is the most valuable commodity we have, so how you use that limited time sends a powerful message to your child. For mothers who work to provide essentials for their children, they convey an important message to their children. That mother indicates by working that she is willing to do the necessary to ensure that her children have essentials. For mothers who work to provide extras for their children, it is important to explain that mom works so that the family can afford that perfect dress for the prom, the cost of tutoring necessary to improve the standardized test scores for each of the kids, for braces, for summer vacations, or even a car. For mothers who work because they love the stimulation and thrill of being engaged professionally, their relationship with their kids is perhaps the most difficult. For those mothers, it is essential that they make the most of their time away from work. By ensuring that time away from work is family time, a professional woman can have great relationships with her children. Whether working out, shopping, or doing chores around the house, it is important for that mother to involve her children as much as possible.

For many women the number and spacing of children is critical to balancing the demands of a profession and a personal life. For me, I found a way to balance the demands of two children and a profession, but the addition of a third child was too overwhelming.

The reality is that as convenient as it might be to precisely plan when to have children, it is more important to realize that the best of plans may require adaptation, depending on circumstances. If a CEO has difficulty getting pregnant, she may be elated to learn she is pregnant, even if the birth coincides with a strategic merger she has been working on for ten years. When I miscarried the first time I was pregnant, my priority changed from trying to plan for a perfect time of year for the child's birthday parties, to simply having a birthday to celebrate.

Finally, it may be important for a couple to strategically plan for the birth of a child. The addition of a child transforms the couple into parents. Work schedules and sleeping schedules will inevitably be changed. If the couple has only recently been married, it may be extremely hard to assimilate a child into the household routine. Just as the timing of a baby may be important to the woman's career, it should be equally important to the husband's career. If the husband is planning to devote himself equally to raising the child, then his job and career path must be considered. If the husband doesn't share responsibilities around the house before the birth of a child, it will be even harder after. As much excitement and jubilation as a baby brings, the practical consequences of adding a new member of the family can be fatal to a marriage.

Most hospitals today have birthing classes for fathers. However, the birthing experience is usually over in a single day. A child care class and a cooking class would be much more useful.

"There is a special
place in hell
for women who don't
help other women."

-Madeleine Albright[360]

CHAPTER XII. EVOLUTION REQUIRES CHANGE

The women on the panel were supposed to introduce ourselves. We were asked to limit our remarks to one minute. The audience knew from the conference brochure that I was an attorney and an author. Some of my proudest accomplishments were not listed. The audience didn't know that I made kick-ass play centers when Anna was in pre-school. I wanted to tell them about the castle I made with a working drawbridge, velvet capes for the kings and queens to match their crowns, and the fake fur covered thrones that were strategically placed in the grand ballroom. I wanted to tell them about the farm I made with a pulley to raise the hay bales into the loft of the barn, and the nests for the chickens complete with life-sized plastic eggs for the kids to gather. Some of the kids still talk about the spaceship that shimmered in its aluminum foil shell. The space craft was complete with a control panel display of levers to pull and buttons to push as the kids pretended to be astronauts blasting off to the moon. It would be hard to describe the pride I felt when I devised a working conveyor belt made with PVC pipe and black spandex fabric. It transported the 200 lbs. of gravel I placed in the cave made from brown butcher paper. It only took 14 days for my back to recover from the ten 20 lb. bags of gravel I carried into school during the creation of that amazing play center. Why would the audience at a Diversity Conference in San Antonio, Texas care about the fun I had watching the kids scoop those rocks onto the conveyor belt to transport the rubble out of the cave?

Maybe I would tell them about my skill making things out of cardboard boxes, using only a box cutter, and some duct tape. Wouldn't they be impressed knowing about the adorable Citizen-ship I made for the 4th grade play? If they knew about the blue and white paint-splattered waves I made for the front of the ship, and the gang-plank covered in wallpaper that looked like rustic old planks of wood, my audience should be impressed. Surely they would be surprised to learn that these creative feats were accomplished by a mother who had no training in art or stage craft. I could mention the spook houses I made in my dining room every Halloween for 6 years, laying refrigerator boxes end-to-end, creating a maze through which the kids in their spooky costumes would crawl. By the 6th year of the spook house the black lights I cleverly positioned made the rubber rats glow.

I thought about sharing my secrets for making smoking green witches brew for the beverage at the Halloween parties, the oozing eyeball cupcakes, and the brownies with creepy spiders crawling across the webs of powdered sugar. Perhaps I would explain how much fun I had creating a separate scrapbook for each of the girls on Katie's varsity basketball team filled with personalized pictures of their individualized contributions during the season.

Could I make the audience understand how much fun it was to see the sparkle in each 3rd grader's eyes as they found their art work displayed on the bulletin board I created in the main hall of the lower school? Would anyone in the audience care that I learned how to crochet blankets, in the appropriate school colors, for each of my kids as they headed off to college? Who would care that my kids covered-up each night in college surrounded with a blanket that reminded them of the softness of mom's caress. Maybe I will just tell them how I have expanded my culinary skills to experiment with new recipes from the internet since I am no longer limited to variations in sauces for chicken nuggets.

No. I don't have time to tell them about any of these things. They didn't come to the seminar to hear from a creative mother talk about what an incredible joy it had been to make things for my kids. They wanted to hear a woman who was a lawyer talk about how to have it all. It was my professional accolades that attracted people to the presentation, not my expertise at making things. They probably wouldn't understand why I was proud of feats for which nobody paid money, no prizes were awarded, and no recognition was received…other than from children. I'll just tell them about the things on my resume. If I told the audience that I've written two books, they might be impressed. If they knew that there were over one million books published in the United State in 2009, they might not be so impressed.[361] They might be interested to know that I've written for national media including the Huffington Post or that my personal blog has over 4,500,000 views. They'd probably be interested to know that my blog is political in nature and doesn't have anything to do with crafts, recipes, or child care. However, I don't get paid to write about politics, so that might not be very impressive. I won't mention that I have M.S., for fear that they will think I want them to feel sorry for me. I won't mention that I am happily married to my first husband of 30 years, for fear that they will think I don't represent real American women.

I won't tell the audience that this is the first time I've engaged in public speaking since I opted out of my job as an attorney 20 years ago. They might think that I forgot how to speak in public, even though I was a trial attorney, taught Business Law at the University of Oklahoma, and gave CLE lectures to hundreds of attorneys around the state. I won't tell them that this is a momentous day for me, because it marks the beginning of what I want to be when I grow up; an advocate for women. I wasn't getting paid to appear on the panel, and my travel expenses weren't even being reimbursed. I didn't expect any public accolades for my presentation at the conference. There was no promotion or new job title awaiting me if I did a good job. I derived no monetary reward from the organizers of the conference. In fact, it cost me $47.00 in gas for the round trip from Dallas to San Antonio. The hotel was nice, but it should have been for the $189.00 they charged me. I couldn't even expect that the conference would bring me fame, as the audience in my break out session was only about 75 people. Yet, speaking at this conference seemed like the right thing to do, just as quitting my job seemed like the right thing to do 20 years ago. If financial reward had been the sole motivator, I would never have quit my job to raise kids. I surely wouldn't be spending time and money now to speak at a conference that wasn't even going to buy me lunch.

As the other women on the panel arrive, I am curious about their backgrounds and life experiences. Two of us are white and two are African-American. Two are divorced with children, and two of us are married with children. One is a single mother with a young child but that mother shares custody with the ex-husband, who has now remarried. The other divorced mother had only recently divorced. Her kids were already grown. Two have young kids, and two of us have adult kids. Two are younger women in their thirties. I am one of the two older women. When I applied to be considered as a speaker at the conference, it hadn't occurred to me that I might be selected to appeal to the old-white-woman demographic.

The session was advertised as *Succeeding at Work & Life 24/7*. Obviously the panel of women would be focused on the daily challenges women face of trying to balance personal and professional life. The break out session was not called *Having it All*, but that was clearly the point of the session. As I met the other women on the panel, I realized that a lot of thought had gone into the selection of members for the panel. We represented a broad cross-section of women who are dealing with the complex issues of trying to have it all.

Before the session began I had an opportunity to visit with the young white woman seated next to me. Try as hard as I might, it was difficult for me to refrain from making any stereotypical judgments about this woman. She was wearing heels that were higher than the combined height of any two heels from any shoes I had ever worn. The bleach necessary to achieve that degree of blond, for that much hair, would be enough to sanitize an entire public restroom. Grey was the color of her dress, so maybe she thought it would convince people she was a professional? However, the dress was tight enough that the location of her naval was unmistakable. The dress was short enough, that the only thing not obvious, was the color of her bikini panties. The money she spent on breast augmentation was worth every penny, as most people wouldn't recognize her again if they saw only a head-shot. They would remember the gargantuan cantaloupes that occupied the top half of her dress.

I tried to give her the benefit of the doubt. Was I a bad person for thinking that those monster breasts, which seemed unusually firm and stiff, were man-made? Who is to say that God-given breasts are any better than those purchased from Naturelle? Haven't I always advocated the importance of women being willing to take responsibility to find ways to achieve what they want? But it wasn't only the girth and rigidity of her breasts that bothered me. The number and size of the rings and bangles on her hands and wrists conveyed in an instant that this woman had different priorities than I. My only ring was a wedding ring. My only watch was a white plastic Baby-G shock that I bought at Wal-Mart. I was wearing pants instead of a short skirt. My jacket covered my breasts, which were the clementines God gave me.

Worried that I was being too quick to judge, I tried to convince myself not to fall into the trap of stereotyping this young woman. However, when she spoke to me, it became clear that my initial impression was correct. Without prompting or warning, Ms. Mammary introduced herself. Immediately after giving me her name, she announced: "I don't make things." What the hell was she talking about? We were not about to give the audience a lesson in the art of decoupage, knitting, scrapbooking, jewelry making, or weaving. Is she explaining to me that she is not an assembly line worker? Is she worried that I am under some misconception that she is an artist? Maybe she doesn't plan to have any more children and she wanted me to be clear that she had no intention of making any more babies. What was it about my appearance that made her feel compelled to warn me that she didn't make things? I didn't have paint under my fingernails. I didn't have a crochet hook resting over my ear. I wasn't wearing an apron. If she had seen my resume in the conference brochure, it only listed professional accomplishments. She wouldn't be able to tell that one of my favorite things to do was making Gak.

Perhaps my delay in responding to Ms. Mammary's remark caused her to be uncomfortable. In response to my silence, she explained that her ex-husband's new wife makes things. Ms. Mammary wanted to make sure that I was under no illusion that she did, or had ever, made things. This woman, with the G Cup size breasts, explained that her daughter makes things with her step-mother. Ms. Mammary was clear that she doesn't waste her time doing anything as trivial as making things. The contempt in her voice was unmistakable. It was clear that she felt a need to disparage any woman who might dare suggest that there was any merit in making things. In the short span of two minutes, Ms. Mammary had conveyed her total disrespect for me because I, like the second wife of her ex-husband, enjoyed making things. What was my problem? Didn't I realize that this woman's approval was of no significance to me? I would probably never see her again. Her respect for me, or a lack thereof, should have been inconsequential to me. Perhaps she couldn't help herself. Maybe I resembled the woman who made things with her daughter? Perhaps that woman also wore pants instead of skin tight dresses? Maybe Ms. Mammary could tell that I hate shopping? Maybe when Ms. Mammary isn't making things, she is shopping?

Ms. Mammary and I were different and the same. We both had careers, and children. We were both passionate about helping women balance careers and home life. She had not given-up her career as I had. She only had one child and I had three. I was still married. She was not. I enjoyed the challenge of making things, she did not. She had large breasts. I did not. She looked hot in her tight fitting dress. I did not.

What was the lesson of this encounter? Ms. Mammary had a problem with women like me who make things. I became defensive as a result of her disparagement of my choice to make things. But my reaction to her began before she commented about making things. I had a problem with her false façade. It was not the size of her breasts that bothered me. It was the fact that while advertising herself as a business professional, her appearance suggested that if she was a professional it was the kind that worked at night. Instead of getting a graduate degree, she got a boob-job. Instead of dressing for success in a board room, she was dressing for success in the bedroom, like a woman I knew at the law firm where I was a summer clerk. Ms. Mammary was like the contestants in the Miss America pageants, who expected men to evaluate her based upon her appearance, and little else. She wasn't drinking shots of liquor like the woman I met on my first date with Prince Charming. However, her jewelry and the size of her breasts reminded me of the woman who covered her sea otters with only a flimsy halter top. Ms. Mammary was critical of me because she perceived that I was not a professional. She thought I wasn't smart enough to find a plastic surgeon to enhance my appearance. I was a frumpy old woman, who made things. I was critical of her because she sought men's approval and acceptance by use of her body, instead of her brain.

Our problems lacked a name. We didn't talk about our problems with each other. Neither of us even acknowledged that there were any problems. Both of us were at the conference, proclaiming our mastery of having it all. Both of us were polite and participated together as fellow panel members, trying to help our audience solve the problems of finding a balance between personal and professional life.

My reaction to Ms. Mammary is a perfect example of the reason that women today are so conflicted about the choices we make to balance professional and personal success. Stay-at-home mothers criticize professional mothers for not doing enough for their children. Professional mothers criticize stay at home mothers for not being smart enough to do anything other than making things. Mothers criticize women who choose not to have children, suggesting that they are too self-centered and ambitious. Women like Ms. Mammary, tend to be judgmental about women like myself, who have no fashion sense, and don't seem to care. I tend to be judgmental about women like Ms. Mammary, who seem more interested in appealing to a man's sexual desires, rather than his intellect. We are all guilty of failing to respect and honor the choices of other women. It was alright that Ms. Mammary prefers shopping instead of making things. It was alright that I prefer to make things. Ms. Mammary felt compelled to disparage women like myself who like to make things. That was her way of being critical of stay-at-home mothers, without actually saying it. By attacking the notion of making things, Ms. Mammary was suggesting that making things was not as important or as worthwhile, as the work she did in her job. Her attack was even more illuminative because it was an indirect attack on the step-mother for spending time with Ms. Mammary's child. That was time that Ms. Mammary wasn't spending with her child because she was busy working at her profession.

Ms. Mammary represented a woman who set her priorities on physical appearance and attractiveness to men. She did not appear to me to be a woman dedicated to her career or to her children. If her resume had included some award from the Little Miss Sunshine pageant, I wouldn't have been surprised. What bothered me was her priorities, and what I anticipated would be her reaction to mine. I was right. She went out of her way to disparage women who make things and to do so with their children. Surely if I was appearing at this conference, proclaiming the importance of every woman making the choices that best suit her unique circumstances, I should be more accepting and less judgmental about Ms. Mammary.

Our problems didn't have names. We weren't talking about them. We didn't even act like we had any problems, so we surely didn't have a solution. We parted ways appearing to be friendly acquaintances. In truth we both felt threatened and inadequate. My breasts weren't as big as hers, so I obviously wasn't as attractive to men, as she was. I made things so I was obviously a better mother than she was. She was dressed provocatively and I was dressed professionally.

Fifty years ago Betty Friedan wrote:

> "Men are not the enemy, but the fellow victims. The real enemy is women's denigration of themselves."[362]

In spite of many advances in women's education and professional achievements, we are still actively involved in denigrating each other. This is the only aspect of feminism in which women have failed to evolve. Perhaps the problem is that we have different standards, against which we evaluate performance. The standards fall into three categories. A mother has one set of standards. A professional has another set. A mother who is a professional has a third set. All three relate to choices women make about job, education, and children.

The second set of standards relates to a woman's appearance and demeanor which is geared toward sexual appeal to men. A woman who has attempted to succeed professionally, by exploiting her sexuality, is the second way to categorize women. Women disagree about the role of women as mothers and professionals. Women also disagree about the most effective way to appeal to men sexually. Some women believe the way to a man's heart is through larger breasts and more jewelry. Other women feel that it is degrading to women to flaunt the size of the sea otters under a halter top. Most women feel vulnerable about the set of standards we have chosen. We are susceptible to, and become defensive about, mastery of our own set of standards. I shouldn't have felt so defensive about enjoyment of making things with my children. Ms. Mammary shouldn't have felt defensive about that fact that she doesn't. I shouldn't have reacted to her style of dress or her goal to make herself as attractive to men as humanly possible. I have a husband, and she didn't.

If we are to evolve to conquer the third wave of feminism we MUST stop being defensive about the standards to which we hold ourselves accountable. If Ariel became Eric's wife because of her red hot hair and monstrous breasts, then we should realize that both Ariel and Eric value sexual appeal in a woman, and little else. If Mary Richards (Mary Tyler Moore) chose to be single, without children, and pursue a professional career, we should respect her choice. Her professional accomplishments in no way minimize the importance of Carol Brady (Florence Henderson) in being a mother to six kids in the Brady family. If Murphy Brown chose to be a single mother, and a professional, she had a completely different set of standards and challenges that should never be compared to those of Carol Brady or Mary Richards. The rewards for Ariel, Mary, Carol, and Murphy were different. The standards by which they evaluated their success were different. The contributions of each to society were important. Instead of disparaging the success of each other, these women should be celebrating the accomplishments of women in every field and in every aspect of our society.

What a powerful force for good in society we could be if we supported each other. If we embrace the accomplishments of other women, even if different than our own, and especially if different than our own, then we enhance the respect of women. Men will only respect women, after women begin to respect other women.

"You have brains in your head.
You have feet in your shoes.
You can steer yourself
any direction you choose.

You're on your own, and
you know what you know.
And YOU are the one
who'll decide where to go...

So be sure when you step,
Step with care and great tact.
And remember that life's
A Great Balancing Act.

And will you succeed?
Yes! You will,
Indeed 98 ¾ percent
guaranteed."

-Dr. Seuss, Oh, the Places You'll Go![363]

CHAPTER XIII: SEARCHING FOR HAPPILY EVER AFTER

Perhaps we are asking the wrong question! Instead of asking how to have it all, maybe we should be asking how to live happily ever after? If having it all causes us to die young, be depressed, or spend our lives being resentful of the people who are the most important in our life, then maybe it's time to re-evaluate. Maybe we missed the point? If we have obedient children, a loving committed husband, a booming career, a beautiful home, make a lot of money, make the costume for our child's part in the school play, make the scenery for that play, organize the sports teams, do all the cooking, cleaning, laundry, pay the bills, meet the repairman, buy the birthday presents, schedule all the doctor appointments, transport the kids to all their activities, plan all the vacations, and exercise five days a week, we might have it all. The problem is that the all wouldn't include sleep. We'd die young. We'd end up divorced. We'd lose custody. When we saw our children we'd be so stressed that we'd communicate only resentment and anger. Instead of the old-folks home, our grandchildren would have to visit us at the mental institution.

If Snow White's mother had encouraged her to get an education, she might have gone to college, majored in geology, and employed the dwarves in her diamond business. If her mother had taught her to be wary of strangers who offered her food, Snow White would never have had to wait in bed for a strange man to rescue her. What if Sleeping Beauty's mother had encouraged her to get a degree in engineering and develop a more efficient way of making yarn? Spinning wheels would have been unnecessary. Sleeping Beauty would be the "Rich, Powerful, Alert Beauty." If Cinderella's mother had promoted a sense of independence in her daughter, Cinderella wouldn't be waiting around for a handsome prince to stop by with the latest in designer footwear. By the time the Prince found his way to Cinderella's castle she might have already grown her house-cleaning business into a Fortune 500 franchise. The Prince, a shoe salesman, would be lucky to get an audience with Cinderella, the CEO of Cinderella's Castle Cleaning Cache. What if Ariel had gotten a degree in Marine Biology? She could have become a professor at the college where Erik attended school. Ariel and Erik might have lived happily ever after, but it would be Ariel supporting Erik, while he finished his education.

Beauty could have supported the Beast from profits from her magic mirror and glass company. The Beast might have had a hard time finding a job due to fear that his gargantuan size might frighten away customers. Even the most politically correct of employers, would not want her customers to run away in fear of the Beast.

Mulan could have hired full-time help to care for her ailing father with the profits from Mulan's Mixed Martial Arts Studios.

Each of the heroines of the Disney movies needed a mother to inspire her to gain an education. Learning to be self-sufficient, each princess could have found her prince, without becoming dependent. Instead of sleeping, the princesses would be awake. Instead of defining their lives by the men they married, they would be enriching an already rich and rewarding life. Instead of defining success by marrying a prince, they would re-define success by being both an independent professional, and the wife of a man they loved. If they chose to have children, each prince might have to assist in raising and caring for the royal babies. If the prince and his bride decided that the better path was for one of them to stay at home and the other to run the kingdom, they could each focus their energy on a single endeavor instead of trying to balance two simultaneously. Either way it would be the choice of the Prince and the Princess, depending on their unique circumstances.

At the time my Prince started his own business, nobody thought of him as opting out of his career as an attorney. He gave up a high paying job and the security of a big firm practice to follow his dream. He did it in part because Cinderella could support him. When Cinderella opted out of her career as an attorney to care for the royal children, she too was following her dream and did it in part because the Prince could support her. Now the royal children have moved into their own kingdoms in search of their life partners. Cinderella hasn't opted out of her job as a mother. She's still a mother, but now she writes books. Even when she becomes a grandmother she will still be a mother. At the time of leaving the practice of law there was no grand scheme or plan to become an author, a blogger, or advocate for women's rights. It was simply the natural progression of Cinderella's evaluation of circumstances at the time and making choices that suited her situation.

When I left the practice of nursing, other nurses were disappointed that I was giving up my commitment to nursing. In fact I was more effective as an attorney elevating the perception of nurses, than when I was a practicing nurse. When I left the practice of law, other women felt betrayed and abandoned because of my departure. However, it is precisely because I moved on that I can today be an advocate for both mothers and professional women. It was that decision that empowered me to have it all. As a mother and a professional, I am a stronger advocate for all women. Opting out bestowed upon me strength that was unimaginable at the time. I didn't opt out so that one day I could write a book. It was simply the next step in my journey.

To conquer the third wave of feminism every woman must ask "What is my happily ever after?" Implicit in this question is the notion that every woman's circumstances are unique to her. The question "What is my happily ever after?" can only be answered by each individual woman, after considering all of the unique factors that impact her life. For example, a woman can determine what will be the most fulfilling course for her life after she considers:

1. What is the potential for higher education?

2. Does she have the ability to pay for higher education or to obtain scholarships?

3. How many children she has or wants, the age at which she begins trying to have children, and will she have difficulty getting pregnant?

4. Is she married? Does she want to be? Does she think she will be? Will her spouse be male or female?

5. Does her spouse earn sufficient income to support her and any children?

6. Does the woman earn enough money to support the family?

7. How much help can the woman realistically expect from the spouse with regard to child care and domestic chores?

8. Are there any elderly parents that must receive care at home, or are there any parents available and willing to assist in child care?

9. Given the type of job or profession of the woman, are the demands of her profession such that it would be impossible to work part-time?

10. Given the type of job or profession of the woman, does she have the ability to work from home?

11. Does the woman have any family members who would be available and interested in child care?

12. Does the woman have any family or other friends who might be available to help with unanticipated illness or emergency needs of her children?

13. Do any of the children have special needs, or require a greater amount of time than typical?

14. How much sleep do you need to feel rested and refreshed?

15. Are any of the children old enough to drive? Do they have a car?

16. How much time do you want to spend with the children? How much time do you perceive is necessary to spend with your children?

17. What would the expected income of the woman be, as compared to the cost of child care?

18. What is the level of stress associated with your job?

19. How flexible and supportive is your employer?

20. What are the ages of your children at the time you return to work?

21. What is the maternity policy of the company for whom you work?

22. What are the expectations you place on yourself for success at work, and at home?

23. Is public recognition of your success important?

24. Are you willing to fill a supportive role? Is it important to you to be in charge?

25. How would your spouse answer each of the above questions?

The answers to these questions will improve your ability to find your "happily ever after." Over time the answers to these questions may change, so it may be time to reevaluate. To answer these questions, and formulate a plan to achieve success, each woman must adapt, discard inaccurate perceptions, accept responsibility for her own happiness, be willing to make choices, gain an understanding of the masculine mystique, never lose her sense of humor, and stop disparaging other women for making choices different than her own. The reason women have the ability to make the choices that best suit their lives is because feminism has evolved. Even though evolution has occurred, and improvements have been made, we're not done yet.

If you are searching for your happily ever after, remember:

✓ Never allow another person to determine success for you. You will never be satisfied if you try to satisfy someone else's definition of success.

✓ Most women will never dominate a man physically. We can compete on equal footing, or even win, if the weapon of choice is wit or intelligence.

✓ Prince Charming might not really be a prince. No man is perfect, even though we may expect him to be. Happiness in a relationship with any partner is ultimately determined by the partner's character, love, and devotion to you. All the rest is secondary. Demand character. Overlook the small stuff.

✓ Identify the goals that are truly important to you and strive to achieve them. Lean in. If your spouse or partner has goals that are annoying, but don't interfere with yours, try to be tolerant.

- ✓ Be willing to modify your goals as circumstances in your life change. Frustration, resentment, and anger are predictable responses when you fail to adapt. They are also deadly to any relationship.

- ✓ Share your success with your spouse, and allow your spouse to share his with you. Success for the team means victory for you but only if you are a member of the team.

- ✓ Realize that you can satisfy many different goals at different times, when the circumstances are right. Even if you spend half of your life getting an education and raising children, the other half remains for you to mold to fit your goals and ambitions at that time, given your new circumstances.

- ✓ The more you take on professionally, at the same time you are attempting to have a family, the more your spouse needs to share in all that you do personally.

- ✓ Professional achievement can be delayed, postponed, or drawn out. Children cannot. If we delay too long, our bodies may not allow pregnancy as an option. If we have children but delay providing the attention they need, when they need it, it will likely be hard to provide it latter. On average, 25% of your life will be devoted to raising children, so don't underestimate the importance of the time you have with them. Time with children is limited. There may be time later in life to pursue other dreams, but the dream of children can't be recaptured. If you are missing your kids, they are likely missing you too. Listen to your heart.

- ✓ Be grateful to a spouse who assists in making a career possible by sharing responsibility for children and household chores. If a spouse isn't willing to help with personal responsibilities, domestic tasks, and child rearing, hopefully you knew that before you married the prince. Hopefully you will trade resentment and anger for an understanding that it is your goal to provide a rich environment in which your children might thrive. There will still be many years ahead to achieve greatness in your profession, but you can never get back those formative years of your children. If your income is essential for the family then you and your children will appreciate and respect that contribution. You may desire more time with your kids, but you won't wonder if you made the right decision to go to work.

- ✓ Don't empower your spouse to take advantage of you. How you spend the time you have is within your control, so you have to have the courage to make the choice that will bring you happiness.

- ✓ Money is not the thermometer of success, but only a barometer. A hug from mom, when the dark clouds envelop the sky is invaluable to the child and to mom. A paycheck lasts for about a month, but a loving relationship can last for an eternity.

- ✓ Sometimes men can be our best advocates. Be willing to accept their help when offered and make them a soldier in your war for happiness.

- ✓ Don't be the Little Red Hen and try to do everything yourself. Take responsibility to either let others have it all with you, or modify your definition of all. Otherwise you may be an old, fat, lonely hen, eating your delicious bread all by yourself.

- ✓ Find something to laugh about every day.

- ✓ You are never too old to change your life and find success.

- ✓ We all die. Modern science has extended our life expectancy. Death, however, is inevitable. The dilemma is what we do with the time we have. Formulate your own definition of success. Only then can you have it all.

- ✓ Find your bliss.

- ✓ Anything worth doing is worth doing well. Participate.

- ✓ The only bad choice is not to make a choice.

- ✓ Be compassionate and warm hearted.

- ✓ Nourish your friends.

- ✓ Failure is an inevitable part of life. The secret to success is how you deal with failure.

- ✓ If you don't get enough sleep, you might fall asleep and fail to appreciate that you had it all.

- ✓ Stop wishing that you could have it all. Instead search for your happily ever after.

- ✓ Be strategic about the timing of having children but be aware that the longer you delay having a family the greater the likelihood that you will have difficulty getting pregnant. If you do get pregnant as an older mother, the risk of health problems for you and the baby increase dramatically. Be aware that postponing the decision to have children may eliminate that possibility or require a much greater commitment of time due to physical problems that may arise.

✓ Don't disparage other women for making choices different than your own.

✓ Be willing to give, and take credit for, an assist.

✓ Don't wait till you are losing it all to realize that you can't have it all at the same time.

✓ Realize that you never lose the experiences of the past. They will always be a part of who you are. By choosing to stop spending time doing one thing, you are necessarily making more time to do something that you enjoy more.

There is a fine line we must walk between wanting more, and being happy with what we have. Ambition is great if you are willing and able to devote 110% of your time, effort, and energy to your profession. If your bliss is limited to your career, then more money, more promotions, and more responsibility may bring you satisfaction and a sense of accomplishment. If your bliss is staying at home with your children, then designing a fabulous birthday cake or building a castle with a working draw bridge, may bring you great pride and happiness. However, if your bliss is a combination of personal and professional success, your happily ever after may mean that you are satisfied to be an attorney with a major law firm, but not a senior partner. You may be happy to attend your child's school play, even though you bought her costume but didn't have time to help build the scenery.

If you find, as I did, that success and happiness could only be achieved through focusing on one aspect of your life at a time, then you may follow a different path. You may opt to work to become a Senior Partner first, and a scenery designer for the school play later. Because we are unable to find more than 24 hours in a day, it is imperative that we find a balance that suits our circumstances, and those of our spouse and children. The all that we achieve is based upon our success perfecting the skills of whichever job or jobs we undertake, or moderating the skills necessary to accomplish both at the same time.

Women today have a life expectancy of 81 years.[364] If we raise children for 20 years of our lives, chances are there will be 61 other years to experience the rest of "all."

We are riding the third-wave of feminism. Women have progressed in the professional world so far that we now have choices. We can have it all, but we have to choose how and when to have it. We can be the CEO, the President, an Olympic Athlete, or a Senior Partner. We can create play centers, build spook houses, sew Halloween costumes, organize sports teams, attend every school event for each of our children, schedule and attend visits of each child with the orthodontist, the eye doctor, the pediatrician, and the speech therapist. But, it's hard to find time to visit the pediatric dentist the same day as closing argument in the $50 Million dollar case you are handling as a Senior Partner. How can we justify spending 10 hours making the perfect Elvis costume if the company retreat is next weekend and we have responsibility for orchestrating that critical weekend? If our spouse has just been laid off, our income may be more important than ever. If our spouse is Prince Charming and makes plenty of money, but has little or no time for domestic chores, then those circumstances may dictate a different choice.

Women of today are lucky. No longer do we have to stay at home and cook and clean if we might be better suited to running a multi-million dollar company or deciding a case before the U.S. Supreme Court. When our mothers read us the *Little Engine That Could* we heard the words "I think I can," and we believed! We learned that we can. However try as hard as we might, as creative as women may be, we have not invented a way to expand the number of hours in a day. Even the Little Engine had to rest at night from his hard journey up the hill.

We can choose to have a family, or not. We can choose to do both at the same time. But if that is our choice, we must do each in moderation. Women who are CEO's, but opted not to have children are highly respected and admired. Those women found their bliss in their professions. Women who are stay-at-home mothers have a support group of other mothers who have also opted out of their professions in order to dedicate themselves to raising the next generation of inhabitants of this earth. Both are important contributions to women, and to society.

The third wave of the women's movement has arrived. It is the strongest, most powerful, and most gratifying wave of the three. It built momentum as a result of the first and second waves. As women fought for the right to vote, we earned the right to influence public policy. Women make up the majority of the electorate, and we vote in higher percentages than our male counterparts. As women mastered the second wave, we earned the right to be treated as equal to our male counterparts in business and in professions. We have established ourselves as powerful executives and accomplished professional women. Now that we have earned respect, we no longer feel compelled to justify our choices. As we master the third wave, we realize that we have choices in our professional and personal lives. All are good choices. Whether our choice is to stay at home to raise the next generation of Americans, or to run companies employing the next generation of Americans, we have earned that choice. We must now have the courage to make the right choice for ourselves if we are to live happily ever after.

Women didn't wait for men to give us the right to vote; we fought for it. We didn't wait to be promoted in our professional lives; we fought for it. Now, as we struggle to master the third wave of feminism, we must be brave enough to make the right choices for ourselves and our families. We must not fight among ourselves, trying to prove that one choice is better than another. Women will learn to surf the third wave of feminism only by working together and respecting each woman as she arrives at shore, in her own way, in her own time, using her own technique. The secret to *having it all* is to determine what is your bliss, to have the courage to make the choices that will optimize your chance of success, and to be willing to adapt, making more changes if the result doesn't make you happy. Once we identify what happiness is, and how to achieve it, we will *have it all*. We will become role models for the men we love, and for the next generation of women. Only then can we find our **happily ever after**.[iii]

Here's to Good Women,
May We Know Them,
May We Be Them,
May We Raise Them.

-Unknown

[iii] https://www.youtube.com/watch?v=fia4HY9pWuo

EPILOGUE

The Compass

Whatever you give a woman, she will make greater.

If you give her sperm, she'll give you a child.

If you give her a house, she'll create a home.

If you give her groceries, she'll cook a meal.

If you give her a smile, she'll give you her heart.

If you give her a sheet, she'll make a costume.

If you give her yarn, she'll crochet a blanket.

If you give her a paintbrush, she'll create a masterpiece.

If you give her a photo, she'll give you a scrapbook.

If you give her a map, she'll show you the way.

If you give her a camera, she'll open your eyes.

If you give her a suitcase, she'll take you on vacation.

If you give her a team, she'll make an assist.

If you give her a gavel, she'll make fair decisions.

If you give her your tax return, she'll get you a refund.

If you give her a computer, she'll make you a "friend."

If you give her a cell phone, she'll call you on your birthday.

If you give her your cold, she'll make you soup.

If you give her a small company, she'll make it larger.

If you give her a failing business, she'll make it profitable.

If you give her an education, she'll become a teacher.

If you allow her to fight, she'll become a hero.

If you teach her to fly, she'll take you to the moon.

If you share your tears, she'll give you a hug.

If you give her respect, she'll give you her loyalty.

If you have an injury, she'll heal your wound.

If you have a disease, she'll find a cure.

If you get old, she'll make you feel young.

If you give her a trumpet, she'll give you music.

If you give her a challenge, she'll rise to the occasion.

If you give her a job, she'll pay for her salary.

If you give her a raise, she'll double her effort.

If you give her maternity leave, she'll help you hire more women.

If you give her an illness, she'll show you courage.

If you learn you are dying, she'll give you a reason to live.

If you give her a conflict, she'll facilitate a compromise.

If you give her a smile, she'll make you laugh.

If you give her a book, she'll share its wisdom.

If you give her advice, she'll take it to heart.

If you give her a chance, she'll make you proud.

If she finds success, she'll share her secret.

If you give her hope, she'll make others believe.

If you give her a compass, she'll show you the way.

If you give her a surfboard, she'll master the waves.

If you teach her about evolution, she'll adapt and survive.

Malia Litman

CITATIONS

1.   Sanderson, Brandon. *Words of Radiance*. Tor Books; First Edition edition, 2014. Print.

2.   Sandberg, Sheryl. *Lean In: Women, Work, and the Will to Lead*. New York: Knopf; 1 edition, 2013. Print.

3.   *Sabrina*. Dir. Sydney Pollack. Perf. Harrison Ford, Julia Ormond. Paramount, 1995. DVD.

4.   Gandi, Mahatma. "Mahatma Gandi Quotes." n.d. *Brainy Quote*. Web. 25 October 2013. <http://www.brainyquote.com/quotes/quotes/m/mahatmagan107894.html>

5.   "Women in the Professional Workforce." August 2013. *Department for Professional Employees, AFL-CIO*. Web. 30 July 2014. <http://dpeaflcio.org/professionals/professionals-in-the-workplace/women-in-the-professional-and-technical-labor-force/>

6.   Huffington, Christina. "Women Stress More Than Men In The Workplace." 13 March 2013. *Huff Post: Women*. Web. 30 July 2014. <http://www.huffingtonpost.com/2013/03/05/stress-at-work_n_2812035.html>

7.   Yapp, Robin. "Working women 'still do housework'." n.d. *Daily Mail*. Web. 30 July 2014. <http://www.dailymail.co.uk/news/article-206381/Working-women-housework.html>

8.   "Women's Safety and Health Issues at Work." 19 June 2013. *Centers for Disease Control and Prevention*. Web. 30 July 2014. <http://www.cdc.gov/niosh/topics/women/>

9.   Huffington, Christina. "Women Stress More Than Men In The Workplace." 13 March 2013. *Huff Post: Women*. Web. 30 July 2014. <http://www.huffingtonpost.com/2013/03/05/stress-at-work_n_2812035.html>

10. Campbell, Denis. "High stress in middle age may increase women's risk of dementia." 30 September 2013. *The Guardian*. Web. 30 July 2014. <http://www.theguardian.com/society/2013/sep/30/stress-middle-age-women-dementia>

11. NoCamels Team. "Let's Relax: Researchers Show Stress Leads To Increase In Autoimmune Diseases." 16 May 2013. *NoCamels. Israeli Innovation News*. Web. 30 July 2014. <http://nocamels.com/2013/05/lets-

relax-researchers-show-stress-leads-to-increase-in-autoimmune-
diseases/>

12. WebMD Medical Reference. "Heart Disease and Stress: What's the Link?" n.d. *WebMD.* Web. 30 July 2014. <http://www.webmd.com/heart-disease/guide/stress-heart-disease-risk>

13. Division for Heart Disease and Stroke Prevention. "Women and Heart Disease Fact Sheet." 22 July 2014. *Center for Disease Control and Prevention.* Web. 30 July 2014. <http://www.cdc.gov/dhdsp/data_statistics/fact_sheets/fs_women_heart.htm>

14. Klein, Sarah. "Heart Disease: 17 Celebrities With Heart Problems." 7 February 2012. *HuffPost Healthy Living.* Web. 30 July 2014. <http://www.huffingtonpost.com/2012/02/06/heart-disease-celebrities_n_1258409.html>

15. "How Does Heart Disease Affect Women?" 21 April 2014. *NIH: National Heart, Lung, and Blood Institute.* Web. 30 July 2014. <http://www.nhlbi.nih.gov/health/health-topics/topics/hdw>

16. Mosca, L., Benjamin, E.J., Berra, K., et al. "Effectiveness-Based Guidelines for the Prevention of Cardiovascular Disease in Women - 2011 Update: a guideline from the American Heart Association." *Circulation* (2011): 123: 1243-262. Web. <http://circ.ahajournals.org/content/123/11/1243.full>

17. Melnick, Meredith. "Job Equality: Stressful Work Raises Women's Risk of Heart Disease Too." 15 November 2010. *Time.* Web. 30 July 2014. <http://healthland.time.com/2010/11/15/job-equality-stressful-work-raises-womens-risk-of-heart-disease-too/>

18. "Stress." 2015. *World Heart Federation.* Web. 28 March 2015. <http://www.world-heart-federation.org/cardiovascular-health/cardiovascular-disease-risk-factors/stress/>

19. Garrett, Danielle. "Declining Life Expectancies Show Why Women's Health Should be a Priority." 22 June 2011. *National Women's Law Center.* Web. 30 July 2014. <http://www.nwlc.org/our-blog/declining-life-expectancies-show-why-womens-health-should-be-priority>

20. Greenfield, Shelly F., et al. "Substance Abuse in Women." *The Psychiatric Clinics of North America* 33.2 (2010): 339-355. Web. 29 July 2014. <http://www.ncbi.nlm.nih.gov/pmc/articles/PMC3124962/>

21. "Substance Abuse." 2014. *Heathy People: 2020 Topics & Objectives.* Web. 30 July 2014. <https://www.healthypeople.gov/2020/topics-objectives/topic/substance-abuse>

22. "Women's Health in Dangerous Decline." 2013. *My Healing Kitchen.* Ed. Jim Healthy. Web. 29 July 2014. <http://myhealingkitchen.com/featured-articles/womens-health-in-dangerous-decline/>

23. Levine, Bruce. "Why the Rise of Mental Illness? Pathologizing Normal, Adverse Drug Effects, and a Peculiar Rebellion." 31 July 2013. *Mad in America.* Web. 30 July 2014. <http://www.madinamerica.com/2013/07/why-the-dramatic-rise-of-mental-illness-diseasing-normal-behaviors-drug-adverse-effects-and-a-peculiar-rebellion/>

24. "Women and Depression: Fact Sheet." October 2009. *The National Alliamce on Mental Illness.* Web. 28 July 2014. <http://www.nami.org/Content/NavigationMenu/Mental_Illnesses/Women_and_Depression/womenanddepression.pdf>

25. "Incarcerated Women: Fact Sheet." September 2012. *The Sentencing Project.* Web. 25 July 2013. <http://www.sentencingproject.org/doc/publications/cc_incarcerated_women_factsheet_sep24sp.pdf>

26. "Women Arrested for Drunk Driving Increases While Men Take More Care." 6 January 2010. *Elements Behavioral Health.* Web. 29 July 2014. <http://www.elementsbehavioralhealth.com/addiction-and-the-law/women-arrested-for-drunk-driving-increases-while-men-take-more-care/>

27. Smith, Jay Scott. "Why are more women arrested for drunk driving? Number increases nearly 20 percent since 2003." 27 April 2014. *MLive.* Web. 28 March 2015. <http://www.mlive.com/lansing-news/index.ssf/2014/04/womens_drunk_driving_arrests_h.html>

28. Innes, Emma. "Women DO need more sleep than men: Multi-tasking means their brains take longer to recover." 24 December 2013. *Daily Mail.* Web. 30 July 2014 <http://www.dailymail.co.uk/health/article-2528920/Women-DO-need-sleep-men-Multi-tasking-means-brains-longer-recover.html>

29. Innes, Emma. "Women DO need more sleep than men: Multi-tasking means their brains take longer to recover." 24 December 2013. *Daily Mail.* Web. 30 July 2014 <http://www.dailymail.co.uk/health/article-2528920/Women-DO-need-sleep-men-Multi-tasking-means-brains-longer-recover.html>

30. WebMD Medical Reference. "Women's Health: How Sleep Loss Affects Women More Than Men." n.d. *WebMD*. Web. 30 July 2014. <http://www.webmd.com/women/features/how-sleep-loss-affects-women-more-than-men>

31. "5 Other Disastrous Accidents Related To Sleep Deprivation." 3 December 2013. *Huff Post: Healthy Living*. Web. 30 July 2014. <http://www.huffingtonpost.com/2013/12/03/sleep-deprivation-accidents-disasters_n_4380349.html>

32. Belkin, Lisa. "More Fathers Are Getting Custody in Divorce." 17 November 2009. *The New York Times*. Web. 27 October 2013. <http://parenting.blogs.nytimes.com/2009/11/17/more-fathers-getting-custody-in-divorce/?_r=0>

33. Grall, Timothy. "Custodial Mothers and Fathers and Their Child Support: 2009." December 2011. *Census.gov*. Web. 27 October 2013. <http://www.census.gov/prod/2011pubs/p60-240.pdf>

34. "Betty Friedan." 2015. *Women on 20s*. Web. 28 March 2015. <http://www.womenon20s.org/betty_friedan>

35. Pogrebin, Letty Cottin. "Women's Rights in the Workplace Blog." 11 September 2013. *Women's Rights in the Workplace Advocacy*. Web. 21 February 2012. <http://www.womensrightsny.com/blog/2013/09/11/when-men-are-oppressed-its-a-tragedy>

36. "The Best Hitters inBaseball History." 2015. *Ranker*. Web. 25 February 2013. <http://www.ranker.com/crowdranked-list/best-hitters-in-baseball-history?page=2>

37. "Cinderella." 22 February 1965. *IMDB*. Web. 11 October 2013. <http://www.imdb.com/title/tt0057950/>

38. Trimarchi, Maria. "Why do feet stink?" 29 January 2000. *HowStuffWorks.com*. Web. 4 October 2013. <http://health.howstuffworks.com/skin-care/information/anatomy/question5142.htm>

39. "Imitation is the sincerest form of flattery." n.d. *The Phrase Finder*. Web. 4 October 2013. <http://www.phrases.org.uk/meanings/imitation-is-the-sincerest-form-of-flattery.html>

40. "Cognitive Development Domain." 27 March 2014. *California Department of Education*. Web. 9 October 2014. <http://www.cde.ca.gov/sp/cd/re/itf09cogdev.asp>

41. Ellwood, Charles A. "The Theory of Imitation in Social Psychology." *American Journal of Sociology* 6.6 (1901): 721-741. Web. 11 October 2013. <http://www.jstor.org/stable/2762020?seq=1#page_scan_tab_contents>

42. Bandura, A., Ross, D., Ross, S. "Transmission of aggression through imitation of aggressive models." 1961. *Holah.co.uk Psychology*. Web. 7 October 2013. <http://www.holah.karoo.net/bandurastudy.htm>

43. Kantra, Dr. David. "'I Want To Be Like You': The Importance of Imitation." 3 April 2010. *PsychDigest*. Web. 7 October 2013. <http://psychdigest.com/i-want-to-be-like-you-the-importance-of-imitation/>

44. "Enjoli - Classic 80's Commercial." 1982. *YouTube*. Web Video. 26 June 2014. <https://www.youtube.com/watch?v=_Q0P94wyBYk&feature=kp>

45. "Nielsen Estimates 115.6 Million TV Homes in the U.S., Up 1.2%." 7 May 2013. *nielsen: Newswire*. Web. 10 October 2013. <http://www.nielsen.com/us/en/insights/news/2013/nielsen-estimates-115-6-million-tv-homes-in-the-u-s---up-1-2-.html>

46. Boyse RN, Kyla. "Television and Children." August 2010. *University of Michigan Health System: Your Child Development & Behavior Resources*. Web. 10 October 2013. <http://www.med.umich.edu/yourchild/topics/tv.htm>

47. Stromberg, Peter G. "Sex, Drugs, and Boredom." 8 November 2009. *Psychology Today*. Web. 10 October 2013. <https://www.psychologytoday.com/blog/sex-drugs-and-boredom>

48. Crupi, Anthony. "The 10 Most Powerful Women in Television." 16 May 2011. *Adweek*. Web. 11 October 2013. <http://www.adweek.com/news/television/10-most-powerful-women-television-131635>

49. Investigation Discovery. "Women Warriors: 27 Females Kicking Ass On TV." 21 August 2013. *Huffington Post*. Web. 11 October 2013. <http://www.huffingtonpost.com/2013/08/21/discovery-women-warriors-27-females_n_3645791.html>

50. Warner, Judith. "The Women's Leadership Gap." 7 March 2014. *Center for American Progress*. Web. 28 March 2015. <https://www.americanprogress.org/issues/women/report/2014/03/07/85457/fact-sheet-the-womens-leadership-gap/>

51. Adams, Carrie. "The Top 10 Worst Toys to Give Your Daughter This Christmas." 21 December 2011. *Sojourners*. Web. 30 July 2014.

<http://sojo.net/blogs/2011/12/21/top-10-worst-toys-give-your-daughter-christmas>

52.　Netherwood, Cathy. "Toys that teach our kids how to learn." 2015. *Mums: Body & Soul*. Web. 28 March 2015. <http://mums.bodyandsoul.com.au/kids+health/health/toys+that+teach+our+kids+how+to+learn,8973>

53.　Simons, Jake Wallis. "Toy companies want your kids to have a gender-specific Christmas." 3 December 2014. *The Telegraph*. Web. 28 March 2015. <http://www.telegraph.co.uk/men/relationships/fatherhood/11268426/Toy-companies-want-your-kids-to-have-a-gender-specific-Christmas.html>

54.　Simons, Jake Wallis. "Toy companies want your kids to have a gender-specific Christmas." 3 December 2014. *The Telegraph*. Web. 28 March 2015. <http://www.telegraph.co.uk/men/relationships/fatherhood/11268426/Toy-companies-want-your-kids-to-have-a-gender-specific-Christmas.html>

55.　"Barbie." 19 August 2015. *Wikipedia*. Web. 20 August 2015. <http://en.wikipedia.org/wiki/Barbie>

56.　Wrzesinski, Philip C. 2006. *How Toys Teach*. Web. 28 March 2015. <http://philsforum.com/pdf/How%20Toys%20Teach.pdf>

57.　Anthony, Susan B. "Biography of Susan B. Anthony." 2013. *National Susan B. Anthony Museum & House.*

58.　"Lucretia Mott." 2015. *Bio*. Ed. A&E Television Networks. Web. 25 October 2013. <http://www.biography.com/people/lucretia-mott-9416590>

59.　"Lucretia Mott." 2015. *Bio*. Ed. A&E Television Networks. Web. 25 October 2013. <http://www.biography.com/people/lucretia-mott-9416590>

60.　"19th Amendment to the U.S. Constitution: Women's Right to Vote." n.d. *National Archives*. Web. 25 October 2013. <http://www.archives.gov/historical-docs/document.html?doc=13&title.raw=19th+Amendment+to+the+U.S.+Constitution:+Women%27s+Right+to+Vote>

61.　"Ida B. Wells." 2015. *Bio*. A&E Television Networks. Web. 25 October 2013. <http://www.biography.com/people/ida-b-wells-9527635>

62.　Baker, Lee D. "Ida B. Wells-Barnett and Her Passion for Justice." n.d. *Duke University*. Web. 25 October 2013.

<http://people.duke.edu/~ldbaker/classes/AAIH/caaih/ibwells/ibwbkgrd.h
tml>

63. Wormser, Richard. "Plessy v. Ferguson (1896)." n.d. *PBS.* Web. 25
October 2013.
<http://www.pbs.org/wnet/jimcrow/stories_events_plessy.html>

64. Wells, Ida B. *Crusade for Justice: The Autobiography of Ida B. Wells.*
Chicago: University of Chicago Press, 1991. Print.

65. "Ida B. Wells." n.d. *Answers.* Web. 25 October 2013.
<http://www.answers.com/topic/ida-b-wells>

66. "Gender and Society". n.d. *Trinity.edu.* Web. 20 March 2015.
<http://www.trinity.edu/mkearl/gender.html>

67. "Exposing Massachusetts' lopsided arrests for prostitution related
crimes." 2014. *Demand Abolition.* Web. 21 March 2015.
<http://www.demandabolition.org/exposing-massachusetts-lopsided-
arrests-for-prostitution-related-crimes/>

68. "A History of Women in Industry." 2007. *National Women's History
Museum.* Web. 21 March 2015. <https://www.nwhm.org/online-
exhibits/industry/womenindustry_intro.html>

69. Moran, Mickey. "1930s, America – Feminist Void?" 1988-89. *Loyno.edu.*
Web. 21 March 2015. <http://www.loyno.edu/~history/journal/1988-
9/moran.htm>

70. "Aftermath of Winning the Vote." 2007. *National Women's History
Museum.* Web. 21 March 2015. <https://www.nwhm.org/online-
exhibits/rightsforwomen/aftermath.html>

71. Moran, Mickey. "1930s, America – Feminist Void?" 1988-89. *Loyno.edu.*
Web. 21 March 2015. <http://www.loyno.edu/~history/journal/1988-
9/moran.htm>

72. "The Great Depression." 2015. *History.* Web. 28 March 2015.
<http://www.history.com/topics/great-depression>

73. "A History of Women in Industry." 2007. *National Women's History
Museum.* Web. 21 March 2015. <https://www.nwhm.org/online-
exhibits/industry/womenindustry_intro.html>

74. "American Women in World War II." 2015. *History.* Web. 28 March
2015. <http://www.history.com/topics/world-war-ii/american-women-in-
world-war-ii>

75. "Partners in Winning the War: American Women in World War II." 2007. *National Women's History Museum.* Web. 21 March 2015. <https://www.nwhm.org/online-exhibits/partners/18.htm>

76. Chafe, William H. "World War II as a Pivotal Experience for American Women." In *Women and War: The Changing Status of American Women from the 1930s to the 1940s,* edited by Maria Diedrich and Dorothea Fischer-Hornung, pp. 21-34. New York: Berg, 1990. Web. 21 March 2015. <http://ic.galegroup.com/ic/uhic/PrimarySourcesDetailsPage/PrimarySou rcesDetailsWindow?query=&prodId=UHIC&contentModules=&display GroupName=PrimarySources&limiter=&disableHighlighting=false&disp layGroups=&sortBy=&search_within_results=&p=UHIC%3AWHIC&ac tion=2&catId=&activityType=&documentId=GALE%7CCX3441600284 &source=Bookmark&u=plant&jsid=4804b7c6323967c31e6d59dcdccdee 30>

77. Chafe, William H. "World War II as a Pivotal Experience for American Women." In *Women and War: The Changing Status of American Women from the 1930s to the 1940s,* edited by Maria Diedrich and Dorothea Fischer-Hornung, pp. 21-34. New York: Berg, 1990. Web. 21 March 2015. <http://ic.galegroup.com/ic/uhic/PrimarySourcesDetailsPage/PrimarySou rcesDetailsWindow?query=&prodId=UHIC&contentModules=&display GroupName=PrimarySources&limiter=&disableHighlighting=false&disp layGroups=&sortBy=&search_within_results=&p=UHIC%3AWHIC&ac tion=2&catId=&activityType=&documentId=GALE%7CCX3441600284 &source=Bookmark&u=plant&jsid=4804b7c6323967c31e6d59dcdccdee 30>

78. "The Great Depression." 2000. *EyeWitness to History.* Web. 21 March 2015. <http://www.eyewitnesstohistory.com/snprelief1.htm>

79. Moran, Mickey. "1930s, America – Feminist Void?" 1988-89. *Loyno.edu.* Web. 21 March 2015. <http://www.loyno.edu/~history/journal/1988-9/moran.htm>

80. "The Great Depression." 2000. *EyeWitness to History.* Web. 21 March 2015. http://www.eyewitnesstohistory.com/snprelief1.htm>

81. Ware, Susan. "Women and the Great Depression," *History Now* 19 (Spring 2009): n. pag. The Gilder Lehrman Institute of American History. Web. 21 March 2015. <http://www.gilderlehrman.org/history-by-era/great-depression/essays/women-and-great-depression>

82. History.com Staff. "American Women in World War II." 2010. *History.com.* A+E Networks. Web. 21 March 2015.

<http://www.history.com/topics/world-war-ii/american-women-in-world-war-ii>

83. Stamberg, Susan. "Female WWII Pilots: The Original Fly Girls." *NPR.* 9 March 2010. Web. 21 March 2015. <http://www.npr.org/2010/03/09/123773525/female-wwii-pilots-the-original-fly-girls>

84. History.com Staff. "American Women in World War II." 2010. *History.com.* A+E Networks. Web. 21 March 2015. <http://www.history.com/topics/world-war-ii/american-women-in-world-war-ii>

85. History.com Staff. "American Women in World War II." 2010. *History.com.* A+E Networks. Web. 21 March 2015. <http://www.history.com/topics/world-war-ii/american-women-in-world-war-ii>

86. History.com Staff. "American Women in World War II." 2010. *History.com.* A+E Networks. Web. 21 March 2015. <http://www.history.com/topics/world-war-ii/american-women-in-world-war-ii>

87. History.com Staff. "American Women in World War II." 2010. *History.com.* A+E Networks. Web. 21 March 2015. <http://www.history.com/topics/world-war-ii/american-women-in-world-war-ii>

88. "Literacy from 1870 to 1979." 1993. *National Center for Education Statistics.* U.S. Department of Education. Web. 21 March 2015. <https://nces.ed.gov/naal/lit_history.asp>

89. Toossi, Mitra. "A century of change: the U.S. labor force, 1950-2050," *Monthly Labor Review* (May 2002): pp 15-28. Bureau of Labor Statistics. Web. 21 March 2015. <http://www.bls.gov/opub/mlr/2002/05/art2full.pdf>

90. "The Rise of Women: Seven Charts Showing Women's Rapid Gains in Educational Achievement." 2013 February 21. *Russell Sage Foundation.* Web. 21 March 2015. < http://www.russellsage.org/blog/rise-women-seven-charts-showing-womens-rapid-gains-educational-achievement>

91. "The Rise of Women: Seven Charts Showing Women's Rapid Gains in Educational Achievement." 2013 February 21. *Russell Sage Foundation.* Web. 21 March 2015. < http://www.russellsage.org/blog/rise-women-seven-charts-showing-womens-rapid-gains-educational-achievement>

92. "Opportunities for Women in 1950s." n.d. *Edith Hornik Beer Digital Scrapbook.* Alanis.Simmons.edu. Web. 21 march 2015. <http://alanis.simmons.edu/edith/opportunities>

93. Hix, Lisa. "Women in the Skies: The Birth of the Stewardess." *Ms. Magazine blog.* Web. 21 March 2015. <http://msmagazine.com/blog/2014/09/16/women-in-the-skies-the-birth-of-the-stewardess/>

94. Vantoch, Victoria. "The Rise of the Airline Stewardess." 5 April 2013. *Slate.* Web. 25 October 2013. <http://www.slate.com/articles/double_x/books/2013/04/airline_stewardesses_through_history_photos.html>

95. Hall, Michelle. "By the Numbers: End of World War II." 2 September 2013. *CNN Library.* Web. 22 March 2015. <http://www.cnn.com/2013/09/02/world/btn-end-of-wwii/>

96. "Publication of "The Feminine Mystique" by Betty Friedan." n.d. *Jewish Women's Archive.* Web. 10 July 2014. <http://jwa.org/thisweek/feb/17/1963/betty-friedan>

97. Friedan, Betty. "The Feminine Mystique Quotes." n.d. *goodreads.* Web. 25 October 2014.

98. McLaughlin, Katie. "5 things women couldn't do in the 1960s." 25 August 2014. *CNN.* Web. 21 March 2015. <http://www.cnn.com/2014/08/07/living/sixties-women-5-things>

99. "Title VII of the Civil Rights Act of 1964." n.d. *U.S. Equal Employment Opportunity Commission.* Web. 22 March 2015. <http://www.eeoc.gov/laws/statutes/titlevii.cfm>

100. Menand, Louis. "Books as Bombs: Why the women's movement needed 'The Feminine Mystique'." 24 January 2011. *The New Yorker.* Web. 21 March 2015. <http://www.newyorker.com/magazine/2011/01/24/books-as-bombs>

101. Reese, Hope. "'Anger Boiled Up, and Betty Friedan Was There': 'Feminine Mystique' at 50." 28 January 2013. *The Atlantic.* Web. 22 March 2015. <http://www.theatlantic.com/sexes/archive/2013/01/anger-boiled-up-and-betty-friedan-was-there-feminine-mystique-at-50/272575/2>

102. "The 1960s-70s American Feminist Movement: Breaking Down Barriers for Women." n.d. *Tavaana.org.* Web. 22 March 2015. <https://tavaana.org/en/content/1960s-70s-american-feminist-movement-breaking-down-barriers-women>

103. "The 1960s-70s American Feminist Movement: Breaking Down Barriers for Women." n.d. *Tavaana.org.* Web. 22 March 2015. <https://tavaana.org/en/content/1960s-70s-american-feminist-movement-breaking-down-barriers-women>

104. "The 1960s-70s American Feminist Movement: Breaking Down Barriers for Women." n.d. *Tavaana.org.* Web. 22 March 2015. <https://tavaana.org/en/content/1960s-70s-american-feminist-movement-breaking-down-barriers-women>

105. Cohen, Sandy. "Birth control pills helped empower women, changed the world." 17 July 2005. *The Religious Consultation.* Web. 22 March 2015. <http://www.religiousconsultation.org/News_Tracker/birth_control_pills_helped_empower_women_changed_world.htm>

106. Haddock, B. "The 1960's hippie Counter Culture Movement." 9 March 2011. *Mortal Journey.* Web. 21 March 2015. <http://www.mortaljourney.com/2011/03/1960-trends/hippie-counter-culture-movement>

107. Cohen, Sandy. "Birth control pills helped empower women, changed the world." 17 July 2005. *The Religious Consultation.* Web. 22 March 2015. <http://www.religiousconsultation.org/News_Tracker/birth_control_pills_helped_empower_women_changed_world.htm>

108. Reese, Hope. "'Anger Boiled Up, and Betty Friedan Was There': 'Feminine Mystique' at 50." 28 January 2013. *The Atlantic.* Web. 22 March 2015. <http://www.theatlantic.com/sexes/archive/2013/01/anger-boiled-up-and-betty-friedan-was-there-feminine-mystique-at-50/272575/2>

109. "American Women: Report of the President's Commission on the Status of Women." 1963. *United States Department of Labor.* Web. 21 March 2015. <http://www.dol.gov/wb/American%20Women%20Report.pdf>

110. "American Women: Report of the President's Commission on the Status of Women." 1963: p 9. *United States Department of Labor.* Web. 21 March 2015. <http://www.dol.gov/wb/American%20Women%20Report.pdf>

111. "American Women: Report of the President's Commission on the Status of Women." 1963: p 12. *United States Department of Labor.* Web. 21 March 2015. <http://www.dol.gov/wb/American%20Women%20Report.pdf>

112. "American Women: Report of the President's Commission on the Status of Women." 1963: p 14. *United States Department of Labor.* Web. 21

March 2015.
<http://www.dol.gov/wb/American%20Women%20Report.pdf>

113. Maslin, Janet. "Looking Back at a Domestic Cri de Coeur." 18 February 2013. *The New York Times.* Web. 22 March 2015. <http://www.nytimes.com/2013/02/19/books/betty-friedans-feminine-mystique-50-years-later.html?pagewanted=all>

114. Rowbotham, Sheila. "Betty Friedan: Feminist icon of the 1960s, renowned for her bestseller, The Feminine Mystique." 6 February 2006. *The Guardian.* Web. 21 March 2015. <http://www.theguardian.com/news/2006/feb/06/guardianobituaries.gender>

115. "Women at work." March 2011. *U.S. Bureau of Labor Statistics.* Web. 21 March 2015. <http://www.bls.gov/spotlight/2011/women/pdf/women_bls_spotlight.pdf>

116. "Women at work." March 2011. *U.S. Bureau of Labor Statistics.* Web. 21 March 2015. <http://www.bls.gov/spotlight/2011/women/pdf/women_bls_spotlight.pdf>

117. Dean, Michelle. "On the 'Anger' of Betty Friedan and 'The Feminine Mystique'." 17 February 2013. *The Nation.* Web. 21 March 2015. <http://www.thenation.com/blog/172963/anger-betty-friedan-and-feminine-mystique>

118. "Betty Friedan Interview." *PBS.org.* Web. 21 March 2015. <http://www.pbs.org/fmc/interviews/friedan.htm>

119. Mabe, Chauncey. "It wasn't enough for Betty Friedan to change the world – she should have perfected it, too". 28 January 2011. *Open Page.* Web. 21 March 2015. <http://flcenterlitarts.wordpress.com/2011/01/28/it-wasnt-enough-for-betty-friedan-to-change-the-world-she-should-have-perfected-it-too/>

120. Friedan, Betty. The Feminine Mystique. New York: Norton, 2001. Print.

121. "Smith History." n.d. *Smith College.* Web. 21 March 2015. <http://www.smith.edu/about-smith/smith-history>

122. "College Profile: Smith College." n.d. *CollegeData.com.* Web. 22 March 2015. <http://www.collegedata.com/cs/data/college/college_pg01_tmpl.jhtml?schoolId=61>

123. "Smith at a Glance." n.d. *Smith College.* Web. 22 March 2015. <http://www.smith.edu/about_justthefacts.php>

124. Klein, Julia M. "Unreal Choices: On The Feminine Mystique." 8 April 2013. *The Nation.* 21 March 2015. <http://www.thenation.com/article/173440/unreal-choices-feminine-mystique>

125. Maslin, Janet. "Looking Back at a Domestic Cri de Coeur." 18 February 2013. *The New York Times.* Web. 22 March 2015. <http://www.nytimes.com/2013/02/19/books/betty-friedans-feminine-mystique-50-years-later.html?pagewanted=all>

126. "Betty Friedan." 19 March 2015. *Wikipedia.* Web. 22 March 2015. <http://en.wikipedia.org/wiki/Betty_Friedan>

127. Kreiser, John. "Betty Friedan Remembered." 6 February 2006. *CBS News.* Web. 20 March 2015. <http://www.cbsnews.com/news/betty-friedan-remembered/>

128. MacPherson, Myra. "She Gained Her Liberty But Lost A Husband." 28 February 1971. *The Tuscaloosa News.* Web. 21 March 2015.

129. Maslin, Janet. "Looking Back at a Domestic Cri de Coeur." 18 February 2013. *The New York Times.* Web. 25 March 2015.

130. "Betty Friedan Interview." *PBS.org.* Web. 21 March 2015. <http://www.pbs.org/fmc/interviews/friedan.htm>

131. Cohn, D., Livingston, G. and Wang, W. "After Decades of Decline, A Rise inStay-at-Home Mothers." 8 April 2014. *Pew Research Center.* Web. 25 March 2015. <http://www.pewsocialtrends.org/2014/04/08/after-decades-of-decline-a-rise-in-stay-at-home-mothers/>

132. Cohn, D., Livingston, G. and Wang, W. "After Decades of Decline, A Rise inStay-at-Home Mothers." 8 April 2014. *Pew Research Center.* Web. 25 March 2015. <http://www.pewsocialtrends.org/2014/04/08/after-decades-of-decline-a-rise-in-stay-at-home-mothers/>

133. Cohn, D., Livingston, G. and Wang, W. "After Decades of Decline, A Rise inStay-at-Home Mothers." 8 April 2014. *Pew Research Center.* Web. 25 March 2015. <http://www.pewsocialtrends.org/2014/04/08/after-decades-of-decline-a-rise-in-stay-at-home-mothers/>

134. Cohn, D., Livingston, G., and Wang, W. "After Decades of Decline, A Rise in Stay-at-Home Mothers." 8 April 2014. *Pew Research Center.* Web. 25 March 2015. <http://www.pewsocialtrends.org/2014/04/08/after-decades-of-decline-a-rise-in-stay-at-home-mothers/>

135. "Third-wave feminism." n.d. *Wikipedia.* Web. 25 March 2015. <http://en.wikipedia.org/wiki/Third-wave_feminism>

136. "Are women the stronger sex?" n.d. *Yahoo answers.* Web. 28 March 2015. <https://answers.yahoo.com/question/index?qid=20100223125506AArX8 Bh>

137. *10 Things Women Can Do Better Than Men.* April 2010. Web. 28 October 2013. <http://wattpad-catalog.blogspot.com/2010/04/10-things-women-can-do-better-than-men.html>

138. *Official: Sick men do complain more.* 9 June 2010. Web. 28 October 2013. <http://metro.co.uk/2010/06/09/official-sick-men-do-complain-more-377741/>

139. —. *Women by the Numbers.* 2007. Web. 12 October 2013. <http://www.infoplease.com/spot/womencensus1.html>

140. *10 Things Women Can Do Better Than Men.* April 2010. Web. 28 October 2013. <http://wattpad-catalog.blogspot.com/2010/04/10-things-women-can-do-better-than-men.html>

141. *90 Years Later: Women Vote More Often Than Men.* 26 August 2010. Web. 12 October 2013. <http://abcnews.go.com/blogs/lifestyle/2010/08/90-years-later-women-vote-more-often-than-men/>

142. *Volunteering in the United States, 2013.* 22 February 2013. Web. 28 October 2013. <http://www.bls.gov/news.release/archives/volun_02222013.htm>

143. Associated Press. *In a first, women surpass men in college degrees.* 26 April 2011. Web. 28 October 2013. <http://www.cbsnews.com/news/in-a-first-women-surpass-men-in-college-degrees/>

144. Wolf, Mark D. *Women-Owned Businesses: America's New Job Creation Engine.* 12 January 2010. Web. 28 October 2013. <http://www.forbes.com/2010/01/12/small-business-job-market-forbes-woman-entrepreneurs-economic-growth.html>

145. State & County Quickfacts. n.d. Web. 28 October 2013. http://quickfacts.census.gov/qfd/states/00000.html

146. Yoba, Akoshia. National Small Business Week 2014: Women-owned Small Businesses Are Making Strides. 13 July 2014. Web. 13 May 2014. <http://www.huffingtonpost.com/akoshia-yoba/national-small-business-w_1_b_5309971.html>

147. Hess, Ph.D., Cynthia and Milli, Ph.D., Jessica et al. "The Status of Women in the United States 2015." N.d. *The Women's Foundation of Colorado.* Web. 22 June 2015. <http://www.wfco.org/file/StatusofWomen2015_FullReport.pdf>

148. "Prostitution in the United States." 2015. *HG.org.* Web. 25 March 2015. <http://www.hg.org/article.asp?id=30997>

149. Redden. Molly. "The GOP Lawmaker Wants a Woman to Get Permission From the Father Before Having an Abortion." 17 December 2014. *Mother Jones.* Web. 25 March 2015. <http://www.motherjones.com/politics/2014/12/republican-wants-women-get-permission-father-having-abortion>

150. Redden. Molly. "The GOP Lawmaker Wants a Woman to Get Permission From the Father Before Having an Abortion." 17 December 2014. *Mother Jones.* Web. 25 March 2015. <http://www.motherjones.com/politics/2014/12/republican-wants-women-get-permission-father-having-abortion>

151. Redden. Molly. "The GOP Lawmaker Wants a Woman to Get Permission From the Father Before Having an Abortion." 17 December 2014. *Mother Jones.* Web. 25 March 2015. <http://www.motherjones.com/politics/2014/12/republican-wants-women-get-permission-father-having-abortion>

152. Kessler, Glenn. "The claim that the incidence of rape resulting in pregnancy is 'very low'". 13 June 2013. *The Washington Post.* Web. 25 March 2015. <http://www.washingtonpost.com/blogs/fact-checker/post/the-claim-that-the-incidence-of-rape-resulting-in-pregnancy-is-very-low/2013/06/12/936bc45e-d3ad-11e2-8cbe-1bcbee06f8f8_blog.html>

153. Millhiser, Ian and Waldron, Travis. "GOP U.S. Senate Candidate Calls Rape Pregnancies a 'Gift From God'". 23 October 2012. *Think Progress.* Web. 25 March 2015. <http://thinkprogress.org/justice/2012/10/23/1078181/gop-us-senate-candidate-calls-rape-pregnancies-a-gift-from-god/>

154. "Mike Huckabee". 2015. *Bio.* A&E Television Networks, 2015. Web. 25 March 2015. <http://www.biography.com/people/mike-huckabee-261446>

155. Petri, Alexandra. "Mike Huckabee and women's uncontrolled libido, or, Uncle Sugar." 23 January 2014. *The Washington Post.* Web. 25 March 2015.

<http://www.washingtonpost.com/blogs/compost/wp/2014/01/23/mike-huckabee-and-womens-uncontrolled-libido-or-uncle-sugar/>

156. Drexler, Dr. Peggy. "Mom And Dad, Please Explain This One to Your Daughters." 2 January 2015. *HuffPost: Politics.* Web. 25 March 2015. <http://www.huffingtonpost.com/peggy-drexler/mom-and-dad-please-explai_b_6406970.html>

157. Miller, Claire Cain. "A Racy Silicon Valley Lawsuit, and More Subtle Questions About Sex Discrimination". *The New York Times.* Web. 24 March 2015. <http://www.nytimes.com/2015/03/07/upshot/a-racy-silicon-valley-lawsuit-and-more-subtle-questions-about-sex-discrimination.html?abt=0002&abg=0>

158. Dangli, Dustin L. "Women officers talk about discrimination, their future". *Star-Telegram.* Web. 24 March 2015. <http://www.star-telegram.com/news/local/crime/article3875173.html#storylink=cpy>

159. Migdal, Ariela. "A Free, Federal College Education – But Mostly For Men". *American Civil Liberties Union.* Web. 24 March 2015. <https://www.aclu.org/blog/womens-rights-national-security/free-federal-college-education-mostly-men>

160. Sadler, A.G. et al. n.d. "Warning: Study says 1 in 3 Women RAPED in the Military". *Arlington West Santa Monica.* Web 24 March 2015. <http://www.arlingtonwestsantamonica.org/MST.html>

161. Sadler, A.G. et al. n.d. "Warning: Study says 1 in 3 Women RAPED in the Military". *Arlington West Santa Monica.* Web 24 March 2015. <http://www.arlingtonwestsantamonica.org/MST.html>

162. Cohn, Marjorie. "The Fear That Kills". 20 January 2006. *Alternet.* Web. 24 March 2015. <http://www.alternet.org/story/31584/the_fear_that_kills>

163. "Human Trafficking." n.d. *Federal Bureau of Investigation.* Web. 25 March 2015. <http://www.fbi.gov/about-us/investigate/civilrights/human_trafficking>

164. "United States of America." 2006. *HumanTrafficking.org.* Web. 24 march 2015. <http://www.humantrafficking.org/countries/united_states_of_america>

165. "Human Trafficking is a Problem 365 Days a Year." 2015. *Polaris.* Web. 24 March 2015. <http://www.polarisproject.org/take-action/365-days >

166. Zurita, Brenda. "Human Trafficking Estimates and Statistics." 10 July 2014. *American Thinker.* Web. 24 March 2015.

<http://www.americanthinker.com/articles/2014/07/human_trafficking_es
timates_and_statistics.html#ixzz3TuaIcmWL>

167. Durando, Jessica. "CDC: Nearly 1 in 5 women raped." 7 September 2014.
      USA Today. Web. 24 March 2015.
      <http://www.usatoday.com/story/news/nation-now/2014/09/07/cdc-rape-
      women-statistics/15239361/>

168. Catalano, Shannan, et al. "Female Victims of Violence." 23 October
      2009. *Bureau of Justice Statistics.* Web. 25 March 2015.
      <http://www.bjs.gov/content/pub/pdf/fvv.pdf >

169. "Empowering Women in Sports." 2014. *Feminist Majority Foundation.*
      Web. 24 March 2015.
      <http://www.feminist.org/research/sports/sports2a.html>

170. Collins, Sarah. "Gender Discrimination in Sports." 13 October 2013.
      Livestrong.com. 24 March 2015.
      <http://www.livestrong.com/article/247625-gender-discrimination-in-
      sports>

171. "Women as religious leaders: priests, preiestesses, pastors, ministers,
      rabbis...." 31 January 2015. *Religious Tolerance.* Web. 24 March 2015.
      <http://www.religioustolerance.org/femclrgy.htm>

172. "What percentage of pastors are female?" 2006. *Hartford Institute for
      Religion Research.* Web. 24 March 2015.
      <http://hirr.hartsem.edu/research/quick_question3.html>

173. Berman, Jillian. "Corporate America's Staggering Sexism, In 1 Chart."
      22 July 2014. *HuffPost Business.* Web. 24 March 2015.
      <http://www.huffingtonpost.com/2014/07/18/women-corporate-
      leaders_n_5600557.html>

174. Jaschik, Scott. "More Women on College Boards." 21 January 2009.
      Inside Higher Ed. Web. 24 March 2015.
      <https://www.insidehighered.com/news/2009/01/21/trustees>

175. Anderson, Nick. "The gender factor in college admissions: Do men or
      women have an edge?" 26 March 2014. *The Washington Post.* Web. 24
      March 2015. <http://www.washingtonpost.com/local/education/the-
      gender-factor-in-college-admissions/2014/03/26/4996e988-b4e6-11e3-
      8020-b2d790b3c9e1_story.html>

176. Chemaly, Soraya. "10 Ridiculously Sexist and Dangerous Laws From
      Around the World." 15 February 2015. *HuffPost Politics.* Web. 24 March
      2015. <http://www.huffingtonpost.com/soraya-chemaly/10-ridiculously-
      sexist-laws-around-the-world_b_6679970.html>

177. "House Floor – Rep. Thompson on Disrespect to Women." 26 May 2011. *YouTube.* Web Video. 22 Fecruary 2014. <https://www.youtube.com/watch?v=QKf-6WiBq_Q>

178. Baker, Joan E. "Employment Discrimination Against Women Lawyers." *ABA Journal* 59 (1973): 1029-32. Web. 26 March 2015. <https://books.google.com/books?id=R4Lsn4QhNPgC&pg=PA1029&lpg =PA1029&dq=how+long+have+law+schools+had+equal+women&sourc e=bl&ots=hUKsOXfTzQ&sig=JsRyd1d8SWNaaTewv9sB60P9ATw&hl =en&sa=X&ei=sRdBVbEfxpc236uB2Ak&ved=0CFsQ6AEwCQ#v=one page&q=how%20long%20have%20law%20schools%20had%20equal%2 0women&f=false>

179. Weiss, Debra Cassens."Men Outnumber Women at Most Top Law Schools, But the Imbalance is Greater at B-Schools." 9 May 2011. *ABA Journal.* Web. 28 March 2015. <http://www.abajournal.com/news/article/men_outnumber_women_at_m ost_top_law_schools_but_the_imbalance_is_greater_at/>

180. Warner, Judith. "Fact Sheet: The Women's Leadership Gap." 7 March 2014. *Center for American Progress.* Web. 27 March 2015. <https://www.americanprogress.org/issues/women/report/2014/03/07/854 57/fact-sheet-the-womens-leadership-gap/≥

181. "Featured Documents: The Emancipation Proclamation." N.d. *U.S. National Archives & Records Administration.* Web. 8 March 2014. <http://www.archives.gov/exhibits/featured_documents/emancipation_pr oclamation/>

182. Kingkade, Tyler. "College Student Survey Suggests We've Made Little Progress Eliminating Racism." 2 February 2015. *HuffPost College.* Web. 7 March 2015. <http://www.huffingtonpost.com/2015/02/07/college-student-survey-race_n_6632854.html>

183. Gettys, Travis. "Black activist explains what white people don't get about race after reporter shares racial slur horror story." 6 April 2015. *Raw Story.* Web. 22 May 2015. <http://www.rawstory.com/2015/04/black>

184. Lee, Jaeah. "Exactly How Often Do Police Shoot Unarmed Black Men?" 15 August 2014. *Mother Jones.* Web. 22 January 2015. <http://www.motherjones.com/politics/2014/08/police-shootings-michael-brown-ferguson-black-men>

185. Grimsley, Edwin. "What Wrongful Convictions Teach Us About Racial Inequality." 26 September 2012. *Innocence Project. Web.* 16 February 2014. <http://www.innocenceproject.org/news-events-exonerations/what-

wrongful-convictions-teach-us-about-racial-inequality#sthash.DvT1BlTU.dpuf>

186. Shasha, Deng, ed. "Ethnic minorities severely discriminated against in US: report." 25 May 2012. *English.news.cn.* Web. 22 August 2013. <http://news.xinhuanet.com/english/china/2012-05/25/c_131611466.htm>

187. Bell, Derrick. "Racial Discrimination Prevails – Minorities Ill Treated." 31 December 2010. *The University of Dayton: School of Law.* Web. 22 August 2013 <http://academic.udayton.edu/race/06hrights/georegions/northamerica/china05.htm>

188. Human Wrongs Watch. "Ethnic Minority Women Face Double Exclusion in Workpace Due to Their Race, Gender." 2 February 2013. *Pressenza.* Web. 22 August 2013. <http://www.pressenza.com/2013/02/ethnic-minority-women-face-double-exclusion-in-workplace-due-to-their-race-gender/>

189. Rickman, Dina. "Black and Minority Ethnic Women 'Discriminated Against at Every Stage' of Recruitment Process." 12 July 2012. *The Huffington Post UK.* Web. 22 August 2013. <http://www.huffingtonpost.co.uk/2012/12/07/bme-women-runnymede-trust-jobs_n_2256589.html>

190. Dodd Vikram. "Ethnic minority women face jobs crisis." 6 December 2012. *The Guardian.* Web. 22 August 2013. <http://www.theguardian.com/world/2012/dec/07/ethnic-minority-women-jobs-crisis>

191. Warner, Judith. "Fact Sheet: The Women's Leadership Gap." 7 March 2014. *Center for American Progress.* Web. 22 July 2014. <https://www.americanprogress.org/issues/women/report/2014/03/07/85457/fact-sheet-the-womens-leadership-gap/>

192. Guerra, Maria. "Fact Sheet: The State of African American Women in the United States." 7 November 2013. *Center for American Progress.* Web. 22 July 2015. <https://www.americanprogress.org/issues/race/report/2013/11/07/79165/fact-sheet-the-state-of-african-american-women-in-the-united-states/>

193. Glynn, Sarah Jane and Powers, Audrey. "The Top 10 Facts About the Wage Gap." 16 April 2012. *Center for American Progress.* Web. 22 July 2015. <https://www.americanprogress.org/issues/labor/news/2012/04/16/11391/the-top-10-facts-about-the-wage-gap/>

194. Fisher, Milia. "Women of Color and the Gender Wage Gap." 14 April 2015. *Center for American Progress.* Web. 22 July 2015. <https://www.americanprogress.org/issues/women/report/2015/04/14/110 962/women-of-color-and-the-gender-wage-gap/>

195. Valenti, Jessica. "The F-card won't wash." 11 September 2008. *The Guardian.* Web. 25 March 2015. <http://www.theguardian.com/commentisfree/2008/sep/12/sarahpalin.fem inism>

196. Slack, Megan. "From the Archives: President Obama Signs the Lilly Ledbetter Fair Pay Act." 20 January 2012. *The White House Blog.* Web. 25 March 2015. <http://www.whitehouse.gov/blog/2012/01/30/archives-president-obama-signs-lilly-ledbetter-fair-pay-act>

197. CBS News. "Transcript: Palin And McCain Interview." 30 September 2008. CBS Interactive Inc. *CBS Evening News.* Web. 25 March 2015. <http://www.cbsnews.com/news/transcript-palin-and-mccain-interview/>

198. "Data Points: Gender Gap in the 2008 Election." 6 November 2008. *U.S. News.* Web. 25 March 2015. <http://www.usnews.com/opinion/articles/2008/11/06/data-points-gender-gap-in-the-2008-election>

199. Jones, Jeffrey M. "Gender Gap in 2012 Vote Is Largest in Gallup's History." 9 November 2012. *Gallup.* Web. 25 March 2015. <http://www.gallup.com/poll/158588/gender-gap-2012-vote-largest-gallup-history.aspx>

200. Borger, Julian and McVeigh, Karen. "Women's vote carries Obama to victory on historic election night." 7 November 2012. *The Guardian.* Web. 25 March 2015. <http://www.theguardian.com/world/2012/nov/07/womens-vote-obama-victory-election>

201. Dailey, Kate. "US election: Women are the new majority." 7 November 2012. *BBC News Magazine.* Web. 25 March 2015. <http://www.bbc.com/news/magazine-20231337>

202. "Gender Differences in Voter Turnout." 2014. *Center for American Women and Politics.* Web. 25 March 2015. <http://www.cawp.rutgers.edu/fast_facts/voters/documents/genderdiff.pdf >

203. Warner, Judith. "Fact Sheet: The Women's Leadership Gap." 7 March 2014. *Center for American Progress.* Web. 22 July 2014 <https://www.americanprogress.org/issues/women/report/2014/03/07/854 57/fact-sheet-the-womens-leadership-gap/>

204. Ireland, Corydon. "Feminism, now stalled." 28 February 2012. *Harvard Gazette.* Web. 22 July 2014. <http://news.harvard.edu/gazette/story/2012/02/feminism-now-stalled/>

205. Ireland, Corydon. "Feminism, now stalled." 28 February 2012. *Harvard Gazette.* Web. 22 July 2014. <http://news.harvard.edu/gazette/story/2012/02/feminism-now-stalled/>

206. Coontz, Stephanie. "Why Gender Equality Stalled." 16 February 2013. *The New York Times: Sunday Review.* Web. 22 July 2014. <http://www.nytimes.com/2013/02/17/opinion/sunday/why-gender-equality-stalled.html>

207. Straus, Tamara. "What Stalled the Gender Revolution? Child Care That Costs More Than College Tuition." Winter 2014. *California Magazine.* Web. 22 July 2014. <http://alumni.berkeley.edu/california-magazine/winter-2014-gender-assumptions/what-stalled-gender-revolution-child-care-costs>

208. NWLC Staff. "Women's Poverty Rate Stabilizes, But Remains Historically High." 12 September 2012. *National Women's Law Center.* Web. 22 July 2014. <http://www.nwlc.org/press-release/women%E2%80%99s-poverty-rate-stabilizes-remains-historically-high>

209. Williams, Joan C. "Jumpstarting the Stalled Gender Revolution: Justice Ginsburg and Reconstructive Feminism." *Hastings Law Journal* 63.5 (2012): 1267-96. Web. 26 March 2015. < http://www.hastingslawjournal.org/wp-content/uploads/Williams-63.5.pdf>

210. Straus, Tamara. "What Stalled the Gender Revolution? Child Care That Costs More Than College Tuition." Winter 2014. *California Magazine.* Web. 22 July 2014. <http://alumni.berkeley.edu/california-magazine/winter-2014-gender-assumptions/what-stalled-gender-revolution-child-care-costs>

211. Rhode, Deborah L. "Why Women Are Conflicted by the Feminist Label." 8 February 2015. Womensenews.org. Web. 24 March 2015. <http://womensenews.org/story/books/150206/why-women-are-conflicted-the-feminist-label>

212. "'Women Against Feminism' Angers Feminazis." 29 July 2014. The Rush Limbaugh Show. Web. 24 March 2015. <http://www.rushlimbaugh.com/daily/2014/07/29/women_against_feminism_angers_feminazis>

213. Woodruff, Mandi. "Marissa Mayer Doesn't Consider Herself A Feminist." 27 February 2013. Business Insider. Web. 24 March 2015. <http://www.businessinsider.com/marissa-mayer-criticizes-feminism-2013-2>

214. "Female Celebrities Who Rejected Feminism." 27 February 2015. Rebel Circus. Web. 25 March 2015. <http://www.rebelcircus.com/blog/female-celebrities-rejected-feminism/>

215. http://www.today.com/news/ohio-middle-school-photoshops-feminist-shirt-t15781

216. Brinker, Luke. "Phyllis Schlafly: Campus sex assault is on the rise because too many women go to college." 6 January 2015. Salon. Web. 25 March 2015. <http://www.salon.com/2015/01/06/phyllis_schlafly_campus_sex_assault_is_on_the_rise_because_too_many_women_go_to_college/>

217. May, Caroline. "Coulter on feminism: 'All pretty girls are right-wingers'." 10 February 2012. The Daily Caller. Web. 25 March 2015. <http://dailycaller.com/2012/02/10/coulter-on-feminism-all-pretty-girls-are-right-wingers/.>

218. May, Caroline. "Coulter on feminism: 'All pretty girls are right-wingers'." 10 February 2012. The Daily Caller. Web. 25 March 2015. <http://dailycaller.com/2012/02/10/coulter-on-feminism-all-pretty-girls-are-right-wingers/.>

219. Rothkopf, Joanna. "Ann Coulter: Women who say they are raped are just 'girls trying to get attention'." 18 December 2014. Salon. Web. 25 March 2015. <http://www.salon.com/2014/12/18/ann_coulter_women_who_say_they_are_raped_are_just_girls_trying_to_get_attention/>

220. Bassett, Laura. "Senate Candidate Joni Ernst Endorses Federal Personhood Bill For Fetuses." 16 October 2014. HuffPost Politics. Web. 25 March 2015. <http://www.huffingtonpost.com/2014/10/16/senate-candidate-endorses_n_5997126.html>

221. Bassett, Laura. "Senate Candidate Joni Ernst Endorses Federal Personhood Bill For Fetuses." 16 October 2014. HuffPost Politics. Web. 25 March 2015. <http://www.huffingtonpost.com/2014/10/16/senate-candidate-endorses_n_5997126.html>

222. Stein, Sam. "Sharron Angle's Advice For Rape Victims Considering Abortion: Turn Lemons Into Lemonade." 8 July 2010. HuffPost Politics. Web. 25 March 2015.

<http://www.huffingtonpost.com/2010/07/08/sharron-angles-advice-
for_n_639294.html>

223. Rhode, Deborah L. "Why Women Are Conflicted by the Feminist Label."
     8 February 2015. WomensNews.org. Web. 25 March 2015.
     <http://womensenews.org/story/books/150206/why-women-are-
     conflicted-the-feminist-label>

224. Rhode, Deborah L. "Why Women Are Conflicted by the Feminist Label."
     8 February 2015. WomensNews.org. Web. 25 March 2015.
     <http://womensenews.org/story/books/150206/why-women-are-
     conflicted-the-feminist-label>

225. Pilkington, Ed. "The hardest, highest glass ceiling': Hillary Clinton on the
     chances of electing a female US president." 21 June 2014. *The Guardian.*
     Web. 22 July 1014.
     <http://www.theguardian.com/world/2014/jun/22/hillary-clinton-hardest-
     highest-glass-ceiling-president>

226. Rucker, Philip. "Clinton: 'Crack every last glass ceiling'." 24 February
     2015. *The Washington Post.* Web. 22 July 2015.
     <http://www.washingtonpost.com/politics/hillary-clinton-previews-2016-
     says-its-time-to-crack-every-last-glass-ceiling/2015/02/24/c5d262c2-
     bc45-11e4-8668-4e7ba8439ca6_story.html>

227. Kumar, Anita. "Race relations arguably worse in 'Age of Obama'." 11
     December 2014. *McClatchy DC.* Web. 22 June 2015.
     <http://www.mcclatchydc.com/2014/12/11/249786/race-relations-
     arguably-worse.html#storylink=cpy>

228. Agiesta, Jennifer. "Under Obama, 4 in 10 say race relations worsened."
     13 March 2015. *CNN Politics.* Web. 22 June 2015.
     <http://www.cnn.com/2015/03/06/politics/poll-obama-race-relations-
     worse/>

229. Slaughter, Anne Marie. "International Men's Day." 8 March 2011. *The
     Huffington Post: The Blog.* Web. 22 June 2015.
     <http://www.huffingtonpost.com/annemarie-slaughter/international-
     mens-day_b_832917.html>

230. Pappas, Stephanie. "5 Ways Motherhood Has Changed Over Time." 10
     May 2013. *Livescience.* Web. 22 June 2015.
     <http://www.livescience.com/29521-5-ways-motherhood-has-
     changed.html>

231. Pappas, Stephanie. "5 Ways Motherhood Has Changed Over Time." 10
     May 2013. *Livescience.* Web. 22 June 2015.

<http://www.livescience.com/29521-5-ways-motherhood-has-changed.html>

232. Pappas, Stephanie. "5 Ways Motherhood Has Changed Over Time." 10 May 2013. *Livescience.* Web. 22 June 2015. <http://www.livescience.com/29521-5-ways-motherhood-has-changed.html>

233. Pappas, Stephanie. "5 Ways Motherhood Has Changed Over Time." 10 May 2013. *Livescience.* Web. 22 June 2015. <http://www.livescience.com/29521-5-ways-motherhood-has-changed.html>

234. Pappas, Stephanie. "5 Ways Motherhood Has Changed Over Time." 10 May 2013. *Livescience.* Web. 22 June 2015. <http://www.livescience.com/29521-5-ways-motherhood-has-changed.html>

235. Knerl, Linsey."What's the true value of a stay-at-home mother?" 6 May 2011. *Today.* Web. 22 June 2015. <http://www.today.com/id/42906705/ns/today-money/t/whats-true-value-stay-at-home-mother/#.VUPmovlVhBc>

236. Fell, Sara Sutton, ed. "15 Surprising Work-from-Home Jobs." 2015. *Working Mother.* Web. 22 June 2014. <http://www.workingmother.com/flexible-work/15-surprising-work-home-jobs>

237. Eleeuw, Vered. "The Financial Price of Being a Stay at Home Mom." 2014. *Money Ning.* Web. 22 June 2014. <http://moneyning.com/money-management/the-financial-price-of-being-a-stay-at-home-mom/>

238. Latvala, Charlotte. "The New Stay-at-Home Mom." N.d. *parenting.* Web. 22 June 2015. <http://www.parenting.com/article/the-new-stay-at-home-mom>

239. Fertility of American Women: 2010-Detailed Tables. June 2010. Web. 28 October 2013. <https://www.census.gov/hhes/fertility/data/cps/2010.html>

240. Fertility of American Women: 2010-Detailed Tables. June 2010. Web. 28 October 2013. <https://www.census.gov/hhes/fertility/data/cps/2010.html>

241. Fertility of American Women: 2010-Detailed Tables. June 2010. Web. 28 October 2013. <https://www.census.gov/hhes/fertility/data/cps/2010.html>

242. Rampell, Catherine. "U.S. Women on the Rise as Family Breadwinner."
      29 May 2013. The New York Times. Web. 27 October 2013.
      <http://www.nytimes.com/2013/05/30/business/economy/women-as-
      family-breadwinner-on-the-rise-study-says.html?_r=0>

243. U.S. Census Bureau. "Newsroom Archive, Facts for Features, Mother's
      Day: May 13, 2012." 19 March 2012. U.S. Census Bureau. Web. 28
      October 2013.
      <https://www.census.gov/newsroom/releases/archives/facts_for_features_
      special_editions/cb12-ff08.html>

244. Rampell, Catherine. "U.S. Women on the Rise as Family Breadwinner."
      29 May 2013. The New York Times. Web. 27 October 2013.
      <http://www.nytimes.com/2013/05/30/business/economy/women-as-
      family-breadwinner-on-the-rise-study-says.html?_r=0>

245. Parker, Kim. "Social Trends: Women, Work and Motherhood." 13 April
      2012. *Pew Research Center.* Web. 28 October 2013.
      <http://www.pewsocialtrends.org/2012/04/13/women-work-and-
      motherhood/>

246. Rampell, Catherine. "U.S. Women on the Rise as Family Breadwinner."
      29 May 2013. *The New York Times.* Web. 27 October 2013.
      <http://www.nytimes.com/2013/05/30/business/economy/women-as-
      family-breadwinner-on-the-rise-study-says.html?_r=0>

247. Kelly, Andrew. "'First time' in history: White deaths ounumber births in
      US." 13 June 2013. *RT.* Web. 22 June 2014 <http://rt.com/usa/us-white-
      births-census-613/>

248. Tozzi, John. "What's Killing White Women?" 5 March 2015. *Bloomberg
      Business.* Web. 22 June 2015.
      <http://www.bloomberg.com/news/articles/2015-03-05/health-what-s-
      killing-white-women->

249. Kelly, Joan B. "The Determination of Child Custody." *Children and
      Divorce* 4.1 (1994): 121-142. Web. 25 July 2015.
      <http://www.princeton.edu/futureofchildren/publications/journals/article/i
      ndex.xml?journalid=63&articleid=414&sectionid=2825>

250. "Marriage and Divorce Act, Model Summary." N.d. *Uniform Law
      Commission.* Web. 25 July 2015.
      <http://www.uniformlaws.org/ActSummary.aspx?title=Marriage%20and
      %20Divorce%20Act,%20Model>

251. Kelly, Joan B. "The Determination of Child Custody." *Children and
      Divorce* 4.1 (1994): 121-142. Web. 25 July 2015.

<http://www.princeton.edu/futureofchildren/publications/journals/article/index.xml?journalid=63&articleid=414&sectionid=2825>

252. "Academy Award for Best Supporting Actress." 23 August 2015. *Wikipedia.* Web. 22 May 2015. <http://en.wikipedia.org/wiki/Academy_Award_for_Best_Supporting_Actress>

253. Bennett, Jessica. "The Brotherhood of the Stay-at-Home Dad." 14 November 2014. *The New York Times.* Web. 22 June 2015. < http://www.nytimes.com/2014/11/16/fashion/the-brotherhood-of-the-stay-at-home-dad.html>

254. Bennett, Jessica. "The Brotherhood of the Stay-at-Home Dad." 14 November 2014. *The New York Times.* Web. 22 June 2015. < http://www.nytimes.com/2014/11/16/fashion/the-brotherhood-of-the-stay-at-home-dad.html>

255. Gazzar, Brenda. "Fathers changing roles: Dads doing more at home." 15 June 2013. *Whittier Daily News.* Web. 22 June 2015. <http://www.whittierdailynews.com/general-news/20130615/fathers-changing-roles-dads-doing-more-at-home>

256. Gazzar, Brenda. "Fathers changing roles: Dads doing more at home." 15 June 2013. *Whittier Daily News.* Web. 22 June 2015. <http://www.whittierdailynews.com/general-news/20130615/fathers-changing-roles-dads-doing-more-at-home>

257. Livingston, Gretchen and Parker, Kim. "A Tale of Two Fathers." 15 June 2011. *Pew Research Center.* Web 22 June 2015. <http://www.pewsocialtrends.org/2011/06/15/a-tale-of-two-fathers/>

258. Gazzar, Brenda. "Fathers changing roles: Dads doing more at home." 15 June 2013. *Whittier Daily News.* Web. 22 June 2015. <http://www.whittierdailynews.com/general-news/20130615/fathers-changing-roles-dads-doing-more-at-home>

259. "It's 2015, and the Picture Has Changed for Working Dads." 9 June 2014. *The White House.* Web. 22 June 2015. <https://www.whitehouse.gov/share/working-dads>

260. Furman, Jason and Stevenson, Betsey. "The Changing Role of Fathers in the Workforce and Family." 9 June 2014. *The White House.* Web. 22 June 2015. <https://www.whitehouse.gov/blog/2014/06/09/changing-role-fathers-workforce-and-family>

261. Oaklander, Mandy. "This Divorce Arrangement Stresses Kids Out Most." 27 April 2015. *Time.* Web. 22 June 2015. <http://time.com/3836627/divorced-parents-joint-custody/>

262. Winfrey, Oprah. "What Is a Good Summary of Oprah's Philosophy of Life?" 29 November 2011. *Forbes.* Web. 20 February 2014. <http://www.forbes.com/sites/quora/2011/11/29/what-is-a-good-summary-of-oprahs-philosophy-of-life/>

263. Megginson, Leon C. "Leon C. Megginson Quotes and Sayings." 2015. *Meetville.* Web. 22 February 2014. <http://meetville.com/quotes/author/leon-c-megginson/page1>

264. Brown, Jim. "Jim Brown Quote." 2015. *iz quotes.* Web. 22 February 2014. <http://izquotes.com/quote/25154>

265. "Sam Walton." 2013. *Bio.* A&E Television Networks. Web. 25 October 2013. <http://www.biography.com/people/sam-walton-9523270#final-years>

266. Kennon, Joshua. "Sam Walton (aka Samual Moore Walton)." 2013. *About.* Web. 30 October 2013. <http://beginnersinvest.about.com/od/samwalton/p/aasamwalton.htm>

267. Anderson, Erika. "10 Quotes From the 'First Lady of the World'." 10 January 2013. *Forbes.* Web. 25 March 2015. <http://www.forbes.com/sites/erikaandersen/2013/01/10/10-quotes-from-the-first-lady-of-the-world/>

268. Clinton, Hillary. "I fought all my life for women." n.d. *Lifehack Quotes.* Web. 20 February 2014. <http://quotes.lifehack.org/quote/hillary-clinton/i-fought-all-my-life-for-women/>

269. "40 Facts About Sleep You Probably Didn't Know...(or were too tired to think about)." n.d. *The National Sleep Research Project.* Australian Broadcasting Corporation 2000. Web. 29 October 2013. <http://www.abc.net.au/science/sleep/facts.htm>

270. Einstein, Albert. "Albert Einstein Quotes." 2015. *BrainyQuote.* Web. 22 February 2014. <http://www.brainyquote.com/quotes/quotes/a/alberteins133991.html>

271. Trudon, Taylor. "Rion Paige, 13-Year-Old 'X Factor USA' Contestant, Wows Judges With Incredible Audition." 12 September 2013. *Huffington Post.* Web. 25 October 2013. <http://www.huffingtonpost.com/2013/09/12/rion-paige-x-factor-usa-audition_n_3916588.html>

272. Gonzalez-Barrera, Ana and Lopez, Mark H. "Women's college enrollment gains leave men behind." 6 March 2014. *Pew Research Center*. Web. 25 March 2015. <http://www.pewresearch.org/fact-tank/2014/03/06/womens-college-enrollment-gains-leave-men-behind/>

273. Steinmetz, Katy. "Study: Why We Think Women Are More Trustworthy Than Men." 13 December 2010. *Time*. Web. 25 March 2015. <http://healthland.time.com/2010/12/13/study-why-we-think-women-are-more-trustworthy-than-men/>

274. Hazell, Kyrsty. "A 'Moral DNA Test' Reveals Women Are More Honest Than Men." 16 April 2012. *The Huffington Post UK*. Web. 25 March 2015. <http://www.huffingtonpost.co.uk/2012/04/16/moral-dna-test-womne-more-moral-than-men_n_1428076.html>

275. *Volunteering in the United States, 2013*. 22 February 2013. Web. 28 October 2013. <http://www.bls.gov/news.release/archives/volun_02222013.htm>

276. Jones, Jennifer. "Jennifer Jones: Biography." 2015. *IMDb*. Web. 22 February 2014. <http://www.imdb.com/name/nm0428354/bio>

277. Wong, Brittany. "The Truth About The Divorce Rate Is Surprisingly Optimistic." 2 December 2014. *HuffPost Divorce*. Web. 25 March 2015. <http://www.huffingtonpost.com/2014/12/02/divorce-rate-declining-_n_6256956.html>

278. Christensen, Darlene and Washburn, Carolyn. "Financial harmony: A key component of successful marriage relationship." April 2008, Vol.13, No. 1. *The Forum for Family and Consumer Issues*. Web. 25 March 2015. <http://ncsu.edu/ffci/publications/2008/v13-n1-2008-spring/Washburn-Christensen.php>

279. Wong, Brittany. "The Truth About The Divorce Rate Is Surprisingly Optimistic." 2 December 2014. *HuffPost Divorce*. Web. 25 March 2015. <http://www.huffingtonpost.com/2014/12/02/divorce-rate-declining-_n_6256956.html>

280. Cape, Anthony. "Maintain Power In Your Relationship." n.d. *askmen*. Web. 25 March 2015. <http://www.askmen.com/dating/curtsmith_60/76_dating_advice.html>

281. Green, Harriet. "Who drives the car – him or her?" 22 November 2013. *The Guardian*. Web. 25 March 2015. <http://www.theguardian.com/lifeandstyle/2013/nov/22/who-drives-car-him-or-her>

282. Thoman, Elizabeth. "Home, Home on the Remote: Why Do Men Control 'the Clicker'?" 2011. *Center for Media Literacy.* Web. 25 March 2015. <http://www.medialit.org/reading-room/home-home-remote-why-do-men-control-clicker>

283. Fussell, James A. "In a man's castle, the remote control is his scepter." 18 August 1993. *The Baltimore Sun.* Web. 25 March 2015. <http://articles.baltimoresun.com/1993-08-18/features/1993230170_1_remote-control-tv-remote-changing-the-channels>

284. Collins, Danica. "Laughter Therapy…Laugh Your Way To Well Being." 2011. *Underground Health Reporter.* Web. 18 November 2013. <http://undergroundhealthreporter.com/laughter-therapy-well-being-and-health/#axzz3QbnEgni4>

285. Segal PhD, Jeanne and Smith MA, Melinda. "Laughter is the Best Medicine." December 2014. *Helpguide.org.* Web. 28 December 2014. <http://www.helpguide.org/articles/emotional-health/laughter-is-the-best-medicine.htm>

286. Fishel, PhD, Anne. "FAQ." n.d. *TheFamilyDinnerProject.org.* Web. 16 July 2014. <http://thefamilydinnerproject.org/resources/faq/>

287. Lawrence, D.H. *Lady Chatterley's Lover.* Herfordshire: Wordsworth Editions Limited, 2005. Print.

288. "The 75 Greatest Women of All Time." 2015. *Esquire.* Web. 22 June 2015. <http://www.esquire.com/entertainment/g514/greatest-women-in-history/>

289. "Eleanor Roosevelt Quotes." N.d. *Brainy Quote.* Web. 22 June 2015. <http://www.brainyquote.com/quotes/quotes/e/eleanorroo161321.html#r10kg3bzjyvtxVUI.99>

290. "The 25 Greatest Female Athletes of All-Time." 24 March 2010. *Sports Pickle.* Web. 23 June 2015. <http://www.sportspickle.com/2010/03/the-25-greatest-female-athletes-of-all-time>

291. Olivera, Monica. "Heroic Mothers: Amazing Tales of Moms Protecting Their Young." 18 July 2012. *Mamiverse.* Web. 23 June 2015. <http://mamiverse.com/heroic-mothers-15521/>

292. Howard, Caroline. "The World's Most Powerful Women 2013." 22 May 2013. *Forbes.* Web. 22 October 2013. <http://www.forbes.com/sites/carolinehoward/2013/05/22/the-worlds-most-powerful-women-2013/>

293. "Barbara Walters Addresses the Class of 2012." 20 May 2012. *YouTube*. Web Video. 17 October 2013. <https://www.youtube.com/watch?v=7llYZ2XqLX4>

294. "Barbara Walters Addresses the Class of 2012." 20 May 2012. *YouTube*. Web Video. 17 October 2013. <https://www.youtube.com/watch?v=7llYZ2XqLX4>

295. Slaughter, Anne-Marie. "Why Women Still Can't Have It All." 13 June 2012. *The Atlantic*. Web. 17 October 2013. <http://www.theatlantic.com/magazine/archive/2012/07/why-women-still-cant-have-it-all/309020/>

296. Sandberg, Sheryl. *Lean In: Women, Work, and the Will to Lead*. New York: Knopf; 1 edition, 2013. Print.

297. Sandberg, Sheryl. *Lean In: Women, Work, and the Will to Lead*. New York: Knopf; 1 edition, 2013. Print.

298. Sandberg, Sheryl. *Lean In: Women, Work, and the Will to Lead*. New York: Knopf; 1 edition, 2013. Print.

299. Sandberg, Sheryl. *Lean In: Women, Work, and the Will to Lead*. New York: Knopf; 1 edition, 2013. Print.

300. Barrow, Becky. "I'm a mother first and a boss second, says Burberry chief as she reveals how she balances career with children." 8 September 2013. *DailyMail.com*. Web. 27 October 2013. <http://www.dailymail.co.uk/femail/article-2415439/Burberry-CEO-Angela-Ahrendts-unusual-recipe-balancing-career-children.html>

301. Kowitt, Beth. "Ursula Burns: 'Chill out a little bit'." 17 October 2013. *Fortune*. Web. 25 July 2015. <http://fortune.com/2013/10/17/ursula-burns-chill-out-a-little-bit/>

302. Lepore, Meredith. "10 Famous Women on 'Having it All'." 24 May 2013. *Levo League*. Web. 27 October 2013. <https://www.levo.com/articles/lifestyle/famous-women-having-it-all>

303. Frankel, Bethenny. *A Place of Yes: 10 Rules for Getting Everything You Want Out of Life*. New York: Touchstone, 2011. Print.

304. Gates, Melinda. "Melinda Gates." 28 August 2014 *Twitter*. Web. 15 June 2015. <https://twitter.com/melindagates/status/505120283507048448>

305. "Melinda Gates." N.d. *Brainy Quote*. Web. 15 June 2015. <http://www.brainyquote.com/quotes/authors/m/melinda_gates.html#sBG74McEeBGoymPf.99>

306. "Melinda Gates." N.d. *Brainy Quote*. Web. 15 June 2015. <http://www.brainyquote.com/quotes/authors/m/melinda_gates.html#sBG 74McEeBGoymPf.99>

307. Goudreau, Jenna. "The CEO Of $5 Billion Ingredion Reveals Her Secret To 'Having It All'." 18 March 2013. *Forbes*. Web. 27 October 2013. <http://www.forbes.com/sites/jennagoudreau/2013/03/18/the-ceo-of-5-billion-ingredion-reveals-her-secret-to-having-it-all/>

308. Houghton, Kristen. *And Then I'll be Happy*. Guilford: Globe Pequot Press, First Edition, 2009. Paperback.

309. Sparkes, Matthew. "Christine Lagarde: 'Women can't have it all'." 26 September 2012. *The Telegraph*. Web. 25 October 2013. <http://www.telegraph.co.uk/finance/jobs/9567198/Christine-Lagarde-Women-cant-have-it-all.html>

310. Belanger, Nicole. "Why I Don't Want Work-Life Balance." 3 September 2013. *Levo League*. Web. 27 October 2013. <https://www.levo.com/articles/lifestyle/why-i-dont-want-work-life-balance>

311. "Welcome to the 2014 40 under 40…" n.d. *Fortune*. Web. 22 June 2015. <http://fortune.com/40-under-40/>

312. "The 25 Most Powerful Women in the World, 2014." n.d. *Forbes*. Web. 22 June 2015. <http://www.forbes.com/pictures/lmh45lfdj/marissa-mayer/>

313. Lutz, Ashley. "Inside the Luxe $300 Million Life of New Yahoo CEO Marissa Mayer." 19 July 2012. *Business Insider*. Web. 22 June 2015. <http://www.businessinsider.com/marissa-mayers-fabulous-life-2012-7?op=1>

314. McKenna, Francine. "Marissa Mayer's Pregnancy: What Does Yahoo Have to Disclose?" 17 July 2012. *Forbes*. Web. 25 June 2014. <http://www.forbes.com/sites/francinemckenna/2012/07/17/marissa-mayers-pregnancy-what-does-yahoo-have-to-disclose/>

315. Pepitone, Julianne. "Marissa Mayer extends Yahoo's maternity leave." 30 April 2013. *CNN Money*. Web. 22 June 2014. <http://money.cnn.com/2013/04/30/technology/yahoo-maternity-leave/>

316. Toren, Matthew. "Marissa Explains It all: 5 Motivating Quotes From Yahoo's CEO." 17 July 2014. *Entrepreneur*. Web. 25 July 2014. <http://www.entrepreneur.com/article/234222>

317. "PepsiCo's strength is its people." N.d. *PepsiCo.* Web. 25 July 2015.
<http://www.pepsico.com/Company/Leadership>

318. "50 Most Powerful Women in Business." N.d. *Fortune.* Web. 25 July 2015.
<http://archive.fortune.com/magazines/fortune/mostpowerfulwomen/2009/full_list/>

319. "50 Most Powerful Women in Business." N.d. *Fortune.* Web. 25 July 2015.
<http://archive.fortune.com/magazines/fortune/mostpowerfulwomen/2010/full_list/>

320. "Indra Nooyi Quotes." N.d. *Brainy Quote.* Web. 25 July 2015.
<www.brainyquote.com/quotes/authors/i/indra_nooyi.html#7WpGtVfOvAc8epbv.99>

321. Forbes, Moira. "Pepsico CEO Indra Nooyi on Why Women Can't Have it All." 3 July 2014. *Forbes.* Web. 25 July 2015.
<http://www.forbes.com/sites/moiraforbes/2014/07/03/power-woman-indra-nooyi-on-why-women-cant-have-it-all/>

322. Lepore, Meredith. "10 Famous Women on 'Having it All'." 24 May 2013.
Levo League. Web. 27 October 2013.
<https://www.levo.com/articles/lifestyle/famous-women-having-it-all>

323. Zeilinger, Julie. "Norah O'Donnell: The Guilt Over Having It All 'Has To End'." 25 July 2013. *HuffPost The Third Metric.* Web. 27 October 2013.
<http://www.huffingtonpost.com/2013/07/25/norah-odonnell-the-guilt-over-having-it-all-has-to-end_n_3647246.html>

324. Winfrey, Oprah. *Oprah Winfrey, Quotes, Quotable Quote.* n.d. Web. 27 October 2013. <http://www.goodreads.com/quotes/11820-you-can-have-it-all-just-not-all-at-once>

325. Lepore, Meredith. "10 Famous Women on 'Having it All'." 24 May 2013.
Levo League. Web. 27 October 2013.
<https://www.levo.com/articles/lifestyle/famous-women-having-it-all>

326. Lepore, Meredith. "10 Famous Women on 'Having it All'." 24 May 2013.
Levo League. Web. 27 October 2013.
<https://www.levo.com/articles/lifestyle/famous-women-having-it-all>

327. Brillson, Leila. "Christine Quinn On NYC & Leaning In." 5 September 2013. *Refinery29.* Web. 25 October 2013.
<http://www.refinery29.com/2013/09/52729/christine-quinn-interview>

328. Lepore, Meredith. "10 Famous Women on 'Having it All'." 24 May 2013. *Levo League.* Web. 27 October 2013. <https://www.levo.com/articles/lifestyle/famous-women-having-it-all>

329. Sandberg, Sheryl. *Lean In: Women, Work, and the Will to Lead.* New York: Knopf; 1 edition, 2013. Print.

330. Fischer, Molly. "When Will We Stop Talking About 'Having It All'?" 7 August 2013. *The Cut.* Web. 26 October 2013. <http://nymag.com/thecut/2013/08/when-will-we-stop-talking-about-having-it-all.html>

331. Slaughter, Anne-Marie. "Why Women Still Can't Have It All." 13 June 2012. *The Atlantic.* Web. 17 Ocober 2013. <http://www.theatlantic.com/magazine/archive/2012/07/why-women-still-cant-have-it-all/309020/>

332. Spar, Debora L. "Why theWoman Who "Has It All" Doesn't Really Exist." 19 August 2013. *Glamour.* Web. 27 October 2013. <http://www.glamour.com/inspired/2013/08/why-women-cant-have-it-all-according-to-barnard-college-president-debora-l-spar>

333. Lepore, Meredith. "10 Famous Women on 'Having it All'." 24 May 2013. *Levo League.* Web. 27 October 2013. <https://www.levo.com/articles/lifestyle/famous-women-having-it-all>

334. Garey, Juliann. "US WEEKLY Meryl Streep." October 1994. *Mary Ellen Mark.* Web. 28 October 2013. <http://www.maryellenmark.com/text/magazines/us%20weekly_new/925B-000-001.html>

335. Nepales, Ruben V. "The deliciously candid Meryl Streep." 20 July 2012. *Inquirer.net.* Web. 29 October 2013. <http://entertainment.inquirer.net/50753/the-deliciously-candid-meryl-streep>

336. Stritof, Sheri. "Meryl Streep and Don Gummer Marriage Profile." n.d. *about relationships.* Web. 28 October 2013. <http://marriage.about.com/od/entertainmen1/p/mstreep.htm>

337. Stritof, Sheri. "Meryl Streep and Don Gummer Marriage Profile." n.d. *about relationships.* Web. 28 October 2013. <http://marriage.about.com/od/entertainmen1/p/mstreep.htm>

338. Stritof, Sheri. "Meryl Streep and Don Gummer Marriage Profile." n.d. *about relationships.* Web. 28 October 2013. <http://marriage.about.com/od/entertainmen1/p/mstreep.htm>

339. "Olympic Gold Medalist Kerri Walsh on "Having It All"." August 2013. *Aol.OnSPORTS.* Web Video. 27 October 2013. <http://on.aol.com/video/olympic-gold-medalist-kerri-walsh-on--having-it-all--517911541>

340. Roth, Eric. "Eric Roth Quotes." n.d. *GoodReads.* Web. 22 February 2014. <http://www.goodreads.com/quotes/469896-for-what-it-s-worth-it-s-never-too-late-to-be>

341. "Michael Jordan." n.d. *NBA Encyclopedia Playoff Edition.* Web. 20 October 2013. <http://www.nba.com/history/players/jordan_bio.html>

342. SwishNBA. "Kobe Bryant vs Michael Jordan 2013 Comparison." 7 June 2013. *Swish NBA Blog.* WEb. 20 October 2013. <http://swishnba.com/2013/06/07/kobe-bryant-vs-michael-jordan-2013-comparison/>

343. "Title IX of the Education Amendments of 1972." 13 November 2000. *Justice.gov.* Web. 16 June 2012. <http://www.justice.gov/crt/about/cor/coord/titleixstat.php>

344. Barra, Allen and Dangerfield, Whitney. "Before and After Title IX: Women in Sports." 16 June 2012. *The New York Times: Sunday Review.* Web. 28 July 2013. <http://www.nytimes.com/interactive/2012/06/17/opinion/sunday/sunday review-titleix-timeline.html?_r=0>

345. Barra, Allen and Dangerfield, Whitney. "Before and After Title IX: Women in Sports." 16 June 2012. *The New York Times: Sunday Review.* Web. 28 July 2013. <http://www.nytimes.com/interactive/2012/06/17/opinion/sunday/sunday review-titleix-timeline.html?_r=0>

346. Henry, Erin Joy. "Do You Have Trouble Accepting Help?" 7 September 2011. *The Huffington Post.* Web. 27 July 2014. <http://www.huffingtonpost.com/erin-henry/trouble-accepting-help_b_951545.html>

347. Allen, Woody. *Woody Allen Quotes.* n.d. Web. July 2014. <http://www.goodreads.com/quotes/87478-if-you-want-to-make-god-laugh-tell-him-about>

348. Rawlinson, Keith. "Is Education Important?" 2012. *Eclectic Site.* Web. July 2014. <http://eclecticsite.com/education&income.html>

349. —. *The Feminine Mystique Quotes.* n.d. Web. July 2014. <http://www.goodreads.com/work/quotes/809732-the-feminine-mystique>

350. Sandberg, Sheryl. *Lean In: Women, Work, and the Will to Lead.* New York: Knopf; 1 edition, 2013. Print.

351. Sandberg, Sheryl. *Lean In: Women, Work, and the Will to Lead.* New York: Knopf; 1 edition, 2013. Print.

352. Sandberg, Sheryl. *Lean In: Women, Work, and the Will to Lead.* New York: Knopf; 1 edition, 2013. Print.

353. McCarthy, Laura F. "Pregnancy at 20, 30, 40." 2013. *Parenting.* Web. 18 November 2013. < http://www.parenting.com/article/pregnancy-at-20-30-40>

354. McCarthy, Laura F. "Pregnancy at 20, 30, 40." 2013. *Parenting.* Web. 18 November 2013. < http://www.parenting.com/article/pregnancy-at-20-30-40>

355. McCarthy, Laura F. "Pregnancy at 20, 30, 40." 2013. *Parenting.* Web. 18 November 2013. < http://www.parenting.com/article/pregnancy-at-20-30-40>

356. McCarthy, Laura F. "Pregnancy at 20, 30, 40." 2013. *Parenting.* Web. 18 November 2013. < http://www.parenting.com/article/pregnancy-at-20-30-40>

357. McCarthy, Laura F. "Pregnancy at 20, 30, 40." 2013. *Parenting.* Web. 18 November 2013. < http://www.parenting.com/article/pregnancy-at-20-30-40>

358. Hope, Jenny. "Children of mothers over 40 are 'healthier and more intelligent and less likely to have accidents'". 21 May 2012. Daily Mail. Web. 18 November 2013. <http://www.dailymail.co.uk/health/article-2147848/Children-mothers-40-healthier-intelligent.html>

359. Beddow, Di. "Women who don't help other women: myth or reality?". 15 September 2014. *The Guardian.* Web. 21 October 2014.

360. Piersanti, Steven. "The 10 Awful Truths About Book Publishing." n.d. Out:think. Web. July 2014. <https://www.google.com/webhp?sourceid=chrome-instant&ion=1&espv=2&ie=UTF-8#q=the%2010%20awful%20truths%20about%20book%20publishing>

361. Epstein, Cynthia F. "Betty Friedan: An Appreciation." March 2006. *American Sociology Association, Footnotes.* Web. 23 October 2013. <http://www.asanet.org/footnotes/mar06/indextwo.html>

362. Dr. Seuss. *Oh, The Places You'll Go!!* New York: Random House Children's Books, 19858. Print.

363. "U.S. Life Expectancy Ranks 26th In The World, OECD Report Shows."
21 November 2013. *The Huffington Post.* Web. 28 October 2013.
http://www.huffingtonpost.com/2013/11/21/us-life-expectancy-
oecd_n_4317367.html

VIDEO LINKS

a.   Chicago: Searching https://www.youtube.com/watch?v=eHD7KekkSLs

b.   Helen Reddy's 1975 *I am Woman*
https://www.youtube.com/watch?v=MUBnxqEVKlk

c.   Katy Perry's *Roar* at the Superbowl
https://www.youtube.com/watch?v=l8612NwFRA0

d.   Grambling State Marching Band
https://www.youtube.com/watch?v=fzgZJlg63aI

e.   Helen Reddy Interview
https://www.youtube.com/watch?v=1xhVxpx7aCQ

f.   Bert Parks Miss America
https://www.youtube.com/watch?v=V6RJY5Isv4Y

g.   Cinderella https://www.youtube.com/watch?v=VtFhREtPdiE

h.   Mr. T https://www.youtube.com/watch?v=7_rBidCkJxo

i.   Miss Teen South https://www.youtube.com/watch?v=lj3iNxZ8Dww

j.   Chatty Cathy Doll https://www.youtube.com/watch?v=f-sYQ8_2v_Q

k.   The Exorcist https://www.youtube.com/watch?v=8QjrBjdb2T8

l.   The Wizard of Oz https://www.youtube.com/watch?v=WnXAl1ntt_4

m.   The Beverly Hillbillies: Ellie Starts School
https://www.youtube.com/watch?v=-8jd-3qBi9g

n.   Green Acres: Hot Water Soup
https://www.youtube.com/watch?v=SzGdDqWJcFU

o.   Roseanne Rosannadanna https://screen.yahoo.com/roseanne-rosannadanna-smoking-000000279.html

p.   Charlie's Angels: Season 1, 1976
https://www.youtube.com/watch?v=PcwPo37Q23w

q.   Enjoli https://www.youtube.com/watch?v=_Q0P94wyBYk

r.   Strong Women: Kicking Ass
https://www.youtube.com/watch?v=HtOKlaXFxwk

s.   Little Mermaid https://www.youtube.com/watch?v=HOFZaW92nhA

t.   Mulan https://www.youtube.com/watch?v=ZSS5dEcMX64

u.   Cinderella Trailer https://www.youtube.com/watch?v=20DF6U1HcGQ

v.   Barbie and Body Image
http://www.nbcnews.com/id/21134540/vp/42643430#42643430

w. Old Fashioned Women https://www.youtube.com/watch?v=lqf6d4ImqvU

x. The Help Trailer https://www.youtube.com/watch?v=5h_-Nu7tiag

y. WWII WASPs https://www.youtube.com/watch?v=jdzI5vEb9yM

z. Meryl Streep: Maskers
    https://www.youtube.com/watch?v=XcH2ppft2Gw

aa. Martin Luther King https://www.youtube.com/watch?v=HRIF4_WzU1w

bb. Women demand more
     https://www.youtube.com/watch?v=xO304aoUAWE

cc. Walter Scott Shooting https://www.youtube.com/watch?v=8nrqFaSRclc

dd. Rush Limbaugh: Feminazis
     https://www.youtube.com/watch?v=CRUKCEj7qqA

ee. Rush Limbaugh https://www.youtube.com/watch?v=jCFySez-4tw

ff. Rush Limbaugh https://www.youtube.com/watch?v=asUrboJyc78

gg. Christine O'Donnell: Masturbating
     https://www.youtube.com/watch?v=RzHcqcXo_NA

hh. Patricia Arquette: Oscar Speech https://www.youtube.com/watch?v=L-EmDy3w1X8

ii. Kramer vs. Kramer https://www.youtube.com/watch?v=re0xt6hDdqE

jj. Dad Catches Ball http://sports.yahoo.com/blogs/mlb-big-league-stew/hero-dad-makes-one-handed-catch-while-holding-baby-181701279.html

kk. Dad Doesn't Miss a Beat
     https://www.youtube.com/watch?v=s5XPD5zWcUY

ll. Commercial: Guinness, Wheelchair Basketball
     https://www.youtube.com/watch?v=0Vxjh6KJi8E

mm. Kevin Durant's Mother
     https://www.youtube.com/watch?v=F1m6g124YOM

nn. X Factor: Rion Paige https://www.youtube.com/watch?v=11oMu365xYU

oo. My Big Fat Greek Wedding: Man is the Head
     https://www.youtube.com/watch?v=8fJoPI-xytM

pp. Men Fails https://www.youtube.com/watch?v=1Ybqsis4A64

qq. Ricky Bobby's First Race https://www.youtube.com/watch?v=riBA-FsJJmY

rr. Male Reporter Electrocutes Himself
     https://www.youtube.com/watch?v=TIy3GqS-cd8

ss. It's Not the Nail https://www.youtube.com/watch?v=-4EDhdAHrOg

tt. Jeanne Robertson https://www.youtube.com/watch?v=-YFRUSTiFUs

uu. Madmen: What? https://www.youtube.com/watch?v=WsJSRP7cZVo

vv. Friends: Difference Between Men & Women
https://www.youtube.com/watch?v=iGoC8FTLKSI

ww. Man vs. Wild https://www.youtube.com/watch?v=QuB3kr3ckYE

xx. Blowing up shit https://www.youtube.com/watch?v=_hdl86mhxMo

yy. Watch me go to work
https://www.youtube.com/watch?v=eVXKKaWJTls

zz. I hate it when that happens https://www.youtube.com/watch?v=fE9_MtJ-1aY

aaa. Mrs. Doubtfire https://www.youtube.com/watch?v=MAp8j4c2LGs

bbb. Twins https://www.youtube.com/watch?v=L49VXZwfup8

ccc. https://www.youtube.com/watch?v=WxUulGkLu4I

ddd. Quads Laughing Table
https://www.youtube.com/watch?v=zZH0sNsaAz4

eee. Dad at Comedy Barn https://www.youtube.com/watch?v=Z4Y4keqTV6w

fff. Oprah Talks: Strong Women Around the World
https://www.youtube.com/watch?v=lANb0BAYupE

ggg. Barbara Walters: Yale https://www.youtube.com/watch?v=7llYZ2XqLX4

hhh. Michael Jordan https://www.youtube.com/watch?v=xQwTJsY50l4

iii. Katie Video http://youtu.be/pfnz3ZopHDI

jjj. Women: Inspirational Video
https://www.youtube.com/watch?v=fia4HY9pWuo